The Moral Culture
of the
Scottish
Enlightenment,
1690–1805

THE LEWIS WALPOLE SERIES

IN EIGHTEENTH-CENTURY CULTURE AND HISTORY

The Lewis Walpole Series, published by Yale University
Press with the aid of the Annie Burr Lewis Fund, is dedicated
to the culture and history of the long eighteenth century (from
the Glorious Revolution to the accession of Queen Victoria). It
welcomes work in a variety of fields, including literature and
history, the visual arts, political philosophy, music, legal history,
and the history of science. In addition to original scholarly work,
the series publishes new editions and translations of writing from
the period, as well as reprints of major books that are currently
unavailable. Though the majority of books in the series will
probably concentrate on Great Britain and the Continent, the
range of our geographical interests is as wide as
Horace Walpole's.

The Moral Culture
of the
Scottish
Enlightenment,
1690–1805

Thomas Ahnert

Yale
UNIVERSITY PRESS
NEW HAVEN AND LONDON

Published with assistance from the Annie Burr Lewis Fund.

Yale University Press books may be purchased in quantity for educational, business, or promotional use. For information, please e-mail sales.press@yale.edu (U.S. office) or sales@yaleup.co.uk (U.K. office).

Set in Fournier type by IDS Infotech, Ltd.
Printed in the United States of America.

Library of Congress Cataloging-in-Publication Data
Ahnert, Thomas.
The moral culture of the Scottish Enlightenment, 1690–1805 / Thomas Ahnert.
        pages   cm.— (The Lewis Walpole series in eighteenth-century culture
and history)
Includes bibliographical references and index.
ISBN 978-0-300-15380-4 (hardcover : alk. paper)   1. Enlightenment—Scotland.
2. Scotland—Moral conditions.   I. Title.
B1302.E65A36 2015
941.106—dc23
                                                                            2014021377

A catalogue record for this book is available from the British Library.

This paper meets the requirements of ANSI/NISO Z39.48-1992 (Permanence of Paper).

10 9 8 7 6 5 4 3 2 1

Contents

Acknowledgments

This is a short book that has taken longer to write than I had hoped or expected. I am very grateful for the support I have received over the past few years. One of my greatest debts is to the late Susan Manning and to Nicholas Phillipson, who appointed me to the postdoctoral fellowship attached to a research project on the "Science of Man in the Scottish Enlightenment." The project, funded by the Leverhulme Trust, ran from 2002 until 2006. Many of the ideas in this book have their origin in discussions that took place at the seminars and workshops related to the project. Susan also commented on early drafts of parts of the book. She is deeply missed. I should like to express my gratitude to the now dissolved Max-Planck-Institut für Geschichte in Göttingen, where I was a visiting fellow in 2005 and 2006. I should also like to thank the Arts and Humanities Research Council, which awarded me a grant for research leave in 2008. I am also most grateful to the Institute for Advanced Study in Princeton, where I was the Rosanna and Charles Jaffin Founders' Circle Member in 2010–2011. At the Institute I profited from conversations with many scholars, in particular Jonathan Israel. I also learned much from discussions with Simon Grote, then at Princeton University. I should also like to thank the School of History, Classics, and Archaeology at Edinburgh for granting me research leave on two occasions. I owe a great debt to the late Istvan Hont, whose encouragement and help over many years have been extremely important. I have also benefited greatly from Knud Haakonssen's support and advice for more than a decade. With Hans-Erich Bödeker, Alexander Broadie, James Harris, Colin Heydt, Colin Kidd, Tony LaVopa, Jim Moore, John Robertson, Silvia Sebastiani, Richard Sher, M. A. Stewart, Paul Wood, and Bill Zachs, I have had many stimulating conversations on various aspects of the eighteenth century. James Harris also read and commented on several draft chapters. Tony LaVopa, Hannah Dawson, Brad Bow, and Bridget Ahnert read the entire typescript, which has been noticeably improved by their suggestions. The comments by the two anonymous readers for Yale University Press were most helpful. Chris Rogers at Yale University Press has been a very patient editor. My greatest debt is to my family. The book is dedicated to my parents.

Introduction:
Religion, Morality, and
Enlightenment

In recent years there has been a growing body of secondary literature concerned with elucidating the relationship of European Enlightenment thought to religion, from the second half of the seventeenth century to the early nineteenth. There were a few well-known atheists during that period, such as the Franco-German Baron d'Holbach or the physician Julien Offray de La Mettrie, and many less famous thinkers whose writings were sometimes so inflammatory that they went unpublished and circulated only as clandestine manuscripts.[1] In general, however, the intellectual elites of eighteenth-century Europe were committed to religious beliefs that were at least broadly Christian. The term "religious" or "clerical Enlightenment" is now firmly established in the historiography.

There is still some debate over the precise meaning of this term, but it is generally agreed that eighteenth-century Scotland, or "North Britain," as it was often known, represents a good example of such a "religious Enlightenment."[2] There were very few Scots thinkers whose ideas could be regarded as irreligious or atheistic. The skeptical philosopher David Hume is probably the most prominent of them, but it is doubtful that he was a genuine atheist, even if some of his contemporaries accused him of being one.[3] Adam Smith's moral theory and economic thought implied no religious beliefs, but he never directly questioned the usefulness and truth of religion, either, and his views on religious matters are in effect difficult to establish.[4] Among the other important representatives of Scottish philosophy and letters, many, possibly even the majority, had studied divinity, and many of those went on to serve as ministers, at least for a period. For example, the moral philosopher Francis Hutcheson had been a student of theology at the University of Glasgow in the 1710s, though he did not go on to hold a parish. Hugh Blair, the first incumbent of the Regius chair of Rhetoric and Belles-Lettres at Edinburgh, was an eminent clergyman whose reputation rested in good part on his published collection of sermons, which appeared in numerous editions during his lifetime and continued to be popular after his death.[5] The historian William Robertson, principal of the University of Edinburgh from 1762 until 1793, was a clergyman and a leading member of the supreme governing body of the Presbyterian Church of Scotland, the General Assembly. Adam Ferguson, author of the influential *Essay on the History of Civil Society* (1767) and professor of moral philosophy at the University of Edinburgh from 1764, had been a regimental chaplain in the Black Watch. Another example is Hume's famous critic Thomas Reid, who had been a minister in the parish of New Machar for several years, before teaching at King's College in Aberdeen and, from 1764, as Adam Smith's successor at the University of Glasgow. In eighteenth-century Scotland, as elsewhere in Europe, clergymen were among the most important participants in the republic of letters, and religion was a central intellectual concern of the Enlightenment, not distinct from it.

The focus of this book is on the connection between religious beliefs and Enlightenment moral thought. In particular, I shall examine one important development that is often associated with the "religious Enlightenment," not only in Scotland, but in Europe more widely. This is the change of emphasis in much of eighteenth-century thought from theological doctrine to moral conduct as the true measure of religious belief. It was thought increasingly that a sincerely pious person was distinguished not by the precise creeds he or she professed, but by practical acts of virtue and a good character. The German philosopher Ernst Cassirer already drew attention to this phenomenon in his *Philosophy of the Enlightenment*, when he observed that, for thinkers such as the German author and playwright Gotthold Ephraim Lessing, the "truth of religion cannot be determined according to purely theoretical criteria; its validity cannot be decided abstractly without regard to its moral effect."[6] The historian Blair Worden has described a tendency of this kind in English thought of the late seventeenth and early eighteenth centuries, suggesting that religious attitudes softened, and theological doctrine gave way to a religion of works. "The test of Christianity," he writes, "became good conduct, not right belief." Although this development was not universally welcomed, it was, he says, an increasing trend.[7] The philosopher Charles Taylor has recently advanced a similar interpretation of eighteenth-century religion in his history of secularization in the West.[8] The emphasis on conduct rather than doctrine does not represent a complete secularization of moral thought, but once religion is justified in terms of its moral, this-worldly effect, it seems to require only a small step to conclude that morality no longer needs a religious foundation at all.[9] Secularization, it is believed, may not have been the intended outcome of these ideas, but it was implicit in them, as a logical, if extreme conclusion that was only waiting to be fully developed.

The interpretations of the reasons for this change in the eighteenth century are varied. It has, for example, been attributed to the growing influence of secular reason in enlightened thought, or to the impact of the intellectual heritage of Greek and Roman classical antiquity. Enlightened clergy were often thought to hold an attenuated form of Christianity, in which the authority of revelation was diminished and replaced largely by a "natural religion," founded on human reason alone and accessible, therefore, to non-Christians. I believe, however, there is a different interpretation possible, and that the shift from doctrine to conduct in Enlightenment religion was related to theological questions, in particular the problematic legacy of Protestant solfideism, the principle of salvation by faith alone. Enlightenment theology has received relatively little attention in intellectual history, but it was of profound significance for Enlightenment thought and culture more generally. The aim of this book is to draw attention to the continuing importance of theological languages in Enlightenment thought, and to integrate them more closely into the wider intellectual history of the eighteenth century.[10]

Religion and Reason

Some of the current explanations for the transformation of religion in Enlightenment culture are still associated with "reason," and it is common to relate changes in eighteenth-century religion to the growing influence of "rationalist" arguments in religious affairs.[11] The titles of works such as John Locke's *Reasonableness of Christianity* seem to confirm the trend toward "rational religion" from the late seventeenth century onward. There is some disagreement over the extent to which rationalism in the eighteenth century could be reconciled with religion. Jonathan Israel, for example, has argued that the Enlightenment was characterized by a set of closely related, rational, and secular ideas defended by the Dutch philosopher Baruch Spinoza as early as the second half of the seventeenth century. Such ideas were fundamentally at odds with religion, and were, Israel argues, the essence of the "radical Enlightenment," which was "Enlightenment" in its true sense.[12] There was also a "moderate Enlightenment" of those thinkers who wanted "a balanced compromise between reason and tradition, or reason and religious authority."[13] They tried to reconcile rational principles with religious belief and a commitment to conservative political and social ideas. Their efforts, however, were in vain. All they produced was an unstable hybrid that was not intellectually viable over time. In the long run, the standard of secular human reason in the Enlightenment was incompatible with religious belief.[14]

Others have argued that the synthesis of "enlightened" reason with religious beliefs was more successful and persuasive than Israel allows. David Sorkin, for example, writes that rational, or "natural," religion had been a radical, dangerous idea for much of the seventeenth century, but by the eighteenth, "religious enlighteners co-opted the idea of natural religion to revealed religion," achieving a harmonious synthesis of Scripture with modern intellectual currents.[15] Taylor has used the term "providential deism" to refer to a synthesis of rational argument with Christian beliefs.[16] The challenge for "religious enlighteners," as Sorkin and others have argued, was to preserve Christian belief, founded on Scripture, while absorbing the impact of Enlightenment rationalism. Various solutions to this challenge existed, but they were all situated on a spectrum between reason and revelation. The more radical enlighteners tended toward upholding the authority of secular reason, while the more conservative tried harder to preserve the authority of revelation in as many of its aspects as possible. All other theorists were somewhere between these two extremes.[17]

Regardless of differences of interpretation, therefore, there seems to be widespread agreement that "reason" played an important role in transforming eighteenth-century religion. Yet I contend that reasonable, or natural, religion was less significant in changing eighteenth-century religion than has sometimes been argued. Natural religion commonly stood for a system of religious belief that was founded on human reason and observation rather than on supernatural revelation. It had, however, been part of traditional Christian thought for a long time.[18] It was not a radical innovation of the seventeenth century that had to be brought under control by religious enlighteners in the eighteenth who were trying to find a middle-way between modern and traditional ways of thinking. Also, enlightened clergymen were not necessarily distinguished by a particularly strong commitment to "natural" or "rational" religion. There were some theorists, such as the deist Matthew Tindal, who declared revelation superfluous because reason alone was sufficient. Christianity, he said, required not doctrinal beliefs derived from Scripture, but virtue founded on a rational religion. Yet many clergymen of the mid-eighteenth century Enlightenment in Scotland— figures such as Hugh Blair, William Robertson, and Thomas Reid, all of whom reduced the importance of doctrine in favor of an emphasis on conduct—were in fact much less confident than someone like Tindal about the usefulness of a natural, rationalist religion. Paradoxical though this may seem, these "enlightened" clergymen in the Presbyterian Church of Scotland were actually more skeptical about a natural religion of reason than their more orthodox, traditional counterparts, and their emphasis on conduct as the proper mark of a genuinely religious person was not based on "reason" or "natural religion."

Another explanation for the changes in Christian beliefs refers to the intellectual legacy of European classical antiquity. Peter Gay argued influentially around half a century ago that the Enlightenment of the eighteenth century was a product of the tension between Christianity and the pagan, classical heritage of ancient Rome and Greece.[19] Eventually, this tension between the two traditions undermined the authority of traditional Christianity, leading, in Gay's famous phrase, to the "rise of modern paganism" in the age of Enlightenment. Other historians have suggested that eighteenth-century Christianity was far better than Gay had believed at integrating the intellectual legacy of pagan antiquity. Ancient Stoicism in particular has been regarded as eminently compatible with Christian teachings, and the enlightened clergy of eighteenth-century Scotland have often been characterized as "Christian Stoics." Jim Moore and Michael Silverthorne have, for example, described Francis Hutcheson as such a Christian Stoic, stating that he refashioned "Christian doctrine, notably the Presbyterian or Reformed doctrine of original sin, by substituting for it a particular variant of Stoicism . . . in which the original or natural constitution of human nature contains something divine within: a heart or a soul that is oriented towards affection for others, good offices, benevolence."[20] Richard Sher, too, in his seminal work on the "Moderate" clergy of eighteenth-century Edinburgh argued that Francis Hutcheson had been the first to put forward a synthesis of Christianity with central tenets of ancient Stoicism. That combination of ancient Stoicism with a less rigid form of Calvinism was then adopted "most enthusiastically and completely" by the "Moderate literati" of mid-eighteenth-century Edinburgh, including Ferguson, Blair, and Robertson.[21] As in the case of secular rationalism, the transformative effect of classical Greek and Roman thought is accepted in principle by different historians, who disagree mainly over the extent to which Christian religious believers were able to adapt successfully to the challenge from pagan philosophers.

Certainly, many of the important thinkers of the Scottish Enlightenment, including its clerical men of letters, admired the intellectual achievements of classical antiquity, and they often reserved their greatest praise for the Stoic school. It is also no coincidence that Hutcheson, together with James Moor, published an edition of the Stoic *Meditations* by Marcus Aurelius, and that Robertson began a translation of the same work, although he did not complete it.[22] Yet, the attitude of enlightened clergymen toward the philosophers of classical antiquity was more critical than the idea of Christian Stoicism implies. Their praise for the Greek and Roman thinkers was often heavily qualified, above all because of their paganism.[23] The references to them did not reflect a belief in the superiority of pagan thought to Christianity, but were used, rather, to warn of the deplorable state of Christianity in the eighteenth century. The point being made was that even pagan philosophers, whose ideas suffered from serious shortcomings because of their ignorance of the Gospel, were often more praiseworthy than many modern-day Christians. The reasons why conduct rather than doctrine became so central to notions of religion and piety in the eighteenth century have less to do with the impact of other, rival standards of judgment or systems of thought, such as secular reason or ancient Stoicism, than with particular theological problems concerning the central question of Christian belief, the conditions of salvation.

Charity, Virtue, and Salvation

The emphasis on conduct rather than doctrine reflected a concern that Christian belief had been defined in too narrowly doctrinal terms, at the expense of the upright conduct that was supposed to characterize a sincere Christian believer. It was often said that too many people professed adherence to the Gospel while living more corrupt lives than any heathen. An indication of this widespread preoccupation was the proliferation of Societies for the Reformation of Manners, one of which was formed in Edinburgh in September 1700. These societies were aimed at reversing the "Deluge of Impiety and Licentiousness" that was supposedly overwhelming Britain.[24]

Underlying these trends was a more technical theological argument that the Protestant belief in salvation by faith alone had gone too far and led to the neglect of the practical holiness of life that ought to be typical of the Christian faithful. It was feared that Protestantism, in rejecting the Catholic belief in the efficacy of good works, had encouraged a belief that the faithful were not required to perform good works, or at least had failed to insist sufficiently on the importance of moral conduct, concentrating too much on defining the specific doctrinal beliefs that were required for salvation.

Such concerns had been raised not just in England, Ireland, and Scotland, but also in European religious culture more generally by the numerous, broadly pietistic, spiritualist religious movements that had emerged in the course of the seventeenth century, which emphasized sincerity and practical "holiness of life" over the precise adherence to any doctrinal system.[25] More orthodox theorists did not deny that Christianity demanded a virtuous way of life from its followers, but they also defended the need for a clear doctrinal standard for Christian religion, because the sincerity of religious beliefs was not sufficient for true faith, if the beliefs themselves were wrong. Their opponents tended, to varying degrees, to place less emphasis on the need for such doctrinal standards. They argued that the essence of Christianity was charity, not in its more specific sense as charity toward the poor, but in its widest possible meaning, the selfless love of God and one's neighbor. Charity was a far more significant and valuable bond among Christians than an exact agreement on particular points of doctrine. Charity constituted the foundation of both genuine devotion and the social virtues that were typical of sincere Christians.

That emphasis on charity and its importance for the social virtues can be characterized as broadly Augustinian. St. Augustine of Hippo had been a prominent influence on western European intellectual culture for a very long time and in all of the major Christian confessions, but a particularly powerful current of Augustinian thought ran through the second half of the seventeenth century. In part, this was probably due to the posthumous publication of the Flemish bishop Cornelius Jansen's extremely influential *Augustinus* in 1640, though it is likely that his work was a symptom rather than a cause of the wider interest in Augustine's ideas. Augustine's intellectual legacy could be interpreted and used in a variety of ways, but one of his most distinctive beliefs was that the truly faithful were distinguished by their charity, their pure and selfless love of God, while sinners were marked by their corrupt love of self, which manifested itself in their desire for worldly goods such as glory, wealth, and sensual pleasure. The pursuit of earthly goods out of love of self was an expression of the most heinous human fault—namely, pride, the idea that human affairs were self-sufficient and did not totally depend on God's grace.[26] These themes appeared in the writings of a wide range of seventeenth-century "Augustinians," who were far from being a unified group of thinkers and, on occasion, could be very hostile to one another. The term "Augustinian" therefore will be used very loosely here, as a descriptive label for certain features that are to be found in the texts of many moral theorists in the late seventeenth and early eighteenth centuries. This is not intended to imply that these "Augustinians" were faithful followers of Augustine in every respect, but the complexities of the debates among them are not of concern here. It is sufficient to note that such "Augustinian" theorists generally considered charity, or the love toward God, to be the proper foundation of virtue, happiness, and faith alike.[27]

It has also been argued that certain aspects of this Augustinian tradition in the late seventeenth century converged with a separate revival of interest in the ancient philosophical school of Epicureanism. However different Augustinianism and Epicureanism may seem, it is said that they were in some respects compatible with, and even very close to each other, because both shared a belief that the selfish passions could provide a foundation for a stable society, though one that was not genuinely virtuous. The affinity of Augustinian and Epicurean ideas was emphasized by Pierre Bayle in the entry on "Epicurus" in his 1697 *Dictionnaire Historique et Critique*, but already in the 1670s French Jansenists such as Blaise Pascal and Pierre Nicole had stressed that fallen humans might be able to live in society not in spite of their sinful, post-lapsarian *amour-propre*, but because of it.[28] That "Augustinian-Epicurean" synthesis, it is argued, was gaining influence among cutting-edge intellectuals in the European Republic of Letters toward the end of the seventeenth century.[29]

It is not necessary, however, to assume any synthesis of "Augustinian" with "Epicurean" ideas in order to explain the concern of "Augustinian" theorists with the regulation of worldly affairs. Although it was certainly not considered feasible for entire human societies to be united by the pure love of God, charity was thought to be capable of motivating the moral conduct of individuals, which was a central concern of the theorists examined here. Jansenist theorists like Pierre Nicole acknowledged the capacity of corrupt *amour-propre* to imitate the main actions of genuine virtue, but they always remained deeply critical of it. As Moriarty, for example, explains with regard to Nicole, Augustine "had freely admitted the temporal benefits it [that is, the Roman lust for glory] conferred on the city as a whole," and Nicole, in a sense was "adapting this insight," but he was doing so without "abandoning the axiological distinction between [charity and cupidity]."[30] Far from ebulliently celebrating the social order created by the selfish passions of corrupt human beings, as Bernard Mandeville had done in his infamous *Fable of the Bees*, the "Augustinian" theorists who will be discussed in this book were exploring the conditions of real virtue, which was not founded on selfish passions, and which was essentially identical to true piety. In the late seventeenth century these Augustinian ideas were to be found among some Episcopalian authors, such as Henry Scougal and George Garden, but, as will be seen, they were also influential among certain groups of Presbyterians from the 1720s.

A key question was how the transformation from corrupt sinner to pious and virtuous Christian would be brought about. Any Protestant author would argue that faith could not be achieved by human effort alone, because saying so would be tantamount to a "papist" belief in the efficacy of good works. The extent and the nature of God's assistance for the individual sinner, however, were the subject of considerable debate. There were in eighteenth-century Britain, including Scotland, strong religious revivalist movements, represented by figures such as the English Methodist preacher George Whitefield. They believed that the regeneration of a sinner had to be effected by a miraculous intervention from God, which manifested itself in an emotionally wrenching conversion experience that changed the individual's nature instantly and completely. Dramatic conversions of this kind were usually believed to have been preceded by a series of "signs," which were sent to the sinner by God over a long period of time, but were stubbornly ignored until a moment of crisis, when the sinner realized the depth of his or her own depravity and complete dependence on divine forgiveness for salvation. A good example of such a conversion narrative is the story of the English colonel James Gardiner, who died at the battle of Prestonpans near

Edinburgh in 1745. The account of Gardiner's life was published in 1747 by the Englishman Philipp Doddridge, who was the head of a dissenters' academy in Northampton, but well known in North Britain, where he received several honorary doctorates in divinity.[31]

According to Doddridge, Gardiner, who had joined the army at a young age, had for many years lived a dissolute life. Although a Christian in theory, who did not mock or criticize religion in public, his faith was superficial. On several occasions Gardiner narrowly escaped death. These events, Doddridge suggests, were arranged by God as a warning to Gardiner, reminding him of the urgent need to return to a state of grace before he died. Gardiner ignored these signs, however, and persisted in his corrupt ways, until late one evening, when, trying to kill the time before an "Assignation with a married woman,"[32] he picked up a devotional work thoughtfully slipped into his portmanteau by a pious aunt. Idly leafing through it because no other book happened to be at hand, Gardiner, who may or may not have been asleep, according to Doddridge, suddenly had a vision of Christ on the cross, who demanded of him whether this was how Gardiner requited the sacrifice he, Christ, had made for him. Doddridge leaves open the question whether or not Gardiner was dreaming or wide awake at that point, but Doddridge is in no doubt that the vision of Christ, whether a dream or not, was sent by God to turn Gardiner into a sincere Christian. Gardiner was thrown into emotional turmoil by his experience. At a single stroke, he recognized the extent of his own sinfulness and his total dependence on Christ's sacrifice in order to be saved. At the same time he was in despair because he felt unworthy of sharing in the benefits of Christ's death on the cross for the faithful. From that moment on, Gardiner was a reformed character, a devout Christian whose upright conduct reflected his newly gained purity of faith.[33]

Doddridge's account is a useful illustration of a view of regeneration and justification, from which "enlightened" clergymen were trying to distance themselves, and which they encountered in mid-eighteenth-century evangelical, revivalist circles in Scotland. The most visible example of these beliefs were the events at Cambuslang in 1742, which followed soon after a visit to Scotland by Whitefield and attracted crowds possibly numbering in the tens of thousands. Many of those who attended claimed to have undergone a conversion and reported hearing voices, seeing visions, and going through extreme emotional states of joy and despair.[34] The members of the "religious Enlightenment" that are the focus of this book, however, considered this kind of conversion experience to be prone to religious "enthusiasm," the naive belief in having some form of direct communication with God.[35] Religious enthusiasm was also thought to be dangerous, because it was associated with the extreme religious sects that had contributed to the social and political upheaval of the English civil war in the seventeenth century, and events such as the Anabaptist movement during the German Reformation. Although the representatives of "religious Enlightenment" discussed in this book believed that genuine piety required a transformation of the individual sinner's nature, and that this transformation had to depend on some form of divine assistance and grace, the process by which it occurred was very different from that of the revivalists, because regeneration, they argued, was not a sudden, miraculous event, but a product of a gradual process, which they described as a "culture."

Morality, Religion, and Culture

The term "culture" in this context did not refer either to the arts, music, and literature, or to the shared beliefs and values of a group, as it is often defined, but to a process of cultivation, an incremental improvement of human nature by which individuals were turned into properly virtuous agents.[36] The idea of a moral culture was indebted to classical authors such as Cicero, who had emphasized that philosophy was not only a form of knowledge, but also an art or discipline of living well, which incorporated knowledge within the entire character and conduct of a person.[37] Philosophy in this sense was a cure for the disordered soul, not just an abstract system of truths. The legacy of classical antiquity was appropriated and reinterpreted in various ways in the early modern era, but a very similar concern with philosophy as a "cure" or "medicine" of the mind is to be found in a range of texts, especially from the seventeenth century on. An important example is the work of Sir Francis Bacon, who, in his *Advancement of Learning* stated that moral philosophy had two parts, one "devoted to the doctrine of the good," and the other concerned with the "practical part of moral philosophy," which he described as the "culture," the "Georgic," the "cure," or the "medicining" of the mind.[38]

This "culture" occupied a prominent place in writings by many eighteenth-century Presbyterian clergymen. They thought of it as a "practical" enterprise, in the sense that it was about the reform of conduct, as distinct from the "speculative," theoretical understanding of certain truths by the intellect.[39] It is remarkable how skeptical many of the theorists discussed in this book were about the value of "speculative" knowledge, because abstract truths, they believed, did not necessarily influence our actions, which were the true measure of both morality and piety. Actions, they commonly argued, were motivated by affections, sentiments, and passions, and not opinions in the understanding. Any attempt at moral reform had to be addressed primarily to transforming these dispositions. Hume had famously stated that reason was "and ought only to be the slave of the passions, and can never pretend to any other office than to serve and obey them,"[40] but even the Moderate clergyman Hugh Blair wrote in one of his sermons that "arguments may convince the understanding, when they cannot conquer the passions."[41] It is significant that many of these authors were university teachers and had a strong interest in the practical pedagogic usefulness of moral doctrines. M. A. Stewart has pointed out that the purpose of instruction in moral philosophy at the Scottish universities in the eighteenth century was above all "practical," in that it was intended to "train students for virtuous living in a society regulated by religious observance."[42]

Virtue and religion were thus closely linked. The incremental moral reform of human nature through a process of "culture" was also the means to achieve regeneration and salvation. Reform might not even be complete in this life, but what mattered was the effort that the individual invested in this process of moral reform, consistently and over a long period of time. This effort could not be sufficient for salvation, for which divine grace was always required, but it was a necessary condition of salvation, and without it a sinner did not merit eternal life. The idea of religion and piety as a form of "culture" was distinct not only from the emphasis by the orthodox on the importance of having a doctrinal standard, but also from the beliefs of the revivalists. The "moderate Enlightenment" of the thinkers discussed in this book was not an attempt to accommodate the principles of secular, enlightened reason with traditional Christianity. Rather, they were trying to position themselves in theological terms between the two extremes of orthodox doctrinal rigor and revivalist enthusiasm.

The purpose in the following chapters is to recover the theological language of the "religious Enlightenment" in eighteenth-century Scotland, and in doing so to reexamine existing accounts of secularization in Enlightenment intellectual culture. There are various ways in which secularization has been defined and measured. The emphasis here is not on criteria such as rates of church attendance or popular beliefs, but on intellectual culture, as it is reflected in the writings of primarily university-educated male authors, among whom, it is often argued, the age of Enlightenment represented a kind of halfway station in the emergence of a secular worldview. Although the participants in the "religious Enlightenment" were not thoroughly secular, the principles they drew on, it is said, were increasingly secular in nature. Enlightenment religion involved the application of secular ideas to religious questions, and although secularization was not intended, it was implicit. It is doubtful, however, whether secularization was even implicit in the arguments that help to explain the change of emphasis from doctrine to conduct in the religious Enlightenment of eighteenth-century Scotland. Those features of the "religious Enlightenment" in Scotland that are usually attributed to the influence of more "secular" principles, such as natural reason, are better explained as attempts to make a theological point, and their theological positions, in turn, influenced the way these thinkers conceived of practical morality in this life. Although this may seem counterintuitive, members of the Scottish clerical Enlightenment believed that even secular morality was, in an important sense, incomplete without some form of divinely revealed faith. If anything, they reasserted the importance of Christianity for secular morality, rather than diminishing it. Christianity could be corrupted, but Christian commonwealths, they believed, were more likely to be virtuous and well ordered than non-Christian, pagan ones.

Many historians writing on religion and Enlightenment have been preoccupied with showing that various eighteenth-century thinkers succeeded in making religion and Enlightenment compatible with each other, but in doing so they imply, first, that there is a fundamental tension between "religion" and "Enlightenment," and, second, that it is possible to provide clear definitions of both. However, defining "Enlightenment" is extremely difficult, and there is no general agreement on its meaning. Robertson has emphasized enlightened thinkers' shared commitment to improvement and betterment in this world.[43] Pocock has characterized Enlightenment as a "family" of intellectual movements, held together by a common desire to prevent a renewal of the wars of religion that had plagued Europe throughout most of the seventeenth century.[44] Israel has argued for the importance of a "package" of radical and secular ideas.[45] In this book the term "Enlightenment" is used in a loose sense, to refer to the sum of the debates and ideas of the period from the late seventeenth to the early

nineteenth centuries. "Enlightenment" in this wide meaning includes mutu-
ally contradictory positions, all of which are equally characteristic of the
period. The approach is, as Paul Giles has put it, to trace "areas of conflict,
tension and crossover, rather than to extrapolate any particular aspect of this
complex scene into a more abstract model of Enlightenment thought."[46]
There were a variety of religious beliefs present in the eighteenth century
even within a single church like the established Presbyterian Kirk of Scotland.
The concern is not so much with showing that religion and secular moral
argument were capable of being reconciled with each other, but with the
particular ways in which different religious arguments were connected to
ideas about morality in Enlightenment thought.

The first chapter examines the state of Scottish Presbyterianism in the
decades immediately following the Glorious Revolution of 1688–89. The
revolution had brought about the restoration of the Presbyterian church, but
for many years its adherents regarded their situation as highly precarious.
Orthodox Calvinists believed themselves to be under threat, from
Episcopalians, Jacobites, deists, enthusiasts, and a range of heretics, such as
the Glasgow professor of divinity John Simson, who was formally accused of
heresy twice, in the 1710s and 1720s. Two late seventeenth-century and early
eighteenth-century Episcopalian authors, Henry Scougal and George Garden,
are also discussed. They were important because their writings are an example
of seventeenth-century "Augustinianism," and were influential among heterodox Presbyterians from the 1720s. The following chapter discusses
Presbyterianism during the period from about 1720 to 1750, when a loosely
defined group of heterodox clergymen emerged within the established Kirk,
who argued that genuine faith was based on practical virtue, motivated by
charity, which was the product of the process of "culture" or "culture of the
mind." They were skeptical of the need for a standard of doctrinal orthodoxy
such as the Westminster Confession, which had become the central document
of Presbyterian faith in Scotland after the Glorious Revolution. This theological context, it will also be shown, is crucial to understanding the moral
thought of Francis Hutcheson, whose frequently applied epithet is that of the
"father of the Scottish Enlightenment." Hutcheson thought of both morality
and faith as the product of a "culture," requiring effort on the part of the individual sinner, but also some form of divine assistance and grace. The classic
representatives of the "religious Enlightenment" in eighteenth-century
Scotland were the so-called Moderates who first emerged as a distinct party

within the Presbyterian Kirk in the 1750s. They are the subject of the third chapter. The Moderate Party had formed first in connection with a dispute in ecclesiastical politics, the question over the role of lay patronage in the appointment of ministers. Yet the Moderates also continued many of the strands of argument that had been prominent among the earlier generation of heterodox Presbyterians between about 1720 and 1750. Although they did not openly oppose the Westminster Confession, Moderates clearly did not believe that adherence to it was necessary for being a Christian, and were concerned largely with practical virtue as the sign of a genuine believer. Also, similar to earlier heterodox Presbyterians, the Moderates thought that such virtue joined with piety was the outcome of a gradual "culture" that involved labor and effort on the part of the individual, but which also required some form of divine support. Scripture was important, they believed, not as a source of doctrinal beliefs, but as a sort of practical manual for regeneration. The Moderates were not distinguished by a greater inclination toward natural religion. In fact, as the fourth chapter will show, the so-called orthodox critics of the Moderates, of which John Witherspoon is the most famous, had, if anything, a far more positive and comprehensive view of natural religion than the Moderates. The differences between them, including their different attitudes toward natural religion, are most convincingly explained in terms of their respective theological outlooks. In a separate section, the views of several thinkers are discussed who are usually grouped together as representatives of a school of "common-sense philosophy," based on their common criticism of Hume's philosophical skepticism, but who were also examples of a Moderate religious outlook. Moderatism is often said to have declined intellectually from the 1790s onward, and to have turned into little more than a conservative, reactionary interest group that was interested primarily in securing access to influential, salaried positions. The controversy over the appointment of John Leslie to the chair of natural philosophy at Edinburgh in 1805 is seen as an illustration of this decline. Leslie was opposed by Moderates and was defended by an alliance of orthodox clergymen and secular university professors, in an apparent reversal of the previous distribution of roles between Moderates and orthodox Presbyterians. In the mid-1750s, for example, orthodox Presbyterians had tried to publicly censure Hume, who escaped condemnation by the General Assembly only because of Moderate support, but in the Leslie affair of 1805 it was the Moderates who seemed the intolerant party, and the orthodox the more "liberal," open-minded one. The change is all the more striking, as the Moderates' case against Leslie was built on his apparent endorsement of Hume's notion of causation. The final chapter examines the issues that were at stake in the Leslie controversy, in relation to the outlook of the Moderate Party at that time. It also highlights some of the continuities between the eighteenth-century debates discussed and nineteenth-century attitudes on the role of religion in moral education and the formation of character, indicating that the connections between the Enlightenment and the Victorian age may be stronger than has sometimes been realized.[47]

1. Presbyterianism in Scotland After 1690

Following the Glorious Revolution of 1688–89, Presbyterianism was restored as the established Church of Scotland. The authority of bishops within the ecclesiastical hierarchy was abolished; the General Assembly was now the supreme governing body; Episcopalian ministers were removed from their parishes, often in violent "rabblings," in which a mob ejected the minister by force;[1] and a visitation commission purged universities of Episcopalian regents, many of whom went into temporary or permanent exile in England or Continental Europe.[2]

Nevertheless, the return to Presbyterianism in Scotland seemed insecure and precarious to many of its adherents, until well into the eighteenth century. One reason was that the support of William of Orange for a Presbyterian establishment had been halfhearted. When he succeeded to the Scottish crown, he had originally intended not to restore Presbyterian church government, but to place the state church in Scotland on a broader foundation that would encompass as many Scots as possible, including Episcopalians. His project failed, mainly because of the intransigence of the nonjuring Episcopalian bishops, who refused to swear the oath of loyalty to their new sovereign, so that William was forced, reluctantly, to accept a purely Presbyterian settlement.[3] Numerous Episcopalian ministers in Scotland did in fact manage to hold on to their livings, with some being defended by their parishioners against the emissaries of the General Assembly who had come to remove them.[4] At the same time, William kept up the pressure on the Kirk to comprehend loyal former Episcopalians. Thus, although there was no legal toleration for Episcopalianism as such until 1712, from 1695 at least a hundred Episcopalian clergy who had not been deprived of their churches during the Revolution were granted statutory toleration.[5] Episcopalian bishops, though no longer part of the established church, also remained in office.

It has sometimes been suggested that the differences between Episcopalians and Presbyterians were negligible. On some matters of doctrine that is the case, but in many respects the divisions between them ran deep, and had, if anything, increased in the period before 1689.[6] After 1690 Episcopalians were suspect because many of them continued to support the exiled Stuart dynasty. Not only had Presbyterians suffered from repression at the hands of the Stuarts at various times during the Restoration period. The Stuarts also remained resolutely Catholic, even though their stubborn adherence to their faith had contributed significantly to bringing about their expulsion. The Stuarts, moreover, found refuge at the court of the Catholic Louis XIV of France, whose aggressive foreign policy was raising the specter of a Catholic "universal monarchy" in western Europe.[7] Hence, one of the most powerful arguments for the parliamentary Union of Scotland with England in 1707 was the perceived need for Protestant states like Scotland and England to unite in the face of what was believed to be a serious and growing threat from Catholic powers to roll back the Reformation.[8] The danger that the exiled Stuarts might, with French help, succeed in recovering the throne was, for some time, thought to be very real. There were several Jacobite rebellions, the most significant of which were those in 1715 and, especially, 1745. The latter culminated in the bloody defeat of the Jacobites at the hands of the Hanoverian army under the Duke of Cumberland, after which Jacobitism ceased to present a credible political threat, however much a loose attachment to it may have persisted in some circles.[9]

Another cause for concern among Presbyterians was the fact that the Union of 1707 had subordinated their church to the authority of a largely Anglican parliament, which, it was feared, would meddle in the internal affairs of the Kirk.[10] The Covenanting wing of the Presbyterian church was in favor of a union with England, but this was to be a religious union on the basis of the Solemn League and Covenant of 1643, the agreement of Scottish Presbyterians with the then Long Parliament in England to extend Presbyterian church government to the rest of the British Isles. The Union of 1707, however, was of the wrong kind. Not only was the authority of the bishops in England left intact, but now a predominantly Anglican parliament, which included a bench of bishops in the House of Lords, might also legislate on matters touching the internal affairs of the Scottish Presbyterian Kirk. When the so-called Patronage Act was passed by the British parliament in 1712, it seemed to confirm the worst fears of Presbyterians about such interference, for the 1712 act restored the right of local patrons to present a candidate for a ministerial post, whom the congregation was then expected to accept. This procedure was contrary to Presbyterian principles of church government, which conferred the right of such appointments on presbyteries and synods. Furthermore, the patron, who was often a local grandee, might not even be Presbyterian himself. Patronage remained highly contentious in subsequent decades. It was the immediate cause of the Secession of 1733, when a group of opponents to patronage decided to form a separate church. It continued to be an issue until well into the second half of the eighteenth century, and even into the nineteenth century, when it led to the Great Disruption of 1843, the separation of the Presbyterian Free Church from the established Kirk.[11]

Deism

While the Catholic Stuarts in France, Episcopalians in Scotland, and the Anglican parliament in London represented external threats to the purity and independence of the Presbyterian Kirk, there were also forces that seemed to be eroding its principles from within, including blasphemy, various kinds of heresy, deism, and atheism.[12] Probably the most famous case of blasphemy was that of the Edinburgh student Thomas Aikenhead, who had been overheard referring to the Old Testament as "Ezra's Fables" and uttering other, similarly egregious insults to the Christian faith.[13] He was tried, found guilty on Christmas Eve of 1696, and hanged on 8 January 1697.[14] Aikenhead was prosecuted under a blasphemy law that had been passed by the Scottish parliament as recently as 1695, but his behavior had also been interpreted by contemporaries in broader terms, as an example of "deism" and atheism. Deism was an amorphous phenomenon that is hard to define.[15] Often it seems to have existed in the polemical literature of its critics rather than as a movement in its own right. It certainly did not stand for a coherent or uniform group of thinkers, but it was considered serious enough to be attacked, repeatedly and often at length. "Deism" usually signified a belief that Holy Scripture and all other forms of divine revelation were superfluous, because human reason was entirely sufficient for all human purposes, including salvation.

Although deism might not be explicitly atheistic, it was often considered to be atheistic by implication, to the extent that the two were regularly conflated. In an act of 4 January 1696, for example, the General Assembly referred to the "Atheistical Opinions of the Deists," stating that deists denied "all revealed religion, the grand mysteries of the Gospel . . . and, in a word, the certainty and authority of scripture revelation" and asserted "that there must be a mathematical evidence for each purpose, before we can be obliged to assent to any proposition thereanent, and that natural light is sufficient for salvation."[16] The problem with deists' excessive trust in human reason was not only that it reflected a failure to realize its insufficiency with regard to the goal that mattered most in life——namely, salvation, which, according to orthodox Presbyterians, was totally dependent on knowledge of the Gospel and divine grace; it was also that the principles of deists seemed to undermine directly some of the most foundational religious beliefs, especially in divine providence and the immortality of the soul. Thus, while Aikenhead was imprisoned in Edinburgh's Tolbooth jail, one of his fellow students, Mungo Craig, who had testified against him at his trial, rushed out a pamphlet entitled *A Satyr against Atheistical Deism*, in which he presented deism as a variety of the Epicurean ideas advanced by the ancient Roman philosopher-poet Lucretius in his poem *De rerum natura*. The deist, according to Craig, was "highly enamoured, with *Aristotel's Eternity of the World, paucis mutatis*, with *Epicure's* Denial of Providence, and the fortuitous production of the Universe, with his denial of the Souls Immortality; and especially with his Assertion that temporal Pleasure is the *Summum Bonum*, or last-end of Mankind." His exemplars were "the excellent Head-pice of *Malmsbury*"—namely, Thomas Hobbes, "the incomparable (for Nonsence to Wit) *Theologue and Philosoph Spinoʒa*, with *Lucretius Redivivus*, I mean *Blunt's Oracles of Nonsense*."[17] These views were regarded as dangerous, not only because they were incompatible with Scripture, but also because they were perceived to threaten secular morality. Without belief in an afterlife and divine providence especially, and the guarantee that all crimes would eventually be punished in the afterlife, morality in this life, it was feared, would be replaced by crude self-interest and libertinism. It is no accident, then, that "pneumatics," the philosophical discipline concerned with the investigation of all forms of spiritual being, including the human soul, was joined with ethics in a new chair of "Pneumatics and Ethics" at Edinburgh University in the early eighteenth century. Its first incumbent, William Law, had declared, some years before he was appointed, that "there can be no moral philosophy, which is firm, stable and joined to human nature, unless it is based not only on the existence and providence of a Deity, but also on the immortality of the soul and the rewards and punishments of a future life."[18]

Deistic ideas of this kind were hardly widespread in 1690s Scotland, yet they were available for those who had an interest in them, and they were available in the writings of "deists" themselves, not just in the shape of polemical summaries by their opponents. The library of the University of Edinburgh, for example, held copies of works by Hobbes and Spinoza. Herbert of Cherbury's *De veritate* had been acquired in 1672. Even after the restoration of Presbyterianism in 1690 controversial deistic works were being purchased, including in 1696 a copy of Charles Blount's notorious edition of *The First Two Books of Philostratus, Concerning the life of Apollonius Tyaneus*. Outside of the university, too, deistic publications were in circulation. Only a few months before Aikenhead's trial, a bookkeeper named John Fraser was accused by his landlord and landlady of defending blasphemous statements from Charles Blount's *Oracles of Reason*. Fraser claimed he had been misunderstood and had mentioned the views of Blount in conversation, without, however, approving any of them. Unlike Aikenhead, Fraser got off lightly and received only a largely symbolic punishment.[19] Yet the dangers of deism continued to be the subject of orthodox Presbyterian polemics. The writings of deists such as Herbert of Cherbury or Charles Blount, for example, were refuted by orthodox divines such as Thomas Halyburton (1674–1712), who had been a classmate of Thomas Aikenhead and in 1711 became professor of divinity at St. Andrews. Halyburton had apparently been tempted by "deistic" thoughts similar to those that had been the undoing of Aikenhead, although unlike Aikenhead he had overcome them, concluding that philosophy was of no real use in religious matters.[20] Later in the century Matthew Tindal's *Christianity as Old as Creation* (1731) reignited the debate. However exaggerated Presbyterians' fear of deism may have been, it is an important element in the explanation for the nervous and defensive attitude that characterized the Kirk after 1690.

"Enthusiasm" and Augustinianism

At the other end of the religious spectrum from deism were "enthusiasts" or "fanatics," those who appeared to reduce Christianity to a matter of immediate divine inspiration and paid no heed to any doctrinal standards or natural reason. These were often described as "Bourignonists," after the Flemish mystic Antoinette Bourignon (1616–80), whose eccentric theological beliefs were generally regarded as highly suspect, and which were condemned by the General Assembly in 1710.[21] Often the term "Bourignon-ism" was applied to a range of spiritualist authors, who, to varying degrees, downplayed the importance of doctrine in religion, emphasizing instead a practical "holiness of life" that was inspired by charity as the foundation of virtue and faith alike. They exemplified the broadly Augustinian revival that was particularly strong in France, but also exerted considerable influence throughout Europe. In seventeenth-century Scotland the most prominent exponents of these views were Episcopalians. Their ideas were, however, shared by some members of the restored Presbyterian church after 1690, who drew on the same intellectual currents as these Episcopalian authors.[22] One of the most influential of these from the Restoration period was the minister and professor of divinity at King's College in Aberdeen, Henry Scougal (1650–1678), author of *The Life of God in the Soul of Man*, which first appeared anonymously in 1677 and was reprinted frequently until well into the eighteenth and even nineteenth centuries.[23] In his work Scougal argued in very Augustinian terms that the condition of a human soul was to be "meas-ured by the object of his love":[24] the damned were distinguished by the fact that their "chief and supream affection is placed on Creatures like them-selves,"[25] whereas the saved directed their love toward God. This love of God was also the foundation of all secular virtue, because "a Soul possessed with Divine Love, must needs be inlarged towards all Mankind in a sincere and unbounded, affection because of the relation they carry unto God, being his Creatures, and having something of his Image stamped upon them: And this is that *Charity* . . . under which all the parts of Justice, all the Duties we our to our Neighbour are eminently comprehended."[26]

The possession of divine love was also the surest foundation of happi-ness in this world, the source of "the highest and most ravishing pleasures, the most solid and substantial delights, the humane Nature is capable of,"[27] whereas those whose affection was placed on creation rather than God were bound to be disappointed and afflicted with misery. Their pursuit of worldly goods was an expression of corrupt self-love, which in fallen man had replaced the love of God. Scougal's hostility to such self-love did not imply the ascetic rejection of ordinary pleasures: "Our natural affections are not wholly to be extirpated and destroyed, but only to be moderated and over-ruled by a superior and more excellent principle";[28] they were not "vitious or blameable" in themselves.[29] What made them vicious was the purpose for which they were used by the corrupt. They were not only going to be among the damned; their pleasures in this life were also invariably less solid and lasting than those of the faithful.

Similar to French Jansenist authors such as Pierre Nicole, Scougal believed that even the unregenerate were capable of something resembling virtue, at least externally, even if their motives were not sincerely and genuinely virtuous. Many people were sunk in "natural or animal life,"[30] and were governed by their most basic, sensual appetites, which were the cause of the many bad passions that rendered life miserable.[31] In that low state of existence, close to that of beasts, humans were motivated by a particularly crass self-love, but if "a man have but so much reason as to consider the prejudice which intemperance and inordinate lust doth bring unto his health, his fortune and his reputation, self-love may suffice to restrain him; and one may observe the rules of Moral Justice in dealing with others, as the best way to secure his own interest, and maintain his credit in the world."[32] Thus, even a corrupt motive, such as worldly self-love, could produce actions that were "fair imitations of Virtue and Goodness."[33] This kind of self-love moderated and guided by reason could even inspire an interest in piety and religion, though without the proper foundation of faith—namely, divine love—this interest would be limited to a narrow concern with defending the particular sectarian opinions of a specific church, something that was far removed from true Christian faith, and indeed irrelevant to it.

It is clear that doctrinal orthodoxy played a minor, subordinate role, if any, in Scougal's notion of religion. Faith was about the reform of the individual's heart and would be expressed in the redirection of his or her love away from creation toward God, and the performance of sincerely virtuous actions which were not motivated by any considerations of self-love, whether this was crass or refined by rational argument. In certain cases, however, self-interest could act as a sort of bridge to Christianity. One example was knowledge of the afterlife and the rewards and punishments that, according to Christian belief, were distributed within it. Of course, the fear of these punishments or the hope of attaining these rewards could not be the motive for a truly virtuous action, but they had the advantage of being suitable to influence a "carnal Mind," restraining natural men "from much Evil" and, in some cases, preparing an individual for "more ingenuous and kindly impressions."[34] Thus, the prospect of the afterlife could never "suffice, to make any person truly good," but it could serve an important educational purpose and create suitable conditions for the reception of divine grace.[35] The regeneration that issued in divine love was a gift of divine grace, yet the individual could prepare for it by means of regular exercises that helped to remove the objects of worldly love from view and reduced the stimulation of the corrupt passions that interfered with morality.

Scougal died in 1678, soon after his work had appeared, but his treatise continued to be influential, especially among Episcopalians in the northeast of Scotland, where Scougal had taught at the University of Aberdeen. Another example of this pietistic intellectual current is the work of George Garden (1645–1726), a professor of divinity at King's College in Aberdeen from 1680, until he was deprived of his professorship in 1697 for resisting the demands of the university visitation commission that he take the oath of allegiance to William and Mary and subscribe to the Westminster Confession.[36] In 1700 Garden published a book entitled *Comparative Theology* in which he drew on the same, broadly Augustinian, spiritualist intellectual traditions as Scougal. According to Garden, the "*Essence* of Religion, or of the Duty which Man owes to God, or which God requires of Man, in whatsoever State, whether that of Integrity and Innocence, or Restoration after the Fall, or consummated Felicity, doth solely consist in the LOVE of GOD."[37] When Adam and Eve abused the freedom that God had conferred on them and ate the forbidden fruit from the tree of knowledge, this was a sign that they had transferred their love from God to his creatures. It was only then that religion began to include more than the love of God and to extend to the various means by which "God was determin'd to restore Man,"[38] though these means were themselves secondary to divine love or charity, which was still the "Chief and Capital part of Religion."[39]

Garden was especially keen to emphasize that proper religious faith did not rest on the "Belief and Profession of . . . peculiar and distinguishing Doctrines."[40] The very fact that "almost every Sect of Christians, at least the Ruling Part among them" imposed such doctrines on its adherents, pretending that their acceptance was a "Necessary Condition of Communion," was evidence for the "*deplorable State of the Christian World.*" Doctrinal orthodoxy was not only unnecessary. The insistence on it was also detrimental to the "UNITY and LOVE, and CONCORD, which our Saviour so earnestly recommended to his Disciples," because it sowed the "Seeds of *Discord*, and *Division*, and Hatred among Christians."[41] For Garden, all elements of ecclesiastical institutions, such as clergymen, church buildings, sacraments, public worship, and church government, were potentially useful for leading individuals toward the charity that was the essence of faith, but they were "neither *necessary*, nor *sure* and *Infallible*."[42]

Garden's relaxed attitude toward creedal orthodoxy and forms of church government is surely related to his unsuccessful attempt to be reinstated as professor of divinity at King's College Aberdeen, in spite of his Episcopalian background and refusal to subscribe to the Westminster Confession of Faith. Yet, Garden's views are not simply a pragmatic response to his particular predicament. The arguments used by Garden predate the political and ecclesiastical situation in which he found himself after the Glorious Revolution, when the status of Episcopalianism in Scotland was uncertain for more than two decades, until the passing of the Toleration Act in 1712.[43] Scougal, for example, died a decade before the beginning of the Glorious Revolution. Also, Garden's difficulties are not sufficient to explain his adoption of these Augustinian and pietistic ideas, because other Episcopalians, who found themselves in very similar situations after 1690, held very different views from Garden. Garden's fellow Episcopalian John Cockburn, for example, was twice briefly imprisoned and deprived of his living in 1690 for failing to read the proclamation of William and Mary as sovereigns, but he was also a strong critic of Garden's reduction of faith to charity. Cockburn, who was Garden's brother-in-law and a cousin of Henry Scougal, and who had studied under Henry's father Patrick in Aberdeen, seems to have sympathized with pietistic forms of Christianity earlier in his career, but by the 1690s had become very critical of them, without, however, seeking to be accepted by the reestablished Presbyterian church of Scotland. Unlike Garden, Cockburn argued that true faith required a belief in the right doctrines, not just charity or purity of heart. In fact, "Error and false Doctrine"[44] was one of the main impediments to Christian faith: "The diversity of Opinions in matters of Faith and Religion should not perplex nor confound us, but rather excite us to search after the Truth more carefully, seeing we are expressly fore-warned of these things."[45] Scripture was the source of these saving truths: it was a "Rule of sound Doctrine, good Manners, and of Acceptable Worship and Service," the end of which was "*to make us wise unto Salvation*,"[46] a reference to 2 Timothy 3:15. "New Lights" (a term commonly used for opponents to creedal orthodoxy within the Presbyterian church in Ireland and Scotland and presumably applied in a similar sense by Cockburn) were always false. Unlike Cockburn, Garden thought of Scripture not as a source of doctrines or rules of worship, none of which, according to Garden, were an essential part of Christian faith. Scripture, in Garden's view, was a sort of practical manual for achieving regeneration and the redirection of the individual's love away from creation and toward God. Once a person had become a regenerate Christian, he or she no longer needed Scripture, but could "live a Christian life without these Sacred Books."[47]

Although Garden was an Episcopalian, orthodox Presbyterians perceived his views as a danger to their own beliefs. For one thing, the legal status of Episcopalians was unclear until 1712, and many, like Garden, were clamoring to be included in the established Church of Scotland. Also, views similar to those of Garden were believed to be present not only among Episcopalians. His "Bourignonist" disregard for the necessity of a doctrinal standard was to be found in other churches too, and might therefore just as easily infect the Presbyterian Kirk. The response of orthodox Scottish Presbyterians was to reassert, on several occasions, the centrality of the main doctrinal standard of their church, the Westminster Confession. This document had been drawn up in 1647, at a meeting of divines in London between 1643 and 1648. In 1690 it became the doctrinal standard of Presbyterianism in Scotland. The status of the Confession was reinforced by the Union with England in 1707, when the Act for Securing the Church in Scotland, which accompanied the Union, ruled that every professor, principal, regent, and master or other person bearing office in universities or burgh and parochial schools had to subscribe to it. In 1711 the terms for subscription became even stricter, when the General Assembly's "Act concerning Probationers, and Settling Ministers" determined that all those admitted to the ministry should accept the "whole doctrine" of the Westminster Confession of Faith, which, it was said, was "founded on the Word of God."[48]

There was, nevertheless, a growing tendency among eighteenth-century Presbyterians to emphasize practical holiness of life rather than adherence to the precise tenets of the Westminster Confession as the real essence of Christianity. This willingness to adopt a less rigid attitude on the need for doctrinal orthodoxy was not unique to Scotland. In the Presbyterian Church of Ireland, for example, the requirement for subscription to the Westminster Confession of Faith had been challenged, from the establishment of the general synod of Ulster in 1690 onward, and throughout the 1720s.[49] In England, too, it was questioned whether subscription to the so-called Thirty-Nine Articles of 1571 ought to be a condition for membership in the Anglican Church.[50] For orthodox Scottish Presbyterians, however, there could be no genuine religion without a clear doctrinal standard.

The Defense of Doctrine

The orthodox defense of the centrality of doctrine was based on federal theology, formulated by Johannes Cocceius (1603–1669), a Reformed theologian at the University of Leiden in the Low Countries. Leiden, like other Dutch universities, was a major destination for Scottish students in the second half of the seventeenth century. Many Scots received their theological training there. Dutch textbooks were used for teaching at Scottish universities.[51]

According to federal theology, God had concluded a juristic pact (*foedus*) with Adam in the state of innocence. The pact stipulated that Adam and his descendants would be rewarded with eternal life, if they obeyed God's commands in all their actions. In the state of innocence, therefore, humans had the opportunity to merit eternal life by means of their works, but this "Covenant of Works" was violated, and its promised rewards were lost as a result of original sin. Because Adam had entered this pact or covenant as the legal representative of his entire posterity, his guilt was transmitted to all his descendants, irrespective of whether they had committed any sins themselves.[52] Thomas Halyburton wrote, for example, "Had he [Adam] stood, in him we all had stood, and retained the Innocency and Integrity of our Natures, the Favour, Love and Kindness of Heaven," but once he had eaten the forbidden fruit, "our infected Parents transfer to us the *Infection of Sin*. Sin runs in a Blood, and our Natures have a natural Inclination *to Evil, only to Evil, and that continually*" (a reference to Genesis 6:5).[53] Humans were of course generally so corrupt that they would commit many particular sins during their lifetime, but the implication of federal theology was that even if somebody managed to abstain from sin throughout his or her life, he or she would still be damned, because of the taint of original sin that was passed on from Adam and Eve to all subsequent generations: "all Men and Women descending from Adam in an ordinary way have sinned, and thereby come short of the Glory of God."[54] The transmission of sin excluded Christ, who was not born "in an ordinary way," but in a non-natural and miraculous manner, from a virgin. Even the "Suckling upon the Breast" therefore was liable for damnation. Although children had not had the same opportunity to sin as adults, yet "Sin enough they have *derived to them from* Adam to *damn, to defile* them."[55] Similarly, heathens who had never had the good fortune of being introduced to the Gospel were rightly damned, though Halyburton did concede that their hell would not be as hot as that of nominal Christians, who had sinned "against the clear Light of the Gospel, not darkned by the Clouds of false Doctrines."[56]

Since humans could no longer achieve salvation through the original Covenant of Works, there had to be a new covenant, that of grace, by which humans were able to reverse the effects of the Fall. The main difference between the Covenant of Works and that of Grace was that in the latter humans did not merit eternal life on the basis of their actions. Nothing they did now could lift the guilt of original sin. It was only through the vicarious merit of Christ's death on the cross that salvation was now possible. Christ's intercession with God on behalf of the sinner was essential for that, but this intercession took place only in favor of those humans who had faith that was not superficial, but sincere. Halyburton argued that there were *"different Degrees of Conviction . . .* as to its *Clearness, Extent* and *Continuance,"*[57] and mere familiarity with the main points of Christian doctrine was not sufficient to bring about salvation, which required a thorough, heartfelt persuasion of the truth of the Gospel message. Although most humans knew in principle that sin was bad, their thoughts about it were "for the most part, like the Thoughts of a Man who never saw a Toad with a *full Light.*"[58] That is, even if they agreed that sin was loathsome, they often failed to appreciate properly quite how loathsome it was. Faith therefore required an effort of human understanding, but that effort, according to Halyburton, had to be supported by divine grace. Only then would the individual sinner realize the extent of his or her sinfulness, accept the impossibility of escaping from the consequences of sin by his or her own efforts, and finally turn to a belief in Christ as the sole remedy.

It was a matter of some dispute whether the Covenant of Works applied to those who were saved. When sinners violated the Covenant of Works they were rightfully punished for doing so, and when they abstained from violating it, they did so only out of fear of that punishment. Punishment, moreover, was an integral part of the law. But there was nothing meritorious in adhering to the commands of the Covenant of Works in order to escape its sanctions.

It was therefore argued, by some, that the faithful could not be acting from this kind of self-interested motive. Their whole nature had to have been transformed in such a way that they no longer needed the threat of punishment in order to act morally. These were the views of a group of clergymen within the Presbyterian church who became known as the "Marrow brethren." They were named after an English devotional text, Edward Fisher's *Marrow of Modern Divinity*, which had originally been published in England in 1645, but which had reappeared in Scotland in 1718 with a preface by the Presbyterian minister James Hog (or Hogg) of Carnock. The text became the subject of a controversy within the Presbyterian church when James Hadow, the principal of St. Mary's College at the University of St. Andrews, attacked the *Marrow* in a sermon before the synod of Fife, which approved of Hadow's statements, so much that they had them printed.[59] The resulting series of exchanges between Hog and Hadow culminated in 1720 in an act by the General Assembly against the *Marrow*. The "Marrow brethren," twelve ministers, had signed a representation against the act in May 1721, but the Assembly reiterated its condemnation in 1722. It had been especially concerned that the *Marrow* appeared to exempt believers from the obligations of the Law of Works, thus opening the door to antinomianism, the belief that the saved could act however they liked, because their faith in Christ freed them from all obligations imposed by the Covenant or Law of Works.[60] The critics of the *Marrow* argued that the acceptance of the Covenant of Grace did not make the duties of the Covenant of Works redundant. While Principal Hadow conceded that the defenders of the *Marrow* were not among the more extreme antinomians, who openly advocated libertinism, he feared that they were too careless about the possible implications of their opinions and the influence these might have on others.

The defenders of the *Marrow* had never meant to suggest that believers were licensed to behave like libertines. Their point was that true believers did not need to be put under any legal *obligation*, reinforced by penal sanctions and promises of rewards, in order to act morally. Performing virtuous deeds out of a hope of reward or fear of punishment could not be considered meritorious because it was based on selfish interest, and distinct from many forms of immorality only in that it was based on long-term, rather than short-term, self-interest. Therefore, while the faithful acted morally, this was not an effect of the Covenant of Works. They performed good works spontaneously, not because of some constraint or out of selfish motives. Indeed, the "legalism" of people like Hadow, their emphasis on the continuing relevance of the Law of Works for the faithful, seemed to turn the performance of particular actions into a condition of salvation, and thus to come dangerously close to a Roman Catholic defense of the efficacy of good works for salvation.

The Marrow brethren's beliefs reflected a concern with practical "holiness of life" that was also characteristic of more heterodox thinkers, but the Marrow brethren did not question the need for doctrinal orthodoxy that was part of federal theology. From the 1710s, however, there was a growing tendency within Presbyterianism to go further than the Marrow brethren in replacing the emphasis on the Westminster Confession with one on conduct and practical righteousness. A key figure among these heterodox Presbyterians was the controversial Glasgow professor of divinity John Simson.

The Trials of John Simson

John Simson was a professor of theology at the University of Glasgow when he became the subject of two separate investigations for heresy, in the 1710s and 1720s, in which he was accused of a variety of heterodox beliefs, ranging from Arminianism, Arianism, and Socinianism to deism. Simson had studied divinity in Glasgow and in the Netherlands, probably at the University of Leiden, and in 1705 was called to the parish of Troqueer, where he served as minister, until he was appointed to the Glasgow chair in 1708. Simson's case is important because it is one of the early indications of broader theological changes within the established Presbyterian Kirk after the Glorious Revolution; it reflects challenges to the status of the Westminster Confession, in particular, and a growing emphasis on conduct rather than doctrine as the essence of Christianity.

Simson was first accused of unsound teaching by an orthodox Edinburgh minister, James Webster, in 1710. In 1714 Webster repeated his charge against Simson, and the matter was then referred to a committee chaired by William Carstares, principal of the University of Edinburgh. The content of Simson's correspondence with another minister, Robert Rowan, published by Webster in 1716, seemed to confirm orthodox suspicions of him and fueled the controversy further. Simson's academic colleagues at the University of Glasgow and the presbytery of Glasgow stood firmly behind him, supporting Simson's claim that he had not put forward any heterodox ideas. When the supreme governing body of the Church of Scotland passed a resolution on the controversy in 1717, it issued only a mild reprimand for Simson. In the mid-1720s a new controversy erupted when the presbytery of Glasgow accused Simson of making statements with an Arian tendency and denying the divine nature of Christ in his lectures to divinity students. This time the consequences for Simson were more severe, though hardly devastating. He was suspended from teaching in 1729, but continued to hold his post as professor of divinity with full pay until his death in 1740.

A study of the Simson case by Anne Skoczylas describes meticulously the course of the legal proceedings against Simson and illuminates the role of the two rival political factions of the Argathelians (associated with the duke of Argyll) and the Squadrone volante (linked to the Duke of Roxburgh, among others) in the outcomes of the various trials.[61] Skoczylas has suggested that the mild sanctions imposed on Simson were a cause of deep frustration for hardline Presbyterians and helped to precipitate their exodus from the established church in the secession of 1733. That event, Skoczylas argues, removed from the Kirk many of its more "reactionary" members and prepared it for the triumph of "Moderatism," the synthesis of Christian religion and polite Enlightenment culture that characterized leading figures of the Kirk in the mid- to late eighteenth century, such as Hugh Blair, William Robertson, and Adam Ferguson. Simson, Skoczylas suggests, was controversial because he was more of a rationalist than his orthodox contemporaries. Simson was even described as a deist by his critics, who accused him of attributing "too much to natural reason and the power of corrupt nature,"[62] but accepting the term "deism" at face value in Simson's case is problematic. Simson himself denied being a deist. Given the fate of Thomas Aikenhead two decades before that may seem a matter of prudence rather than principle, but an examination of Simson's own writings strongly suggests that he did not in fact hold particularly deistic views. He did not, for example, believe that "the means of salvation . . . could be discovered through the exercise of reason," as has been suggested.[63] Simson believed that natural religion was not sufficient for salvation; it was useful only insofar as it could act as a stimulus for the further discovery, in revelation, of full religious truth.[64] Yet, even if Simson steered clear of deistic principles in his theological views, the implications of his theories, according to his opponents, were probably indistinguishable from those of professed deists, thus justifying the accusation of deism. In particular, Simson appeared to reduce Christian faith to a form of morality focused on human actions rather than salvation by faith. One reason for his emphasis on conduct was Simson's skepticism of federal theology, as it had been proposed by figures like Halyburton, for example, especially the belief that Adam had been the legal representative of all his descendants, and that this legal status meant that Adam's original sin was imputed to the rest of humanity. His most tenacious critic, James Webster, complained that Simson, in effect, denied that Adam "was our Federal Representative Head,"[65] because "the Professor [Simson] . . . makes our being corrupted, by our Descent from Adam, our Natural Head, to be the Effect of Adam's first Sin, by the Laws of Generation, and not as the Effect of our sinning in Adam, and breaking a proper Covenant made with him and us; and this is all the Imputation that the Professor owns."[66]

Simson was certainly more cautious about the extent to which Adam's own sin in the state of innocence was imputed to his descendants. Although it was possible for humans to be condemned by God for the original sin of their first ancestor, Simson thought it more likely that they would be damned on the basis of their own particular sins—a view that his opponents condemned as "GROSS ARMINIANISM."[67] Humans' sinfulness, Simson wrote, was the consequence of Adam's fall from grace, because it led to their corruption, which was then passed on to all of Adam's posterity through natural procreation, not because Adam represented all his descendants in a juristic sense. The main obstacle to salvation, therefore, was not the legal penalty for Adam's first sin, but the corrupt nature of humans, which prompted them continually to commit further particular sins. Justification had to concentrate on reforming the believer's conduct, rather than removing a legal penalty that had been imposed on all humans for Adam's violation of the original covenant. Simson's view seemed to imply that salvation was about acting morally and avoiding particular sins, not about belief in Christ's sacrifice for humankind. But, the orthodox argued, human actions, however good they were, could never free humans from the legal liability for original sin: moral actions might be fruits of justification, but they were not part of it.

It was feared by his opponents that Simson's argument turned saving faith into a matter of good works rather than faith, and thus, by implication, of moral philosophy and human merit rather than theological doctrines. Webster, for example, argued, that "justifying Faith," according to Simson, "includes in its formal Conception and Nature, Good Works and Obeidence." But this was "with the Professor's good Leave, SOCINIANISM, and condemned in the Scriptures which makes a continual Opposition of Faith to Works in the Business of Justification, which could not be, if Justifying Faith included Works in its very Nature."[68] The implications of Simson's views for the traditional, orthodox idea of the two covenants, of works and of grace, were profound. His views on these matters appeared to be the "Reverse of the Sentiments of Orthodox Divines," in that he denied the relevance of the Covenant of Works altogether, because humans, according to him, were condemned for their particular sins, not Adam's violation of the original covenant. At the same time, he seemed to make salvation depend on the reform of conduct, rather than faith in Christ, which would mean that in principle salvation was available to those who had never heard of the Gospel or refused to believe in it, such as "TURKS, JEWS and PAGANS."[69]

If salvation did not depend on the belief in truths that were revealed in the Gospel, then faith did not require an orthodox doctrinal standard, such as the Westminster Confession, for which absolute truth could be claimed, either. In one of his responses to Webster's accusations, Simson made clear that he attributed less importance to doctrine in religious faith than many of his opponents. He thought that the religious doctrines of the Presbyterian church were provisional and liable to change and modification, since human knowledge in divinity had not yet arrived at perfection and the "Spirit is not Restrained now more than formerly." Prohibiting debate of established doctrinal beliefs would, Simson said, be contrary to "*Protestant* principles." Instead, "Endeavours to find out what may yet ly hid in the Word of God, and to see *Gospel Truths* in a Clearer Light, and to Refute more Convincingly the Objections and Cavils of it's Adversaries, ought to be Encouraged, and even any thing *New* ought to be Calmly and Impartially Weighed."[70] Simson did not downplay the importance of divine assistance in achieving salvation. Humans were not able to achieve it by their own efforts. But this assistance did not necessarily require knowledge of the Gospel message, let alone adherence to an orthodox doctrinal standard such as the Westminster Confession. The purpose of Scripture was to provide humans with a kind of practical manual for spiritual regeneration, rather than a set of doctrines that had to be received and accepted by the understanding in order to be granted forgiveness. Simson was an influential figure among a group of younger, heterodox Presbyterians who were concerned with the question of doctrine from the 1720s.

2. Conduct and Doctrine

A number of heterodox Presbyterians held views similar to Simson's from the 1720s onward; Simson had taught some of them when he was professor of divinity at Glasgow, although others had not initially been influenced by him. They did not necessarily agree with Simson in every respect, but shared his skepticism of federal theology and creedal orthodoxy, and valued righteous conduct above doctrinal accuracy. Often, their emphasis on actions rather than doctrinal opinions in matters of religion can seem similar to the beliefs of deistic authors like Matthew Tindal, who said that "True Religion" consisted "in a constant Disposition of Mind to do all the Good we can."[1] However, the heterodox Presbyterians were not, as was Tindal, defending the sufficiency of natural reason for religion, but making a theological point about the role of conduct in justification, and reacting against the perceived excesses of "solfideism," the belief that salvation was achieved by faith alone, not works. They were very skeptical of the usefulness of natural reason in religious matters, and their theological views were indebted, rather, to the broadly Augustinian, spiritualist currents discussed in Chapter 1, which were prominent throughout European religious culture in the second half of the seventeenth century, and which were characterized above all by the idea that faith and virtue were founded on the right form of love, and that disordered forms of love or desire were to be blamed for irreligion and immorality alike. In late seventeenth-century Scotland, these views were exemplified most clearly by Episcopalian authors such as Henry Scougal and George Garden, and the evident interest of certain eighteenth-century heterodox Presbyterians in them is reflected in the republishing of Scougal's work with a recommendatory preface by a heterodox Presbyterian, William Wishart the younger, in 1739.[2]

This group of heterodox Presbyterians was active especially from the 1720s; most of its members were connected with each other, in various ways. Archibald Campbell (1691–1756), for example, who became professor of ecclesiastical history at St. Andrews in 1731, had been taught by Simson at Glasgow between around 1712 and 1718, when Simson was first put on trial.[3] Campbell openly associated himself with Simson in the 1733 preface of his *Enquiry into the Original of Moral Virtue*, claiming that Simson had read and approved of the manuscript of the book.[4] In 1735–36, Campbell's views were the subject of an inquiry by the Kirk's Committee for Purity of Doctrine.[5] Simson had also taught Francis Hutcheson, who became professor of moral philosophy at Glasgow in 1730. William Wishart the younger had been the only member of the Glasgow presbytery to oppose the prosecution of Simson in 1729, and published a defense, *A Short and Impartial State of the Case of Mr John Simson* (1729). When Wishart served as Scots minister in London from 1730 to 1737, he acted as Francis Hutcheson's book purchasing agent in the capital.[6] Wishart was also a member of the Rankenian Club in Edinburgh, an informal society named after its meeting place in Ranken's tavern, founded by Edinburgh divinity students around 1717. Its members included Robert Wallace (1697–1771), a clergyman who was later involved in a controversy with David Hume over the populousness of the nations of classical antiquity. Other influential members were George Turnbull, who taught at Aberdeen before obtaining a clerical appointment in the Anglican Church, and the Newtonian mathematician Colin MacLaurin. The Rankenians are known especially for their close interest in, and admiration for, the moral writings of the third Earl of Shaftesbury. They were also in regular contact with intellectual and literary circles in Ireland: they discussed critically the philosophical writings of the Irish bishop George Berkeley, and according to a much later author, Berkeley was "heard to say, that no persons understood his system better than this set of young gentlemen in North Britain."[7] They corresponded with the Irish Lord Viscount Molesworth, a Whig and author of the anti-absolutist *An Account of Denmark, as it was in the Year 1692*.[8] They were also known to have been skeptical about the value of creeds, such as the Westminster Confession, and followed the debates over subscription in Ireland, where it was not made mandatory for students entering the ministry until the 1690s, because the precarious existence of Irish Presbyterian congregations in the late seventeenth century had meant that no clear ecclesiastical structures had formed. The general synod of Ulster was established in 1690, but even then the requirement of subscription was contested and remained the subject of controversy at successive meetings of the Ulster synod and in pamphlets throughout the 1720s.[9] The critics of subscription in Ireland were not concerned merely to offer an attenuated and less rigid version of traditional Calvinist doctrinal beliefs, but to question the very place that doctrine—any doctrine—was thought to have in the process of justification and salvation. As one of the most prominent Irish opponents of subscription, John Abernethy, argued, no human being could pretend to understand matters of faith with absolute certainty, but nor was it essential for the members of a church to arrive at a consensus concerning either doctrines or rituals. The true, proper foundation of Christian belief was charity and personal righteousness, which could coexist happily with differences in judgment of the mysteries of faith.[10]

Although there was no similarly open controversy about subscription in the Scottish Presbyterian church of the early eighteenth century, the Rankenians in the 1720s and 1730s were not only in touch with Irish anti-subscriptionists but also deeply interested in the same questions concerning the relative importance of doctrinal orthodoxy and conduct in religion. Other figures in Edinburgh, outside of the Rankenian Club, held similar views, including the cautiously heterodox professor of divinity at the university, William Hamilton (1669–1732), whose only publication, a sermon preached in 1732 on *The Truth and Excellency of the Christian Religion*, shows a reluctance to insist on doctrinal orthodoxy as a condition of Christian faith.[11] Hamilton, moreover, taught William Leechman, who would become a close associate of Francis Hutcheson and, later, professor of divinity and principal of Glasgow University, where in his lectures he emphasized the importance of practical religion and was reticent on doctrinal matters. Like Simson, some heterodox Presbyterians were subjected to heresy trials or investigations by the Kirk, which had, however, little effect on those investigated. Campbell was made to answer to the Kirk's Committee for Purity of Doctrine in 1735–36, but was only urged to speak less incautiously. When William Wishart was nominated principal of Edinburgh University in 1736, the local presbytery tried, unsuccessfully, to block his appointment because they considered him theologically unsound.[12] The Glasgow presbytery tried and failed to prosecute Francis Hutcheson in 1738,[13] and the appointment of Hutcheson's protégé, William Leechman, to the Glasgow chair of divinity was fiercely opposed by the same body. In the end, Leechman and his gang of supporters outmaneuvered the presbytery by appealing to the next higher level in the ecclesiastical hierarchy, the synod of Glasgow and Ayr.[14]

Here, I shall first examine these heterodox Presbyterians' arguments about the importance of charity and a "moral culture," rather than doctrinal beliefs, for salvation, before turning to the orthodox position. Although it may seem paradoxical, the orthodox emphasized natural, reasonable religion to a much greater degree than clergymen like Wishart or Campbell, who are usually considered representatives of an early Enlightenment within the Church of Scotland. In fact, it was precisely because orthodox Calvinists emphasized the importance of doctrinal beliefs that they also defended a more extensive natural religion than their opponents. In the final part of this chapter I examine the thought of Francis Hutcheson. In many ways, Hutcheson exemplified the heterodox Presbyterian beliefs of thinkers like Wishart and Campbell, and yet his close relationship to these intellectual currents has so far received very little attention.

Charity and Doctrine

There were of course some differences between the respective views of these heterodox Presbyterians, but the similarities are at least equally striking. They all believed that Christian faith did not require a fixed, doctrinal standard such as that propounded in the Westminster Confession to which ministers, or anyone else, should be forced to subscribe; rather, the essence of true religion was charity, which was expressed in a practical holiness of life that set apart the genuinely faithful from hypocrites, whose observance of religious principles was superficial and insincere. A full, complete knowledge of the matters of faith which theological doctrine referred to was anyway impossible in this life, because of the weakness of human understanding. A passage from Paul's first letter to the Corinthians, 13:12, was often cited in this connection: "For now we see through a glass, darkly; but then face to face: now I know in part; but then shall I know even as also I am known." The Irish nonsubscriber John Abernethy, for example, who was also a friend and associate of the moral philosopher Francis Hutcheson, made this passage the subject of a sermon in which he argued that all theological doctrine, like that enshrined in the Westminster Confession, should be open to inquiry and debate. Our understanding of religious truths in this life was necessarily limited and imperfect, though it progressed over time, from one historical age to the next. This gradual improvement was believed to be part of a divine providential plan to reveal successively more and more extensive truths until we acquired a complete understanding of matters of faith in the afterlife. For now, however, any belief relating to questions of faith had to be provisional. That ignorance was not a problem, because God did not "absolutely require of us as the Condition of pleasing him an infallible Certainty in understanding his Word and the strict Conformity of our Sentiments to the Truth: If it were so how unhappy would the condition be of the best upon earth, since all are liable to errors; and God knows, they are inevitable!"[15] To be justified before God and achieve salvation, there was no need for an exact and complete knowledge of any particular truths. What mattered was charity, not in its more specific sense as charity toward the poor, but in a much wider sense as the selfless love of God and one's neighbor, as opposed to the love of self that was characteristic of fallen humankind. "The love of God and our fellow creatures," wrote George Turnbull, "is the whole duty of man."[16]

That charity was a far more important and valuable bond among Christians than exact agreement on particular points of doctrine. Even within the same church differences of opinion over doctrines were acceptable. This did not mean *any* belief could be tolerated, but there was no need to restrict Christianity to a single set of doctrinal opinions. This is what the Rankenian Robert Wallace, for example, argued in a manuscript treatise, written sometime before 1720, "Against imposing creeds of confessions of faith."[17] Uniformity of beliefs and practices, Wallace observed, might be desirable, but it was not feasible at present, when Christians often differed over doctrinal issues, each side being convinced that its own "sceme" was exclusively true. In the meantime, we should follow the advice of the apostle Paul, who had recommended "love and charity and forbearing of one another under different opinions."[18] A rigid insistence on doctrinal orthodoxy only bred sectarian conflict, without contributing anything to establishing religious truth. Yet that was precisely how religion was generally taught. The "Care of Parents," as Wishart complained, "or Instructors, about the religious Part of Education, is almost wholly spent in inculcating upon young Ones the *Shibboleth* of a Party; making them acquainted with, and instilling into them a Regard for the particular Doctrines or peculiar Forms of their own Sect; in which there may oft-times be found a Mixture of Things absurd or trifling."[19] George Turnbull referred in a similar vein to the "proud domineering pedantic Priests whose interest it is to train up the youth in a profound vener-ation of their Senseless metaphysical Creeds and Catechisms,"[20] and Wallace suggested that the concern for doctrinal orthodoxy represented a historical aberration from the original teachings of Christ. Like other Protestant authors, he argued that the church had been corrupted in late antiquity, when practical holiness of life had been displaced by a rigid and misguided emphasis on doctrine. That corruption had led to the emergence of the papal church and Roman Catholicism, but Wallace believed also that even Protestant churches had not been completely purged of that fault since the Reformation.[21] If charity were established universally (an aim that Wallace regarded as unre-alistic) all religious sectarian strife would thereby cease, and Christianity would be returned to its original foundation.[22]

The same love or charity that was the essence of religion was also the foundation of secular virtue. Wishart wrote that charity included "Universal Benevolence; and the prevailing Love of Goodness,"[23] which led us to a sincere desire for the welfare and happiness of other rational beings. The "true love of God" was "no other than the highest exercise of that same prin-ciple of benevolence and the love of goodness which leads us to be kind and beneficent to our fellow creatures."[24] Or, as he wrote elsewhere, the "Great Design of Christianity" was the promotion of both "Virtue & Charity,"[25] while his fellow-Rankenian Robert Wallace said that Christianity, being founded on the "love of God and men," taught "substantial goodness and solid virtue."[26] William Hamilton made a very similar point: the Gospel tied us "in the strongest Manner to all Sort of Acts of Benevolence; Love and Goodness towards our Fellow Creatures,"[27] and Archibald Campbell declared that no article of faith or ritual was of any value that did not, above all, "teach us to *deny ungodliness, and worldly lusts, and to live soberly, righteously, and godlily*."[28] The cause of immorality, all these theorists argued, in profoundly Augustinian terms, was the same as that of irreligion—namely, a disordered form of love that directed the human passions and affections away from God and one's fellow human beings toward selfish ends, and which was itself a consequence of the corruption of human nature because of original sin.

Religion and virtue were so closely associated with each other by these heterodox Presbyterians that they considered morality an essential means of obtaining salvation. Turnbull believed that the "sincere and steady practice of virtue is every where inculcated by our SAVIOUR and his Apostles as what only can recommend with any advantage to the Divine favour and approbation here, or hereafter."[29] Similarly, Abernethy argued that the "condition of our title to the final happiness Christ has promised to his disciples is a persevering stedfastness in obeying the immutable moral laws of God; or in practising the virtues of sobriety, godliness, justice and mercy."[30] This emphasis on the role of conduct was problematic and somewhat controversial, because it seemed perilously close to a Catholic belief in the efficacy of morality, or "good works," for justification and salvation. Campbell even used the term "good works" to describe the purpose of Christian religion.[31] Although an orthodox Presbyterian would never doubt that Christians ought to be as moral as corrupt human beings could possibly be, salvation itself was not achieved by being moral. Rather, it required the knowledge of and sincere belief in certain religious truths, above all the importance of Christ's sacrifice on the cross, because sinners were not justified and saved by their actions. No matter how virtuous an individual was, everyone had committed some sins and therefore merited damnation. And since the taint of original sin was transmitted from Adam and Eve to all of humankind, even the newborn child who had not yet had an opportunity to commit any particular trespass was guilty. Divine forgiveness could be obtained only by faith. However, when authors such as Campbell spoke of the role of "good works" in salvation, they did not mean that actions themselves justified sinners, but that virtuous actions were a necessary expression of the kind of reform of human nature and of its affections that was the real condition of salvation—which did not exclude the possibility that actions which were outwardly indistinguishable from virtuous deeds might be the result of corrupt motives, and therefore not contribute to salvation.

Such a change in attitude was achieved incrementally, over a long period of time. Heterodox Presbyterians like Wishart and Wallace were keen to separate themselves from revivalist "enthusiasts" who believed that religious belief was brought about by a sudden, dramatic transformation. They were skeptical of the conversion stories of revivalists. Although they believed that faith required a transformation of the believer's nature, they emphasized the gradual and non-miraculous nature of this regeneration, which they described as the product of a long process of education and discipline, a "culture" or "culture of the mind," quite unlike the abrupt transition expected by the revivalists. The "culture" did not even have to be complete in temporal life for it to contribute to salvation. As Wishart observed, for example, "When first we receive the happy turn and disposition, to set about this culture and improvement in good earnest, we are then *entered* on the true way to happiness: but a great part of our work remains, to carry forward these good beginnings."[32] Nobody would acquire a morally perfect character before they died; what mattered for the purposes of divine forgiveness was the sincere repentance that stimulated the desire for regeneration, and the constant effort that an individual devoted to his or her moral improvement.

The dispositions that underpinned a moral character were formed gradually, through constant practice, until they grew "into a fixed habit and principle."[33] Virtue did not necessarily depend on understanding why a certain way of acting was virtuous. Indeed, theoretical, or "speculative," truths about morality were usually powerless to change the dispositions that were the cause of moral and immoral conduct alike. It was the habitual nature, and hence stability, of a person's dispositions toward virtue, not the decision to act according to virtue on particular occasions, that made this person properly moral. The idea of virtue as a habit may seem odd, because it implies that virtuous conduct is not the result of a deliberate, conscious choice, but an unreflective and almost involuntary act. It could therefore be asked whether a habitual action of this kind could be morally imputed to the agent. Yet, the formation of these habits involved persistence on the part of the agent, over a long period of time, and it was this sustained, concentrated effort by the individual that made such a "culture of the mind" genuinely meritorious.

The more frequently virtuous actions were performed, the easier it became to perform them: "Virtue," wrote Turnbull, "must become natural in the same way that any habit becomes natural, that is, by practice, before it can have that pleasant effect in its exercises, which that alone can have, that is, become habitual or natural, in proportion as it is such."[34] The more progress an individual had made toward acquiring these moral habits, the more spontaneous and unforced—and, in that sense, sincere—did virtuous conduct become. First, however, the habitual attachment to vice had to be broken before moral reform was possible. He also stated,

> As in learning any art or science we distinguish two periods, the first
> of which is harsh, and attended with a great mixture of uneasiness,
> but the other exceeding pleasurable: so is it with regard to virtue, the
> first steps to it, like the first steps towards science or art, are painful,

laborious, and in a great measure irksome; especially when the appetites to be subdued are very imperious, and the evil habits to be
destroyed are very firmly rooted; but as science or art becomes
easier and pleasanter in proportion to the advances made in it, so
likewise does virtue; and, at last, when any considerable degree of
perfection is attained to in it, then all goes very smoothly and very
easily on.[35]

In the initial stages of moral reform the motives for acting according to virtue
need not even be entirely virtuous. We might begin by doing the right thing
for the wrong reason.[36] Sincerely moral dispositions might take root only after
the habit of acting according to virtue had, to a great extent, already been
established for other reasons. The fear of some sort of punishment, especially,
could serve as a kind of educational tool to break our bad habits when more
genuinely moral motives were still too weak to direct us toward virtue.

The most powerful threat of punishment, at least in theory, was that of
divine retribution in the afterlife. Fear of the afterlife was not itself morally
meritorious, let alone did it contribute to justification, but it could help in
breaking our habitual dispositions toward immorality and allow more
genuine virtue to emerge. This idea was somewhat contentious, because the
motives of actions inspired by self-interested fear could seem very different
in kind from those of sincerely moral behavior. French Jansenist theorists
like Blaise Pascal or Pierre Nicole, characterized by Jennifer Herdt as "hyper-
Augustinians," thought that the transition from hypocritical to sincere virtue
involved such a fundamental transformation of a person's basic dispositions
that it could be achieved only through the extraordinary workings of divine
grace, not by natural, incremental means.[37] "Hyper-Augustinian" authors
did not believe that performing outwardly virtuous actions for the wrong
motives could help to develop a truly moral and virtuous character, let alone
contribute to justifying a sinner before God. Such an insincere type of virtue
might have some very limited benefit, because it helped to preserve order
and discipline within human society, but it was worthless with regard to the
goal that really mattered to humans—namely, salvation. The same general
sentiment was shared by evangelical revivalists, for whom there were no
differences in degree between a corrupt and a regenerate character, in whom
the transformation was instant, complete, and miraculous. In contrast to
these "hyper-Augustinians," heterodox Presbyterians, including Wallace or

Wishart, believed there to be a much greater continuity between the hypo-critical virtue inspired by fear, and the real virtuous conduct that was the mark of a regenerate character. They appear to have believed that a more gradual, natural evolution from insincere to genuine virtue was possible because, for them, virtuous dispositions were always part of the natural constitution of humankind, though they were, under normal circumstances, too weak to overcome the contrary impulses of the corrupt passions that had gained the upper hand since original sin. The self-interested fear of the after-life therefore did not have to be transmuted, by some mysterious process, into a more properly virtuous motive; rather, this fear created a sort of protective shell, within which the genuinely virtuous dispositions could develop and grow in strength, until they were able on their own to counter-balance the corrupt passions, and the prospect of an afterlife was no longer needed as a crutch for virtuous conduct.

These heterodox Presbyterians also thought that knowledge of the afterlife could not be derived from unassisted, natural reason alone; it required some form of divine revelation, such as the Gospel. Campbell, for example, commented that the works of the best pagan philosophers of clas-sical antiquity made it clear how far unaided reason fell short of proving the two truths of religion that were most important for morality: the immortality of the soul and the government of the world by divine providence. The philosophers of ancient Rome and Greece had often suspected that the soul survived the death of the body, but when called upon to prove it, either produced absurd arguments, or were forced to admit their inability to provide conclusive evidence.[38] In these matters humankind therefore was dependent on "foreign instruction" by divine revelation, especially Scripture.[39] The writings of the prophets and the apostles were far superior to those of any pagan philosopher and, indeed, anything natural reason had to offer. George Turnbull argued similarly that even the best "heathen moralists" of classical antiquity, such as Socrates or Cicero, had struggled to explain to the mass of the population why they ought to be virtuous. The Gospel, however, "sets before us certain truths which are powerful motives to moral obedience; that the Law, or Light of Nature, cannot discover"—namely, the immortality of the soul and divine justice in an afterlife.[40] Leechman, professor of divinity at Glasgow University from 1744, is another example. He wrote that pagan notions of a supreme deity were insufficient to promote "virtuous practice in the common train of life."[41] The writings of the heathen philosophers did "contain many excellent truths, fine sentiments, and precepts both of the moral and devout kind, which are very worthy of the serious attention and perusal of Christians,"[42] but the problem was that these philosophers lacked all effective means of inculcating their principles in the minds of their fellow heathens, because they had no knowledge of the superior religious truths vouchsafed in Christian revelation concerning the afterlife. And once Christianity had been introduced into the world, there had not been "any one kingdom, great or small, any one city, village, or community" that had "attained to just notions of the Divine perfections, to comfortable views of Divine providence, to purity of worship, *to a perfect system of morals, or to steady hopes of immortality, without the aid of Gospel-light* [my italics]."[43]

Although pagan philosophers had often invented various theories to buttress morality, these were generally so abstruse that they were of little use to an uneducated "plowright" or "mechanick."[44] The writings of Plato and other philosophers were "only in the Hands of the Learned," and ordinary people drew no advantage from them, whereas the "*moral Doctrines contained in the* Bible, *are delivered in so plain and familiar a Manner that they are adapted to the Understanding of* common *Men, and are of* publick Use and Benefit."[45] George Turnbull wrote that the doctrine of an afterlife in which rewards and punishments would be distributed was so useful because it was sufficiently clear and striking to "excite the inferior herd of mankind to the practice of virtue,"[46] even those who could not follow the complex arguments of philosophers like Socrates. The social usefulness of religion was so great that pagan rulers in classical antiquity often "pretended to inspiration, or an extraordinary intercourse with some revered Deity, or heavenly Being," though none of their fictitious religious beliefs could match the political and social benefits of Christianity.[47] Of course, Christianity did not need to be justified by its utility, but its superior advantages, compared with those of pagan religion, offered further proof of its divine origin and truth.

Skepticism about the capacity of natural reason to prove the immortality of the soul in particular was not new. The broadly Aristotelian philosophy at the University of Padua in the Italian Renaissance, including the *De Immortalitate Animae* (1516) of Pietro Pomponazzi,[48] who maintained that natural reason was insufficient to inform humans with any certainty about the afterlife, is an example. There were also the controversial writings of Giulio Cesare Vanini around the turn from the sixteenth to the seventeenth century.[49] In his 1689 *Essay concerning Human Understanding* John Locke had argued that reason did not inform us of the nature of the soul.[50] And in Enlightenment Scotland the most famous statement on this matter was probably that of David Hume, who declared that there were no philosophical, rational grounds for believing in the immortality of the soul.[51] Although Hume's skepticism on this question was extreme, it was not that far removed from the earlier views of several of the Rankenians, or of Archibald Campbell, who also believed that natural reason did not offer any certainty concerning the nature of the soul and its continued existence after death.

Natural Religion and the Orthodox Defense of Doctrine

The more conventional view, however, was that divine justice in an afterlife and the survival of the soul after death were, indeed, known through natural reason, and did not require revelation. The arguments from natural reason for the immortality of the soul were usually believed to rest on proof of its immaterial or spiritual nature. Spiritual beings, such as the soul, it was argued, were different in kind from material bodies. The latter were extended in space; they were composed of many smaller, material parts; and they ceased to exist when they were disaggregated into their constituent elements. Thus, the human body was a material being of this kind, and death its physical dissolution. The soul, like all spirits, on the other hand, was a simple, indivisible substance that could be destroyed only by means of complete annihilation, not through disaggregation into smaller parts. A complete annihilation of any created substance, however, was not possible within the ordinary course of nature, and there was thus no reason to suppose that the physical disintegration of the body in death would necessarily affect the continued existence of the soul.[52] Natural reason therefore led us to believe that the soul would survive the dissolution of the material body.

There were also strong moral arguments for the existence of some system of divine justice after death. It was a matter of fact that, in this life, sometimes the virtuous suffered undeserved misfortune, while the wicked prospered. If there were no guarantee that eventually all would receive the rewards or punishments they deserved, then everyone would end up pursuing his or her narrow self-interest, and morality in this life would soon be reduced to "Epicurean" considerations of crude utility. It would also be difficult, if not impossible, to reconcile the absence of such rewards and punishments with belief in the providential government of creation by a perfectly just and omnipotent God. Without a future state it was not clear what sanctions, if any, reinforced moral obligation in this life.[53] Vicious behavior might be attended by some kind of disadvantage on earth, especially in the long run, as it provoked hostility from others, but this disadvantage was a result of reciprocity, not a punishment that was inflicted visibly by a superior in each particular case. John Locke had been aware of this problem when he put forward his "strange doctrine"[54] that, in the state of nature, prior to the institution of a human sovereign, "every Man hath a Right to punish the Offender, and be Executioner of the Law of Nature," precisely because the existence of divine punishments in an afterlife was not known without an explicit act of revelation from God.[55] Another representative of this concern was the German jurist and philosopher Samuel Pufendorf, whose textbook on natural law, the *De Officio Hominis et Civis* (1673), was widely used in moral philosophy courses at Scottish universities in the first half of the eighteenth century. Pufendorf, too, believed that the immortality of the soul was not evident from natural reason, but this meant that the law of nature had no proper sanctions attached to it: "the impious" were often "abundantly provided with those things by which the vulgar measure happiness." The disadvantages the wicked suffered occasionally were not clearly connected with their actions, and were not, therefore, genuine and effective punishments, the purpose of which was to signal the displeasure of a legitimate superior.[56] The remedy, according to Pufendorf, was to establish a state, but the absence of punishments prior to the creation of a human sovereign was considered dangerous, because it conjured up the anarchic state of nature associated with the "Epicurean" theory of Thomas Hobbes.[57] The German polymath and philosopher Gottfried Wilhelm Leibniz, for example, commented:

> I find it very bad that celebrated people, such as Pufendorf . . ., teach that one knows the immortality of the soul, as well as the pains and rewards which await us beyond this life, only through revelation . . . All doctrines of morals, of justice, of duties which are based only on the good of this life, can be only very imperfect. Take away the [natural] immortality of the soul, and the doctrine of providence is useless, and has no more power to obligate men than the gods of Epicurus, which are without providence.[58]

Similarly, in the first half of the eighteenth century, orthodox Scottish Calvinists often argued that a coherent theory of natural morality had to include punishments that were inflicted by God in the afterlife. A crime might be attended with some disadvantages in this life, especially in the long term, but these disadvantages were not real punishments, because they were just general consequences of certain types of action, not evidently imposed by God in each particular case. The orthodox John Erskine, for example, argued that moral duty required the threat of sanctions. It was not enough, he wrote, to rely on a "natural tendency to excite in us love to God, or benevolence to men, or some other particular duty,"[59] as Wishart or Campbell had done. Although something might naturally prompt us to act morally, a natural *effect* of this kind did not amount to a proper moral *duty:* any duty required sanctions that were not just natural consequences of certain actions, but were evidently inflicted by the respective legislator in each particular case, outside of the normal course of nature. In this life, however, there were no guaranteed punishments of this kind for immorality. If humans were to be under a moral obligation by nature, it was essential that they were conscious of the rewards and punishments of the afterlife without being informed of these though divine revelation. Erskine set out to prove precisely this in his 1741 dissertation, "The Law of Nature sufficiently Promulgated to Heathens," which was directed against Archibald Campbell. Heathens were capable of discovering the immortality of the soul by means of their unassisted reason.[60] Although some pagan beliefs concerning the afterlife, such as the transmigration of souls, might seem absurd, these were only signs that "they [the pagans] advanced things in relation to that notion [of immortality] which reason could not support," not that the notion of immortality itself could not be supported by natural reason.[61]

Heterodox Presbyterians tended to believe that a notion of moral obligation in this life did not necessarily require knowledge of the rewards and punishments of the afterlife: there was plenty of evidence in this life that certain kinds of actions merited divine approval or retribution, even if divine justice was not always complete before death. One such sign of divine approval was the fact that, on the whole, acting morally was in the interests of the agent. Although there might be occasional exceptions, honesty was generally the best policy. This convergence of virtue with utility was morally significant, because it was thought to be willed by God and to reflect his providential ordering of the world. Contrary to later utilitarian moral theories, utility in this case was considered to be good, not because it benefited the individual, but rather, morally good actions also happened to be

useful because God, who was all-powerful and just, had arranged nature
accordingly. Moral actions would not be moral if they were performed
simply out of a desire to further one's own interests, but the fact that moral
actions generally promoted those interests was an indication that they
enjoyed divine approval. The universe, wrote Turnbull, was "governed by
excellent general laws," which meant that, by and large, virtue was rewarded
with prosperity and well-being, for "if we own a blind fortuitous dispensation of goods, and much more, if we own a malignant disposition of them
more in favour of vice than of virtue, we deny a providence or assert bad
administration," and to do so would reflect an "Epicurean" belief that the
world was governed by chance.[62] Occasionally, moral duties and interests
might conflict, but these instances were not failures on the part of God to
associate virtue and interest with each other consistently. They were partly a
reflection of the inevitable imperfections of creation, which, on the scale of
being, was necessarily inferior to the creator. They were also intended by
God as tests of our goodness and strength of moral character. Although
interest was largely served by being moral, it must never become the reason
why moral actions were performed. Those situations in which interest and
morality diverged were opportunities for us to prove that we were capable of
being virtuous from disinterested motives. They were therefore part of a
theodicy, or theory designed to make sense of the presence of evil and hardship in a world created by a supposedly omnipotent and benevolent God.

The most famous theodicy of the early eighteenth century is that of
Leibniz, which first appeared in 1710,[63] but the theodicy of figures such as
George Turnbull is closer to the views of Leibniz's contemporary, arch-
bishop William King of Dublin, who published his influential treatise
De Origine Mali (On the Origin of Evil) in 1702, some years before the publication of Leibniz's *Theodicy*.[64] King's views were echoed and reinforced by
the Englishman John Clarke, the younger brother of Samuel Clarke, whose
correspondence with Leibniz was published in England in 1717. John Clarke's
Boyle lectures, published in 1719–20, were known to Scots including George
Turnbull, who explained that he closely followed Clarke's views.[65] According
to Clarke, evil and hardship in creation were not a sign of God's malevolence
or weakness, but a positive opportunity to exercise moral choice, without
which virtue would not represent a real achievement at all. God's plans were
to some degree inscrutable and did not have to be entirely comprehensible
for humankind to believe in a divine providence, for even if not everything

could be explained in providential terms, the evidence within the natural order for God's benevolence and justice was overwhelming.

In addition, it was argued, some natural rewards and punishments of a certain kind were distributed in this life, and it was not necessary to wait until after death. These were not perhaps rewards and punishments in the strict sense of the word, because their connection with certain types of conduct was not immediately evident, and God did not mete them out directly and publicly. They were, in fact, pleasures and pains within the mind, which were founded in human nature, as it had been created by God. They were thus part of God's providential order, too, but unlike the external, worldly benefits that usually accompanied a life of virtue, these pleasures and pains within the mind occurred invariably, without any exception at all: "We are so constituted," wrote George Turnbull, "that the exercises of virtue, and the conscience of it, are our highest enjoyment, and vice, whatever pleasure it may afford of the sensual kind, always creates bitter remorse, and almost always great bodily disorder."[66] Although these pleasures and pains were not strong enough to deter individuals from wrongdoing, they were a more than sufficient indication of the kinds of action that merited divine approval. Even without knowledge of the rewards and punishments of the afterlife, it was clear to all humans, including non-Christians, that certain actions were not morally indifferent.

The reason, however, for orthodox thinkers to argue that the immortality of the soul was part of natural religion was not only that they thought this was essential for having a coherent notion of moral obligation. Their arguments about the afterlife and natural religion were also closely related to their theological views on salvation. All humans, including non-Christians, had to be able to realize their guilt before God and the inadequacy of their own efforts for achieving salvation. If heathens did not recognize their utter dependence on divine forgiveness, they would not feel compelled even to seek the remedies offered to humankind in the Gospel, let alone adopt them. It was precisely because these thinkers were orthodox that they emphasized the importance of natural religion for secular morality. If secular morality required knowledge of the Gospel, pagans could not be justly damned. In the state of innocence, of course, obedience to the natural moral law (or "Law of Works") would have been sufficient to merit eternal life, but since the fall from grace no human being had been capable of living in a perfectly moral way: everybody had committed sins, any of which deserved to lead to damnation. Nobody could achieve salvation by means of works any longer. It was achieved by means of faith, which was founded not in a certain set of dispositions or "love," as heterodox thinkers believed, but in the sincere assent of the understanding to certain key truths, which were founded on Scriptural revelation. This was why orthodox authors considered it so important to have a clear standard of doctrinal truth, such as the Westminster Confession. However important charity was, it was not sufficient by itself, but had to be informed by correct beliefs in order to play any part in salvation. The main belief which secured divine pardon was that "all saving mercies are dispensed through the blood and merits of Christ."[67] Intellectual assent to the truth of Christ's sacrifice produced trust (*fiducia*), the fruits of which were holiness of life and virtue. While Erskine believed that faith was joined to practical virtue, he was concerned to show that this practical virtue was not the essence of Christian faith, but its consequence. The assent to the key truths of revelation had of course to be sincere and heartfelt. It was possible to hold entirely orthodox ideas in the mind and yet be a "self-deceiver," who lacked true faith, because the appropriate dispositions in the heart were missing.

Although this may appear to be counterintuitive, orthodox Calvinists like Erskine, therefore, defended a much more extensive idea of natural, reasonable religion than heterodox fellow-churchmen such as Wishart, Wallace, Campbell, or Turnbull, who are more likely to be considered representatives of an early Enlightenment within the Scottish Presbyterian Kirk. Yet it was precisely because they were orthodox that theorists like Erskine emphasized natural religion, believing that without knowledge of the immortality of the soul and the existence of an afterlife, moral obligation in this life was incomplete. Moreover, unless this afterlife was known from natural reason, without the assistance of revelation, pagans could not be held accountable before God for their crimes. They would not be aware of their guilt, and they would not be impelled to seek out and accept the remedies offered by Christ in the New Testament. Natural religion, for such orthodox theorists, was an important stepping-stone on the way toward accepting the superior truths of the Gospel. Salvation was then achieved through sincere faith in these truths. The heterodox Presbyterians discussed here, however, believed that it was not the sincere belief in certain doctrinal truths that procured salvation, but the reform and regeneration of the believer's nature. Unlike revivalists and "hyper-Augustinian" authors, however, they did not believe that the change that was necessary was brought about by some instant, emotionally wrenching transformation, but incrementally, in a process of moral culture. Their concern was to avoid the extremes of rigid doctrinal orthodoxy on the one hand, and religious "enthusiasm" on the other. Although human efforts were necessary to achieve a reform, they were not in themselves sufficient. Heterodox theorists believed, as much as the orthodox, that salvation was impossible without divine grace and support. The revelation of the immortality of the soul, which was not known from natural reason, was one way in which the Gospel supported the "moral culture" that was the essence of genuine, salvificatory piety. Although it was not meritorious to act out of fear of the punishments in a future state, the prospect of these punishments fulfilled an important practical and educational purpose. It provided a balance to the corrupt impulses of human nature, and allowed the morally better dispositions that were present to gain in strength through exercise. Good actions could eventually become habitual, so that they no longer required the additional support of a future state.

Christianity and the Culture of Mind: Religion and Francis Hutcheson's Moral Philosophy

The heterodox authors discussed were associated with the most important figure of the early Enlightenment in Scotland, Francis Hutcheson. His relation to their theological outlook is examined in this section. In modern literature on the history of philosophy, Francis Hutcheson is known mainly for his idea of a "moral sense," a natural capacity of humans to distinguish between moral and immoral qualities, similar to the ability of the eye to distinguish between different colors. Much of the discussion on his thought has focused on the epistemological status of the judgments made by this moral sense. In particular, it has been asked whether the judgments of the moral sense are best described as noncognitivist and matters of feeling, or whether they represent a form of "moral realism," involving the perception of real qualities of external objects and actions. However, James Harris has argued convincingly that the epistemological status of moral judgments was not Hutcheson's main concern in his moral philosophy. He suggests that Hutcheson was interested primarily in the *naturalness* of morality, the degree to which the preference for good over bad actions was a natural feature of the human constitution.[68] Hutcheson considered morality to be part of the natural order that had been created by God and that reflected his justice and benevolence toward humanity. The reality of moral distinctions seems to have been regarded as self-evident by Hutcheson. The problem, however, was moral motivation. How could individuals be made to act morally, consistently, and for the right reasons? Exercising the moral sense and being virtuous, Hutcheson argued, produced feelings of pleasure in the agent that were far superior to the crass pleasures that followed from the satisfaction of selfish and immoral desires—and yet many people chose to act immorally nevertheless.

One of Hutcheson's concerns in his moral theory was to refute the Anglo-Dutch satirist Bernard Mandeville's infamous interpretation of human society in his *Fable of the Bees* (1714), and his view of moral actions as forms of selfishness (or "self-liking"), masked by hypocrisy.[69] Hutcheson was also keen to differentiate his account of moral motivation from that of the third Earl of Shaftesbury. Although Shaftesbury, like Hutcheson, had used the term "moral sense," and Hutcheson often praised him because his views were contrary to Mandeville's,[70] Hutcheson also believed that Shaftesbury had placed too much emphasis on interest and self-love as the motive of moral action.[71] Hutcheson may in fact have been misreading Shaftesbury, but to Hutcheson, Shaftesbury appeared to be arguing that true self-interest and morality converged, and that therefore a person's interest was best served by being virtuous. Although Hutcheson agreed that, on the whole, honesty was the best policy, he was reluctant to admit the pursuit of individual interest and happiness as a legitimate motive of moral action. There were several other moral theorists, whom Hutcheson also opposed, who turned self-love into the foundation of morality, such as John Clarke of Hull (1687–1734).[72] Hutcheson wanted to show that human nature did not need self-love as a motive to perform the social virtues, and indeed that self-love was incapable of acting as a consistent motive for virtue, though it might be compatible with virtue and, in some cases, even reinforce it. Hutcheson also distanced himself from those theorists who claimed that the foundation of morality was conformity to rational truth, a view defended by, for example, Gilbert Burnet (a son of the latitudinarian bishop of the same name), John Balguy or William Wollaston, author of *The Religion of Nature delineated*.[73] Hutcheson's theory was also distinct from the teachings of Samuel von Pufendorf, whose compendium *De Officio Hominis* had become the standard textbook on natural law at northern European Protestant universities, and was used by Hutcheson and his predecessor Gershom Carmichael in their teaching as professors of moral philosophy at the University of Glasgow. Hutcheson disagreed with Pufendorf's voluntarist moral theory, according to which the precepts of natural law were binding because they were the commands of God, as these were known through natural reason. For Hutcheson, as we shall see, the existence of a moral obligation did not require the command of a superior. The existence of certain natural pleasures and pains attached to moral and immoral actions, respectively, was enough.

Aside from his engagement with these moral and legal theorists, Hutcheson also faced criticism from representatives of Calvinist orthodoxy in Ireland and Scotland, who were probably even more immediately important opponents than a figure like Mandeville, because they had key roles in the ecclesiastical and educational institutions of which Hutcheson was a member. This point has been made by Luigi Turco and reaffirmed by Thomas Mautner, who have argued that Hutcheson's intention was to find a middle-way between the flippant wit of "polite" culture, exemplified by publications such as Addison's and Steele's *Spectator* on the one hand, and the dogmatic and gloomy religiosity of orthodox Presbyterianism on the other.[74] Yet Hutcheson's response to his more traditional co-religionists involved more than a desire to avoid the extremes of religious fanaticism and secular irreligion. Hutcheson's opposition to orthodox Presbyterianism reflected particular theological views that were similar to the beliefs of contemporaries such as William Wishart the younger, Wallace, Campbell, or Turnbull.

Hutcheson had been trained as a clergyman, and was closely associated with various heterodox figures within the Scottish Kirk and the Presbyterian church in Ireland. He had been educated at a dissenting academy in Ireland, before studying philosophy and then theology at the University of Glasgow under professor John Simson, during the period when Simson was first put on trial for heresy. On his return to Ireland in 1718 Hutcheson was licensed as a probationer by the presbytery of Armagh in Ulster (1719), although he was never appointed as a minister. In the following years he became involved in the controversy over subscription to the Westminster Confession in the Irish Presbyterian church. Subscription to the Confession had not been made compulsory there until 1705, a decade and a half after Scotland. Even then, subscription continued to be the subject of debates at successive meetings of the Ulster synod and in numerous pamphlets in the 1720s. Several ministers,

led by Samuel Haliday of Belfast, chose to defy the 1705 rule. The nonsubscribers tended to champion the right of private judgment in religious
matters, which could not be removed by political or ecclesiastical institutions.[75] While Hutcheson avoided direct involvement in the controversy, he
remained a close friend of leading nonsubscribers such as Haliday and James
Kirkpatrick of Belfast, John Abernethy of Antrim, Michael Bruce of
Holywood, and Thomas Drennan, who was also his assistant at the Dublin
dissenting academy of which Hutcheson became head. Hutcheson was also
acquainted with the influential Robert, Viscount Molesworth, who not only
was in touch with the Rankenians in Edinburgh, but was at the center of an
intellectual and literary circle in Dublin, and an international network of
correspondents that included the third Earl of Shaftesbury, the deist John
Toland, and various Glasgow students who were protesting against their
institution's "scholastic" and "pedantic" intellectual culture.

In Dublin, Hutcheson wrote his first two treatises, the *Inquiry into the
Original of our Ideas of Beauty and Virtue* (1725) and the *Essay on the Nature
and Conduct of the Passions and Affections* (1728). Following the death of
Gershom Carmichael, the first professor of moral philosophy at the University
of Glasgow, Hutcheson was elected as his successor in 1729, taking up the
post in 1730. He was chosen against the opposition of some, who would have
preferred Carmichael's son to succeed to his father's chair. In the following
years Hutcheson came into conflict with orthodox Presbyterians, some of
whom had him put on trial for heresy in 1738. After his death in 1746, his close
associate, the clergyman William Leechman, later principal of the University
of Glasgow, published a biography of Hutcheson as a preface to the posthumous *System of Moral Philosophy*, based on Hutcheson's lectures at Glasgow.
One of the interesting comments by Leechman was that Hutcheson's most
popular lectures in Glasgow were those he gave on Sunday afternoons, not on
moral philosophy, but on the excellence of Christian religion. Although
Hutcheson's post was that of professor of moral philosophy, it is clear that he
continued to have an interest in, and even lecture on, revealed religion. He
also advised divinity students on the preparation of their sermons, a "distinct
and scarcely legitimate addition to the methodology of Moral Philosophy,"
wrote Hutcheson's biographer W. R. Scott.[76] Hutcheson's views on the role
of affections in moral philosophy, and the question of moral reform and
improvement, exemplify many of the same theological arguments that are to
be found among contemporary heterodox Presbyterians in that he presented

conduct founded on charity rather than doctrinal orthodoxy as the essence of genuine religion and virtue alike. Christianity, Hutcheson wrote, was a religion "which gives us the truest Idea of Virtue, and recommends the Love of God, and of Mankind, as the sum of all true Religion."[77] All people, of course, acted immorally, at least occasionally, because the nature of humankind had been corrupt since original sin. The main duty of humans in this life was to make progress toward moral reform and regeneration. That progress was the effect of "culture" or the "culture of the mind," the same incremental improvement of human nature that Wishart and Wallace had turned to in their attempt to mediate between the "enthusiasm" of evangelical revivalists and the rigid, doctrinal orthodoxy of more traditionalist Presbyterians. Although "culture" required effort on the part of the individual agent to be meritorious, that effort by itself was not sufficient but had to be supported by divine revelation and grace to be successful and to terminate, eventually, in moral improvement and salvation.

Morality and the Affections

Morality, according to Hutcheson, was rooted in affections that were "but different modifications" of love and its opposite, hatred, the "Affections which are of most importance in Morals."[78] Elsewhere in the same work he wrote that the true spring of moral actions was "some Determination of our Nature to study the Good of others; or some Instinct, antecedent to all Reason from Interest, which influences us to the Love of others; even as the moral Sense . . . determines us to approve the Actions which flow from this Love in our selves or others."[79] Although the intellect did play a role in morality, it was mainly as an instrument, subordinated to the affections, a view he defended against the rationalism of Gilbert Burnet in a series of exchanges in the *London Journal* during the summer of 1728. "*Speculative Truth* or *Reason*," Hutcheson explained, "is not properly a *Rule* of Conduct."[80] Burnet, following Samuel Clarke on this matter, was concerned that "feeling" was no sufficient guide to virtue, which had to rest on rational argument. Yet Hutcheson argued that, while "*Reason* must find out the *Means*" of performing a moral action, it was our "*Moral Sense* and Affections" that determined the kinds of ends toward which our actions were directed.[81] The capacity for morality was innate in human nature. It did not require any theoretical understanding of the nature of virtue, let alone abstract, speculative reasoning about it: "the *natural Dispositions* of Mankind will operate regularly in those who never reflected upon them, nor form'd just Notions about them. Many are really *virtuous* who cannot explain what *Virtue* is."[82] The existence of these moral affections was an empirical matter of fact: however corrupt humans might often be, there were genuinely moral actions that could not be explained in terms of human pride or secret expectations of selfish gain, contrary to Mandeville's infamous satire on virtue in modern commercial societies in the *Fable of the Bees*. "Never," wrote Hutcheson, "was there any of the human species, except ideots, to whom all actions appeared indifferent."[83]

Like all passions, the moral affections were accompanied by "a pleasant Sensation of Joy" whenever they were gratified,[84] but the pleasures that attended the gratification of the moral affections were the highest possible in this life, so that it was "by the moral sense that actions become of the greatest to our happiness or misery."[85] That connection of virtue with happiness, Hutcheson believed, was also the basis for a certain kind of moral obligation, which existed even in the absence of explicit laws and sanctions. For "if by Obligation we understand a Determination, without regard to our own Interest, to approve Actions, and to perform these; which Determination shall also make us displeas'd with our selves, and uneasy upon having acted contrary to it; in this meaning of the word Obligation, there is naturally an Obligation upon all Men to Benevolence."[86] Here Hutcheson differed significantly from Pufendorf, whose *De Officio Hominis* both he and his predecessor Gershom Carmichael used in their moral philosophy classes at Glasgow. Pufendorf had argued that there could be no moral obligation without the command of a legitimate superior. In the case of natural law or natural morality, which existed prior to the establishment of a human sovereign, this superior was God, "the Creator and supreme governor of the human race, who by virtue of his sovereignty over men, His creatures, has bound them to its observance."[87] The difficulty with a view like Pufendorf's was that a command of this kind, in order to be binding, had to include the threat of sanctions by the superior in case of violation. Pufendorf, however, had not identified a system of rewards and punishments in natural law that was effective in the absence of a human sovereign.[88] In his *De Officio* he said that violations of natural law might lead to disadvantages, especially in the long term, but a disadvantage was not the same as a punishment by God. A punishment, in Pufendorf's view, had to be clearly and directly connected to the crime and to be inflicted visibly by the relevant superior in each particular case. The natural, regular effect of an action was not a sanction in Pufendorf's sense of the word. Hutcheson, by contrast, argued that the natural consequences of certain actions were also to be considered rewards and punishments. The "Sensations of *Joy* or *Sorrow*, upon the Success or Disappointment of any Pursuit, either publick or private," he wrote, had "directly the Effect of *Rewards* or *Punishments*" reinforcing our moral duties. Such natural consequences had a moral meaning, because they reflected God's government of creation by means of general laws, wherein all the separate parts of nature formed a harmonious system in which all was "full of power, activity and regular motion, wisely and exquisitely adapted to the uses of the living and sensible parts of creation."[89] This order had to be the work of a "superior *all-ruling Mind*."[90] Even the existence of occasional "imperfection, indigence, pain, and . . . moral evil in nature"[91] did not contradict the overall evidence of God's benevolent and providential rule. Following the theodicy of the Irish archbishop William King (whom Hutcheson knew personally) in his *De Origine Mali* (1702), Hutcheson argued that particular evils were even a part of God's design.[92] They were necessary to provide humans with opportunities to exercise their moral faculty and prove their moral worth. Doing so allowed them to experience the joys of virtue, which would be largely absent in a state of inaction. Moreover, "our sense of many high enjoyments, both natural and moral is exceedingly heightened by our having observed or experienced many of the contrary evils."[93] Indigence made possible liberality, danger, fortitude, and the "lower appetites or passions" allowed for temperance.[94] The peculiar joys of virtue were experienced regardless of external disadvantages, because "the most heroick excellence, and its consequent happiness and inward joy, may be attained under the worst circumstances of fortune, nor is any station of life excluded from the enjoyment of the supreme good."[95]

Virtue, therefore, produced a kind of superior happiness, but Hutcheson emphasized that it was not a selfish pursuit. It was not possible to will benevolence toward others out of a selfish desire to experience the happiness associated with it because the virtuous affections toward others were the result of spontaneous natural motions of the human soul, and our "desire therefore of the pleasure of self-approbation, or of divine rewards, can only make us desire to have these affections, and to act a suitable part. But these affections cannot be directly raised by the will."[96] There were people, Hutcheson writes, who in certain situations, like danger, for example, wished that they had a virtuous disposition, which would help them cope with the situation they were in, but could not raise this disposition, for an "inward temper and a set of affections do not start up at once upon a wish or command."[97] Morality was never, according to Hutcheson, founded on some species of self-love, contrary to the arguments of a theorist such as Campbell, who had argued that self-love drew us toward society. Campbell had distinguished between good and bad forms of self-love, believing that the former not only was compatible with our social duties toward others, but promoted them. Immorality, on the other hand, was founded on corrupt forms of self-love, not self-love itself.[98] Hutcheson, by contrast, considered self-love itself to be morally indifferent. It never excited moral approbation. "The Actions which flow solely from Self-Love, and yet evidence no Want of Benevolence, having no hurtful Effects upon others, seem perfectly indifferent in a moral Sense, and neither raise the Love or Hatred of the Observer." In some respects, acting contrary to self-love was wrong, for "our Reason can indeed discover certain Bounds, within which we may not only act from Self-Love, consistently with the Good of the Whole, but every Mortal's acting thus within these Bounds for his own Good, is absolutely necessary for the Good of the Whole; and the Want of such Self-Love would be universally pernicious."[99] In some cases self-love might reinforce moral actions; in others it might interfere with them. Yet self-love itself was never morally meritorious, and the approbation due to a moral action was reduced according to the extent to which self-love was involved in motivating it.

Virtue, on the whole, served our external advantage. Hutcheson also believed that honesty was generally the best policy. Morality and interest usually were compatible, and even converged with each other. Yet self-interest, like self-love (which was different from self-interest because it might be founded on a delusion and cause harm to ourselves), could not be the motive of genuinely moral actions, and it could not be used directly to persuade us of the need to have moral affections. Although it was possible to have a sincere desire for the well-being of others as a means of furthering our own interest, such desires "have nothing virtuous in them."[100] The "main question is, whether the affections reputed benevolent are subordinated to some finer interest than worldly advantages, and ultimately terminate upon them."[101] External actions may be influenced by hopes or fears depending on other human beings, but these hopes or fears cannot be considered virtuous motives, since they do not spring from "any inward good-will or desire of their happiness."[102] Arguments based on self-interest could strengthen our moral dispositions indirectly by removing any perceived conflict between virtue and interest. Immoral behavior might be the result of false opinions: "however our Desires, when our *Opinions* are true, and the Desire is proportioned to the *true Opinion*, are all calculated for good, either publick or private; yet *false Opinions*, and *confused Ideas*, or too great a *Violence* in any of them, above a due Proportion to the rest, may turn the best of them into destructive Follies."[103] That kind of reasoning, Hutcheson believed, could not create a moral sense, but it removed obstacles to its proper functioning by demonstrating that there was no real conflict between morality and interest. There was, he argued, "a perfect consistency of all the generous motions of the soul with private interest . . . and a certain tenor of life and action the most effectually subservient to both these determinations."[104]

Moral conduct therefore was natural, pleasurable, and generally advantageous, but it was not the "ordinary condition of mankind."[105] Although real malice was rare compared with acts of virtue and benevolence, no one was capable of adhering perfectly to the "standard of virtue set up in our hearts."[106] The moral powers of humankind had to compete with the attractions of a variety of other, inferior passions. The lowest of these offered "an immediate sense of pleasure, such as the brutes enjoy, but no further satisfaction," and they are "at best beheld with indifference" and are often a "matter of shame, and the cause of contempt."[107] The early years of humans' lives, Hutcheson lamented, were spent in the gratification of sensual appetites, unless there was a "careful education,"[108] and "our selfish passions early gain strength by indulgence."[109] There were also the pleasures of the imagination, which were more lasting than those of the senses. Such were "the beholding beautiful forms, the curious works of art, or the more exquisite works of nature; the entertainments of harmony, of imitation in the ingenious arts; the discovering of the immediate relations and proportions of the objects of the pure intellect and reason."[110] Both these kinds of pleasures were inferior to the joys of sympathy, for which we would willingly forgo any of the pleasures of the senses or the imagination. Yet the "sympathetick pleasures" were subject to uncertainty, because they depended on the "fortunes of those we love," which are unstable, so that "in this we wholly depend on providence."[111] The pleasures of morality, however, were the highest possible in this life. The problem was that it was extremely difficult to persuade the wicked to reform themselves, because they have lost all relish for the supreme joys of virtue, have "stupified consciences . . . insensible of remorse, and live in affluence of all the pleasures they relish," however inferior these may be to the pleasures of the moral sense. Thus, "the minds of a nobler relish see indeed that the vicious have lost the supreme enjoyments of life; but the vicious have no taste for them, nor regret for the want of them, and wallow in what they relish."[112] Their reform required not so much intellectual persuasion and theoretical, "speculative" understanding, which most people were not capable of anyway, and which had no direct influence on the direction of our affections, as a practical program of education—namely, a "culture of the mind" (*cultura animi*).

Morality, Religion, and the "Culture of the Mind"

Hutcheson thought that the "culture of the mind" would allow the moral sense to assert itself against the impulses of the inferior powers and senses. That culture depended on the formation of habit, which was acquired and strengthened through discipline and repeated exercise. The more progress an individual had made toward acquiring these moral habits, the more spontaneous and unforced—and, in that sense, sincere—did virtuous conduct become. But in the initial stages of moral reform, the motives for acting according to virtue need not even be entirely virtuous. We might begin by doing the right thing for the wrong reason.[113] Sincerely moral dispositions might take root only after the habit of acting according to virtue had, to a great extent, already been established for other reasons. Like other heterodox Presbyterians, Hutcheson believed that the fear of some sort of punishment could especially serve as a kind of educational tool to break our bad habits when more genuinely moral motives were still too weak to direct us toward virtue. In many cases, a "Law with Sanctions, given by a superior Being, of sufficient Power to make us happy or miserable, must be necessary to counterbalance those apparent Motives of Interest, to calm our Passions, and give room for the recovery of our moral Sense, or at least for a just View of our Interest."[114] Again, the most powerful threat of punishment, at least in theory, was that of divine retribution in the afterlife. Hutcheson shared Shaftesbury's reservations about "mercenary virtue,"[115] which was motivated only by the prospect of the rewards and punishments of the afterlife, and he did not believe that these rewards and punishments were necessary for the existence of natural moral obligation in this life. Yet he was also convinced that the threat of punishment in a future state fulfilled a useful moral educational purpose. It acted as a temporary support, which allowed the naturally virtuous dispositions of humans to function without interference from the baser passions, and thereby to be trained and strengthened through continual exercise, analogous to the muscles of an athlete preparing for a competition. The prospect of an afterlife was also important because virtue in this life was not invariably rewarded. In this life, Hutcheson wrote, many virtuous people were afflicted with bad fortune, whereas many wicked people escaped all temporal punishments. It might be argued that these wicked people suffered the agonies caused by acting against their moral sense, and that material goods such as wealth were not the reason why the virtuous act morally. Even so, Hutcheson evidently felt that it was unjust for virtue to suffer material distress, while the wicked were blessed with, for example, material prosperity. All injustices of this kind would be remedied by the distribution of rewards and punishments in an afterlife. Although the prospect of this afterlife could not be the reason why moral actions were performed, it offered additional support to virtue, which was often "born down and defeated in this world,"[116] and strengthened trust in divine justice.[117]

Hutcheson believed that natural reason offered at least some probable grounds for belief in such an afterlife. "Mankind in all ages and nations have hoped for it, without any prejudice of sense in its favour, The opinion is natural to mankind, and what their Creator has designed they should entertain," and even the "boldest Epicurean," Hutcheson argued, "never attempted direct proof that a future state is impossible."[118] There were also arguments "which shew the subject of thought, reason, and affections not to be a divisible system of distinct substances, as every part of matter is."[119] Here Hutcheson is referring to standard ideas and texts on this question, including, in a footnote, to Andrew Baxter's "ingenious book on this subject."[120] The soul, it was often said, could not be a material entity, because it was capable of thought, which could not be the result of the rearrangement of particles of matter, because matter was stupid and inert. Unlike corporeal entities, the soul was not composed of smaller elements, but was simple and indivisible. This meant that whereas physical bodies perished when the union of material elements of which they consisted was dissolved, there was no reason to assume that the soul could ever disintegrate in the same way. In theory the soul could be annihilated, but the complete annihilation of any created being, whether material or spiritual, was possible only by an act of God, not within the ordinary course of nature.[121]

But all that these metaphysical and pneumatological arguments could prove was the *possibility* of a continued existence of the soul after death, not that it necessarily did survive the physical disintegration of the body.

Hutcheson, like other heterodox Presbyterians, evidently believed that Christian revelation could at the very least lend philosophical religious beliefs in an afterlife and divine providence additional certainty. In his overview of the history of philosophy, published as a preface to his student textbook on logic, the *Logicae compendium*, the pagan philosopher whom Hutcheson praised most was Socrates, because it was he who had come closest to forming an accurate idea of the relationship between human beings and God and of the implication this relationship had for moral actions. Hutcheson declared Socrates to have been "the founder or author of true philosophy" ("verae philosophiae instaurator aut inventor"), who had turned his mind away from "physical and occult things that contribute little to making a happy life" ("rebus corporeis et occultis, parum ad vitam beatam facientibus") and directed it entirely toward "true piety, the knowledge of God, and the cultivation of every virtue" ("veram pietatem Deique cognitionem, et omnem virtutem excolendam"). Socrates taught that the souls of humans were immortal and that they would be happy or miserable after death, depending on how they had conducted themselves before they died.[122] Hutcheson did, however, always stress the limitations of natural reason in regard to the key truths of religion, especially concerning knowledge of the immortality of the soul and the afterlife. His attitude toward the great philosophers of classical antiquity, who did not have the benefit of Christian revelation, was less favorable and more ambivalent than is perhaps sometimes suggested.[123] In the preface to his *Short Introduction to Moral Philosophy*, he urged his students to go to the "grand fountains of all the sciences, of all elegance; the inventers and improvers of all ingenious arts, the Greek and Roman writers." But while "drawing from them what knowledge you can," his students ought to "have recourse to yet purer fountains"—that is, the Scriptures. They alone gave to sinful mortals "any *sure* hopes [my emphasis] of an happy immortality."[124] In the introduction to his translation of the *Meditations* of the Roman emperor Marcus Aurelius, Hutcheson notes that pagan philosophers clearly suspected the existence of a future state, yet "it was customary among the best philosophers, in imitation of Socrates, to speak upon this subject with such alternatives, even when they were persuaded that there would be a future existence. They thought this highly probable; and yet, as they had not full certainty, they suggested proper supports and consolations even upon the contrary supposition, and endeavoured to give strong motives to virtue independent of future rewards."[125] The full benefits of knowledge of the afterlife were limited to Christians, though pagans might have an inkling of it. Humans did not have to have revelation in order to be moral. It was not as if the desire to act morally and the ability to distinguish between moral and immoral actions depended on the knowledge of Scripture, but humans would only fully understand morality and also be able to benefit from the support that religion provided to morality if they knew the key truths of revelation. The truths of Christian religion, therefore, were important for the sort of moral education that would produce a moral culture of the mind.

Scriptural revelation concerning the afterlife was one form of supranatural assistance given to morality, but there was another. Hutcheson suggests that truly virtuous dispositions in pagans are the result of Christ's merit, which may be effective even in those pagans who have never heard of Christ:

> 'Tis but a late doctrine in the christian church, that the grace of God, and all divine influences purifying the heart, were confined to such as knew the christian history, and were by profession in the christian church. The earliest Christians and martyrs were of a very different opinion. However, they maintained that it is by the merits of our Saviour alone, men can either be justified or sanctified; yet they never denied these blessings could be conferred on any who knew not the meritorious or efficient cause of them. To maintain they could not, is as absurd as to assert, that a physician cannot cure a disease, unless the patient be first instructed in the whole art of medicine, and know particularly the physical principles by which the several medicines operate. Nay, the early Christians believed the spirit of Christ operated in Socrates, Plato, and other virtuous heathens; and that they were Christians in heart, *without the historical knowledge* [my emphasis].[126]

Hutcheson's use of the term "historical knowledge" is significant here. It refers not to knowledge of the historical circumstances of Christ's life, but to the knowledge of doctrinal truths, which was known as "historical faith," as opposed to the reform of the heart. True religion, according to Hutcheson, consisted in the sanctification of the heart rather than doctrinal beliefs. This sanctification of the heart could not be achieved by human efforts alone. It depended on the merit of Christ and on the transformation of corrupt human nature by grace, but it did not require knowledge of the existence of Christ, his life story and death on the cross. The essence of Christian religious faith lay not in doctrinal beliefs, but in virtuous conduct, which depended on Christ's merit, even in those who lacked "historical knowledge" or "historical faith." This was how Hutcheson was understood by the authors of a pamphlet defending him against his orthodox opponents, published in 1738, when there was an attempt to have him put on trial because of his supposedly heterodox religious opinions. Hutcheson's apologists noted that he had "never said there was any Salvation to any of fallen Mankind, except by the Merits of Christ, but often said, he saw no Proof, that none could reap the Benefit of his Merits, but those who actually knew him." And nor, they added, "do we see it."[127] A critic might respond that this view reduced faith to a matter of good works, but Hutcheson would reply that the virtuous deeds of a sanctified believer were distinguished by their motives from those actions that conformed to law externally, but were performed out of fear of punishment or a desire for crude forms of rewards. Hutcheson was saying that while the sanctified took pleasure in acting morally, such pleasure was not only not of the coarse, sensual kind sought by the corrupt; the sanctified did not act morally for the sake of the pleasure these moral actions produced.

Hutcheson's moral theory exemplifies a broader heterodox Presbyterian emphasis on charity, or the "Love of God, and of Mankind,"[128] as the foundation of virtue and faith alike. While he believed morality to be "natural," he also doubted the ability of humans to achieve it without some kind of supranatural assistance, in the form of either Scripture or divine grace. At the same time, genuine religion, according to Hutcheson, was about moral reform, because salvation depended on the redirection of our nature toward the sincere love of God and fellow humans, away from the selfish and corrupt ends that permeated the conduct of fallen humankind. Of course, the individual believer was not the passive recipient of divine grace; moral regeneration required the cooperation of the sinner, and had to be merited by constant effort and labor on his or her part. But those who had never heard of Christ were not necessarily excluded from salvation. Should they be sincerely contrite, God could support their efforts at moral reform directly, without the mediation of Scripture. Hutcheson also seems to have believed that some degree of divine influence was in any case necessary for this moral reform to be possible. Yet he also appears to imply that Christians enjoy certain advantages over others. Christians alone are informed reliably of the existence of an afterlife, which, while it is not essential to moral obligation and cannot provide a truly meritorious motive for moral action, could serve as a protective shell, within which the natural moral dispositions of humankind could be exercised more freely, with less distraction from inferior, selfish passions. Christianity was uniquely useful for furthering the "culture" that moral reform and salvation required in equal measure. That "culture," as in the writings of figures like Wishart the younger, or Wallace, represented a middle-way between the doctrinal rigidity of the orthodox and the "enthusiasm" of the revivalists. There did not have to be some quasi-miraculous transformation of a believer's nature, but rather moral reform and salvation were the products of an incremental process, without dramatic turning points, in which the natural good dispositions that were already present in the human frame were cultivated and reinforced.

3. Moderatism

In the early 1750s there emerged from within the established Presbyterian Kirk a group of clergymen who came to be known as the "Moderates." They included several of the most prominent contributors to Enlightenment culture in the mid- to late eighteenth century. Among them was Hugh Blair, one of the rising stars in the Presbyterian church of the 1750s and a minister at St. Giles's Cathedral from 1758, who was also the first incumbent of the newly created Regius chair of Rhetoric and Belles-Lettres at the University of Edinburgh from 1762. Another example is William Robertson, moderator of the General Assembly in 1763 and principal of the university from 1762 until his death in 1793. Robertson was also Historiographer Royal in Scotland from 1763 and one of the most famous historians of his age; his works earned him widespread fame, as well as a very substantial income. There was also Adam Ferguson, who had been a regimental chaplain in the Black Watch before becoming professor of moral philosophy at Edinburgh and, in 1767, publishing his famous *Essay on the History of Civil Society*. Later, the so-called common-sense philosophers such as Thomas Reid, James Beattie, and George Campbell are also often described as "Moderates."

Moderatism is generally thought to be Scotland's version of a "religious Enlightenment" in the mid- to late eighteenth century. The exact nature of Moderatism, however, remains a matter of debate. As Colin Kidd has pointed out, historians tend to use the term rather casually and in at least two distinct senses. The first of these describes "a more polite, ecumenical outlook" in religious matters. The term "Moderate" had acquired this meaning well before the emergence of the Scottish Moderate Party, as it first appeared in seventeenth-century texts.[1] Johnson's *Dictionary* defined "Moderate" with regard to religious affairs as "not extreme in opinion; not sanguine in a tenet," and "placed between extremes; holding the mean."[2] This reflected an already well-established usage on which eighteenth-century Scots were also drawing. The term "Moderate" was probably first applied to a distinct group within the Presbyterian Kirk by the orthodox clergyman John Witherspoon in 1753, who used it to refer to the group's perceived laxity with regard to the doctrinal standards of the Westminster Confession. Witherspoon's intended meaning of the term there was heavily ironical, even sarcastic, yet, as often happens with terms of abuse, once it had been introduced it began to be used in a positive sense, to describe these Moderates' lack of dangerous and excessive religious zeal and "enthusiasm."[3]

There is, however, another, separate meaning of the term. When Witherspoon first used the term "Moderate," it was during a debate that was prompted by a particular issue in the government of the Presbyterian church, the so-called patronage question. Briefly, this concerned the authority of certain lay patrons to nominate candidates for ministerial posts in parishes.[4] The Moderates as a clearly defined party within the Presbyterian Kirk first formed in relation to this issue of patronage, which they supported more strongly than their opponents in the General Assembly, the "orthodox" or "Popular" party. The second main sense in which the term "Moderate" is used, therefore, is to describe these Moderates' position on ecclesiastical polity and the patronage question.[5]

It is often assumed that these two meanings of the term "Moderate" are, in fact, connected in that the Moderates' position on patronage—that is, their willingness to accept the authority of laymen in ecclesiastical affairs—was said to be an expression of the same broad principles as those that underpinned their flexibility on doctrinal matters. Moderates, it has been said, were characterized by a comparatively Erastian view of the relationship between church and state, which meant that they were more willing to subordinate the Kirk to the requirements of secular society. Although they identified themselves as Calvinists, their Calvinism was an attenuated, less rigid version, which could be accommodated more easily to the demands of secular society than the principles of traditional Presbyterians. Their doctrinal flexibility and their pro-patronage position, therefore, are seen to have an affinity with each other.

These two aspects of Moderatism and their relationship to each other are the subject of this chapter. The reasons for the Moderates' position on patronage will be examined first. The grounds on which they defended, or at least accepted, patronage were complex. Although it is generally acknowledged that they do not represent an example of a full-blown "secular" or "Erastian" view, the secular character of their position on patronage has been emphasized.[6] Yet the conflict between Moderates and the orthodox over patronage was not one between secularizers and anti-secularists. Second, the Moderates' views on doctrine and conduct, and on their respective roles in achieving salvation, will be analyzed. The arguments of leading Moderates like Blair on these questions were in many respects a continuation of those of earlier heterodox Presbyterians like Wishart the younger or Archibald Campbell. Mid-century Moderates believed that Christianity was a matter of practical moral behavior rather than the exact profession of certain orthodox doctrines. And, as in the case of the earlier heterodox Presbyterians, the emphasis of the Moderates on conduct was not simply a watered-down version of more traditional Calvinist beliefs mixed with secular moral philosophical arguments, but the result of a particular theological position, designed to avoid the excesses of solfideism and incorporate good works into the process of salvation, without lapsing into "papism." And, as in the case of the earlier heterodox Presbyterians discussed above, the idea of a gradual, incremental culture of the mind played a central part in their account of salvation.

It is important, therefore, to emphasize the continuities between the Moderates and the earlier generation of heterodox Presbyterians, even if their respective outlooks were not entirely identical. The Moderates were a later generation than the Rankenians or Campbell, and their literary and philosophical interests were more extensive and varied. Robertson's and Ferguson's writings especially reflected the emergence of new "conjectural" and "stadial" models of history, which had played no role in the thought of authors such as Wishart, Wallace, or Campbell. Blair's appointment as the first professor of rhetoric and belles-lettres at the University of Edinburgh similarly reflected more recent intellectual trends that had not been present earlier in the century. The secular intellectual interests of Wallace, Wishart, or Campbell had, on the whole, been confined to moral philosophy.

It has, however, also been argued that there were other, more fundamental intellectual differences between earlier heterodox Presbyterians such as Wishart and later Moderates like Hugh Blair. Evidence for such differences is derived mainly from the two groups' respective attitudes toward David Hume, which became especially apparent on two separate occasions, in 1745 and again in 1755. In 1745 heterodox Presbyterians like William Wishart, Francis Hutcheson, and William Leechman had been the primary source of opposition to Hume's candidacy for the Edinburgh chair of moral philosophy. Ten years later, in 1755, the Moderate Party in the General Assembly prevented a vote of censure against David Hume and Lord Kames. Their support for the two philosophers is sometimes interpreted as a sign of a more enlightened and liberal intellectual attitude among these younger clerics.[7] There was, it is argued, a generational shift between an earlier group of heterodox clergymen, who began the task of reforming and modernizing the Presbyterian Kirk but could have gone further, and a younger group of Moderates, who "finished the job."[8] Yet the significance of these different reactions to Hume's philosophy in 1745 and 1755 appears limited. Not all heterodox Presbyterians in 1745 had joined in the opposition to Hume. Wallace, for example, had not wanted to veto Hume's candidacy and appears to have been scandalized by the "inquisitorial zeal" of Hume's detractors.[9]

More significantly, the circumstances in 1755 are not comparable to those of ten years earlier: the motion of censure was a very different issue from Hume's candidacy for the moral philosophy chair. In 1745 the concerns about Hume focused on his philosophical doctrines, especially his views on justice, which seemed to make him unfit for instructing impressionable young students. It is indeed hard to imagine Hume occupying a chair of "Pneumatics and Ethics," as it was officially known, which would have normally required him to lecture on subjects like natural religion and the immateriality of the human soul. By contrast, the Moderates in 1755 were not supporting Hume's appointment to a university chair, but were only shielding him and Kames from censure by the General Assembly. Moderates also disagreed with Hume's opinions, however much they praised his personal virtue. Hugh Blair, for example, wrote that "every fair reader must admit, and regret, that there are to be found in the writings of this elegant Author [that is, Hume] some principles by no means consistent with sound doctrine."[10] It is difficult to know how Wishart and Hutcheson, the two people who had been largely responsible for Hume's failure to secure the chair in 1745, would have reacted to the proposed motion of censure since they were both no longer alive by 1755. Yet, at the very least, it is likely that even in 1755, electing Hume to a university chair in moral philosophy would have been far more controversial than preventing the General Assembly from passing a motion of censure against Hume and Kames. For example, when Hume was thought to be a possible candidate for another chair, that of moral philosophy at Glasgow University, some years earlier, even his close friend Adam Smith was reluctant to endorse him, because, as Smith explained, he feared that opposition to Hume would be too great. Eventually, Smith succeeded to the chair himself.[11] The apparent differences in attitude between Moderates and the earlier generation of heterodox Presbyterians toward Hume can therefore be explained, at least to some extent, as a reflection of different circumstances. On the other hand, the intellectual similarities between the views of the Moderates and those of the earlier heterodox Presbyterians are often striking. Before turning to these similarities, however, the position of the Moderates in the patronage controversy will be discussed, because their attitude toward patronage is often believed to reflect their broader intellectual outlook. The Moderates, it is argued, were socially and politically conservative, and although they were not full-blown Erastians, their arguments are often thought to represent a concession to more secular principles than their opponents were willing to condone.

Moderatism and the Patronage Question

It was in relation to the patronage question that the Moderates first appeared as a faction within the established Presbyterian Kirk. They emerged in 1751, when a group of young clergymen assembled in an Edinburgh tavern to consider a recent case of insubordination by a presbytery toward the decisions of the General Assembly. Among the fifteen persons present were the clergymen William Robertson, Hugh Blair, and John Home, author of the play *Douglas,* which caused a furor in Edinburgh a few years later. The insubordinate presbytery in question was that of Linlithgow, which had refused to install the Reverend James Watson in the parish of Torphichen, even though he had all the necessary qualifications and had been lawfully presented by the patron for this parish, Lord Torphichen. The presbytery refused to accede to the patron's wishes even when they were instructed to do so by the next higher level in the ecclesiastical hierarchy, the Synod of Lothian and Tweeddale. Instead, they asked to be excused on grounds of conscience from installing the proposed candidate, while making it clear they did not plan to resist, if Watson were inducted by a so-called riding committee, composed of ministers and elders from other parishes for the occasion. In the end, that was the solution adopted, and on 30 May 1751 a riding committee that included the Moderates William Robertson, Hugh Blair, and John Home among its members inducted Watson in Torphichen.[12]

The right of patrons such as Lord Torphichen to present candidates to presbyteries had been controversial ever since it was restored by the 1712 act of Parliament. It was viewed by many to be a breach of the safeguards offered to the Scottish established church in the articles of the Treaty of Union,[13] and an unjustified interference by the predominantly Anglican Parliament in London in the internal affairs of the Presbyterian Kirk. For some time patronage did not become a controversial issue. Most patrons refrained from exercising their right extensively until the 1730s. It was then that disputes about settlements of ministers became more common, prompting Francis Hutcheson to publish a pamphlet in 1735, the *Considerations on Patronage,* in which he was very critical of the 1712 act, writing that the right of patronage was a remnant of Scotland's Catholic past. After the Reformation it had continued, though it was modified in that some concurrence "of the Congregation, of the Heretors and Kirk-Session" was required before a minister could be installed. In the case of conflict between patrons and presbyteries, the final decision was committed by an act of Parliament in 1567 to the supreme governing body of the Kirk, the General Assembly.[14] In 1649 patronage was abolished entirely, and the right to nominate and elect ministers was transferred to the kirk-sessions or elders, who "in those days of universal Sobriety, and, outward Appearance at least, of Religion among the Presbyterians, were generally the Gentlemen or Heretors of best Condition in the Parishes, who were in Communion with the Church." Patronage was reestablished at the Restoration, though the General Assembly retained the right to resolve disputed cases; it was abolished again in 1690, when the right of presentation was transferred to the heritors and elders of the parish under the oversight of the presbytery, to the annoyance of the nobles and gentry who had formerly been the patrons.[15] When patronage was introduced again, in 1712, Hutcheson believed that it was part of an anti-Hanoverian plot by Queen Anne, because, knowing that the Presbyterian gentry firmly supported the Protestant succession, she wanted to weaken their influence by reviving the right of patronage, which would allow the crown to exercise considerable control over the composition of the Scottish clergy. Of the 950 parishes, Hutcheson wrote that the crown held the patronage in 550. Of the remaining churches, around 200 were in the hands of "some Lords, who some-times have not one foot of Land in the Parishes" and had no other real connec-tion with it either.[16] There were "not 150 Parishes in *Scotland*, where the Patronage is in any Gentleman of considerable Estate, or natural Interest in the Parishes, to whom it is of any real consequence, as to himself, whether the Minister be a Person of Sobriety, Diligence, or good Abilities in his Office, or not."[17] Hutcheson was not defending the unadulterated right of the populace to choose its ministers, as some other, more extreme Presbyterians were. There was a need, he believed, to control the zealots.[18] Ministers were to be chosen by "the Men of Property in the several Parishes, in conjunction with the Elders as Representatives of the People."[19] Patronage, however, handed the power to influence the appointment of ministers to people who had no real interest in choosing competent and conscientious candidates, but were liable to use their patronage for selfish and corrupt political ends.

Patronage had not, of course, prevented the Protestant succession, as Queen Anne, according to Hutcheson, had hoped, but he argued that even under the Hanoverian kings patronage gave rise to systematic abuse. Patrons often had no real interest in the parish for which they exercised the right of patronage. They were thus likely to be swayed by considerations that had nothing to do with the qualifications of the candidate for his proposed office. Hutcheson was evidently playing on fears that, under the Walpolean regime of the 1730s, in which government patronage of all kinds was used to secure electoral support for the government, clerical appointments would become a matter of political interest—a fear that seemed all the more plausible because he argued that the crown exercised the right of patronage in well over half of the Scottish parishes.[20] Hutcheson's solution was to repeal the law on patronage, thus "putting Settlements [back] chiefly into the hands of the principal Men of Interest in the Parishes."[21]

When Hutcheson published his *Considerations on Patronage* in 1735, the issue of patronage had come to be particularly controversial. Only two years earlier, in 1733, the minister Ebenezer Erskine had seceded from the estab-lished church over the issue of patronage and formed his own congregation. When Hutcheson was writing the *Considerations*, a bill to repeal patronage was pending in Parliament,[22] and the aim of his pamphlet was to persuade the landowning gentry to lend its support to the proposed repeal, which, however, failed, in part it seems because of a lack of interest on their part. Patronage remained in place, but the view that the selection and nomination of ministers ought to be in the hands of the local gentry rather than patrons who had little involvement in the affairs of the parish did not disappear. It was also the preferred solution of the dominant faction within the so-called Popular Party in the Kirk in the second half of the eighteenth century, who were not the theocratic zealots they have sometimes been portrayed to be.[23] James Oswald, for example, who may even be considered a Moderate in certain respects,[24] was a critic of patronage, and served as moderator of the General Assembly during the so-called Schism Overture in 1766, which blamed the secessions from the established Kirk that had taken place since the split of Ebenezer Erskine in 1733 on the harsh practice of the law of patronage. Oswald argued that patronage might have been justifiable in former times, when the danger of religious enthusiasm and zealotry was still very real, but the "object of terror which drove the laity, and many of the clergy into this scheme, has lost its force." None of the supporters of the Schism Overture countenanced "popular usurpation."[25] Now it was appropriate for the landed gentry to reassume their proper role in the selection and appointment of ministers, as it had been set out in the law of 1690, which, Oswald pointed out, had in fact never been repealed.[26]

The difficulty with the Patronage Act of 1712 was the lack of an agreed procedure for resolving a deadlock between the patron and the presbytery. In principle the General Assembly wielded supreme authority within the Kirk and could decide disputed cases of this kind; in practice, however, this was not straightforward, because some presbyteries refused on grounds of conscience to carry out the injunctions of the General Assembly. When the number of disputed settlements grew in the 1730s, the General Assembly was compelled on several occasions to resort to riding committees, composed of elders and ministers from neighboring presbyteries to install a new minister. Yet riding committees were a second-rate expedient because they were in direct violation of the laws of the church, which stipulated that the candidate for the ministry had to receive a "call" from the presbytery of his parish, not that of another.[27] The disputed settlement of Torphichen in 1751, which precipitated the formation of the Moderate Party within the General Assembly, was such a case of a settlement in which the presbytery resisted the demand from the General Assembly to comply with the patron's wish. The Moderates' main concern in this instance was that the insubordination of presbyteries questioned the supreme authority of the General Assembly, which, they believed, ought to have the power to resolve such controversies without the use of a riding committee. Presbyteries such as that of Torphichen should not just submit passively to the decisions of the General Assembly, but put them into effect. The principle defended by the Moderates, therefore, was not patronage itself, although they did believe patronage had brought some benefits with it. Robertson, for example, in a speech to the General Assembly, suggested that the standard of ministers had been raised as a result,[28] but the key issue for the Moderates was the preservation of the hierarchy of church judicatures within the Presbyterian Kirk, in which the General Assembly wielded final authority in all matters that could not be resolved by provincial synods, presbyteries, or, at the lowest level, the Kirk sessions. "Obedience in inferior courts to the orders of Assembly," declared the Moderate John Hyndman, "is implied in the very nature of our constitution, and in that subordination of judicatures which is here established,"[29] and if a person did not carry out the orders of a superior judicature, then he should withdraw from the Kirk, as one should from any kind of society whose rules one did not accept. Passive submission to the decisions of the General Assembly was not enough, if the authority of the General Assembly within the Kirk was to be preserved intact. Presbyteries had to prove their active obedience by carrying out the resolutions of the General Assembly. A similar problem had surfaced in 1752, in the parish of Inverkeithing. Here the relevant presbytery, of Dunfermline, was refusing on grounds of conscience to induct the Reverend Andrew Richardson, who had been lawfully presented by the patron of the parish, so that eventually he had to be installed by another riding committee. The authority of the General Assembly, according to the Moderates, was weakened even further by the repeated failure of the General Assembly to impose sanctions on disobedient presbyteries. In the Torphichen case, for example, the Moderate John Home had demanded that the presbytery of Linlithgow be suspended for six months, but his motion to that effect was not carried in the General Assembly. The presbytery of Dunfermline had even been threatened with "very high censure" by the General Assembly in November 1751 if it continued to be disobedient. Nevertheless, although they were still refusing to cooperate in March 1752, they escaped censure from the Commission, which managed General Assembly business between sessions. William Robertson, who was emerging as the leader of the Moderate Party within the Assembly, declared that the failure to impose a punishment after it had been announced in case of disobedience was not only inconsistent, but illegal.[30]

A respondent to Robertson, probably John Witherspoon, wrote that the exercise of the presbyters' rights of conscience did not undermine society. Their passive submission to the measures taken by the General Assembly was enough to preserve unity within the church. There was no reason to force them into active obedience. Nor was the Commission obliged to carry out its threat of punishing the disobedient presbytery. There was a value to leniency and mercy, in ecclesiastical as much as in civil government, and presbyters should not be forced to act against their consciences. That sentiment was also expressed by the Synod of Glasgow and Ayr, which transmitted the following statement to the General Assembly concerning the case of Inverkeithing in April 1753:

> 1. That the authority of the Church shall not be interposed to oblige ministers, under pain of deposition, to have an active hand in carrying into execution, such settlements as they shall declare, by their votes, or otherwise, appear to them to be contrary to the Word of God, the present standing rules of this Church, and her constantly avowed principles . . . 2. That no minister shall be deposed, without a libel first given him, making special condescension on the rules transgressed by the facts libelled; and these such rules, the transgression of which is already declared to infer deposition; and that in case such a libel, the accused have sufficient time allowed them, ten free days at least, to make their defences, except in cases referred to in the form of process. 3. That the Assembly would be pleased to take off the censures from Mr Gillespie, and the other brethren of the Presbytery of Dunfermline, upon a proper application from themselves, and in a manner that may be consistent with the authority and honour of the Church; hoping this may contribute much to the maintaining the peace of the Church.[31]

Yet even commentators such as Witherspoon who were critical of Moderates' demands for an active obedience from presbyters agreed with Moderates on the supreme authority of the General Assembly concerning disputed settlements. William Wishart the younger, for example, argued in relation to the Torphichen case that the General Assembly should have shown more respect for the consciences of the presbyters. But he did not dispute the right of the Assembly to make the final decision. On the whole, critics of patronage do not seem to have opposed patronage out of a principled belief in popular elections, which were not generally endorsed, but because of the way in which patronage was exercised. All too often, it was said, the wishes and reservations of the congregations were ignored by the patron, who might be pursuing his own particular interests in urging the appointment of one individual. Also, too often the General Assembly proved itself partial to the wishes of the patron. When Witherspoon complained in his satire on the Moderate Party, the *Ecclesiastical Characteristics*, that the Moderates were full of contempt for ordinary people, he was proposing not that the people should choose their ministers, but that the wishes of the people should be taken into account to a greater degree than was usually the case under the system of patronage. And James Oswald argued some years later that the exercise of the right of patronage did not have be the cause of discontent: "The exercise of the right of patronage began early in the Church of Scotland, and never was held a grievance, whilst the interest of all concerned was duly regarded, and controversies about the settlement were subjected to the judgment of ecclesiastic courts." Everything depended on the way in which it was practiced, in particular, if the opinions of the congregation were properly considered.[32] At the same time, Moderates were not explicitly defending the principle of patronage within the church. Robertson did declare, in his "Reasons of Dissent," that there "can be no union, and, by consequence, there can be no society where there is no subordination."[33] That principle certainly applied to both civil and ecclesiastical societies. "In a numerous society," explained Robertson,

> it seldom happens that all the members think uniformly concerning the wisdom and expedience of any public regulation: but no sooner is that regulation enacted, than private judgment is so far superseded, that even they who disapprove it, are notwithstanding bound to obey it, and to put it in execution, if required; unless in a case of such gross iniquity and manifest violation of the original design of the society, as justifies resistance to the supreme power, and makes it better to have the society dissolved, than to submit to established iniquity.[34]

It is, however, important to stress that the Moderates were using the principle of subordination to justify not patronage, but rather the subordination of church judicatures. The Moderates were certainly socially and politically conservative, and their emphasis on subordination was compatible with a conservative outlook, but the social deference due to those kinds of people who were generally patrons was not the means by which patronage was justified within the church.

It is also apparent that critics of the Moderates accused them not of defending the principle of patronage, but for being too partial to the patron's wishes in practice, and thereby neglecting the more essential qualifications of the candidate. Their "politeness" especially was interpreted as an attempt to pander to the worldly, frivolous tastes of patrons. In his *History of a Corporation of Servants*, Witherspoon mocked this regard for superficial manners over substantial abilities when he caricatured the examination of a candidate for the ministry, first by an orthodox minister, who gives up in despair, when the candidate offers a series of nonsensical answers to his questions. Then,

> when this discontented zealot had dropped the discourse, some other moderate men asked him [the candidate] a few polite and fashionable questions, such as, what is the genteelest lining for a red coat? in what manner should you present a glass of wine to a lord, and how to a farmer? whether is hunting or fishing the pleasantest diversion? whether should the servants or the children of a family have the best lodging, diet, &c.?

"After a few minutes" the candidate passes, with flying colors.[35]

Witherspoon's description was, of course, a caricature. Ian Clark has pointed out that even Moderates were concerned to maintain the independence of the Kirk from government managers.[36] In his life of Hugh Blair, James Finlayson stressed Blair's attempts to preserve the Kirk from slavish dependence on civil power.[37] Of course Moderates were more willing to accept patronage than members of the Popular Party, but it is important to emphasize that patronage itself was not a matter of principle for the Moderates. Their main intention was to defend the hierarchical subordination of church judicatures. At the same time, the dominant faction within the Popular Party was far from being in favor of an unadulterated right of popular choice of ministers. Most of the critics of patronage looked to the selection of ministers by heritors and elders. The two sides' positions on patronage say little, therefore, about their willingness to adapt Calvinism to the demands of secular society. Their dispute centered on the religious and ecclesiological problem, how to maintain the proper balance between preserving the authority of the General Assembly within the Presbyterian Kirk and respecting the tender consciences of individuals who objected to a particular candidate for a ministerial post. Just as the position of the Moderates on patronage is less clearly "secular" or "Erastian" than it may at first seem, their theological outlook and views on morality are also perhaps less influenced by secular principles than has sometimes been argued.

Moderates on Morality, Salvation, and the Culture of the Mind

Moderates, similar to the generation of heterodox Presbyterians before them, emphasized charity as the essence of Christianity; like them, they argued, in broadly Augustinian terms, that faith was founded on the love of God and one's fellow human beings. Doctrine, on the other hand, hardly played a role in their concept of religion. Although they did not openly resist or seek to abolish the Westminster Confession, Witherspoon was correct when he characterized their commitment to doctrinal orthodoxy as lukewarm at best. They thought that far more important than adhering to certain views on matters such as the Trinity was the sincere moral goodness of the individual, which was the real expression of genuine piety. The "whole of the divine commandments," wrote the Aberdeen professor George Campbell, "are summed up by our Saviour in the love of God, and the love of our neighbour."[38] James Oswald wrote that "religion does not consist in solemn rites and sublime sentiments, but in a conformity to the will of God; and the perfection of virtue consists in sacrificing our own will to his."[39] Lord Kames, who was not a clergyman but a close ally of many leading Moderates, wrote that religion did not require the belief in certain doctrines. "All who have a good heart with a clear conscience, will meet with the same reward. It is not material in the sight of the Almighty whether the religion they have been taught is or is not orthodox, provided they be sincere."[40] The virtuous, he added later, "are acceptable to God, however erroneous in point of belief."[41] There was no obstacle to prevent different Christian sects that were distinguished only by their doctrinal beliefs from living together in peace and harmony.[42] Kames even declared himself to be "far from thinking, that Christianity is the only road to heaven."[43] Christianity was an especially powerful practical means of instilling the sincere love of God and our fellow human beings that was the essence of true religion, but theoretical, speculative "articles of faith," whether these separated Christians from non-Christians, or different sorts of Christians from one another, were not essential to piety.

Moderates believed that it was very common for religion to be restricted to the profession of such doctrinal articles, and that this tendency reflected a basic misunderstanding of the nature of Christianity, in at least two respects. First, they argued, the entire purpose of faith was not speculative truth, which was addressed to the understanding, but practical truth, which was aimed at the reform of conduct. Thus Alexander Gerard wrote that God gave revelation to humanity to "purify and improve their hearts."[44] Christ had promulgated a "pure, simple, practical doctrine," not a complex system of speculative truths, which had no influence on conduct, because "abstract ideas are too frigid to warm the heart; too weak to draw out good affections; too dim to be kept in view in the moment of action."[45] Similarly, George Campbell wrote that "the ultimate end both of knowledge and faith is practice, or, in other words, the real improvement of heart and life."[46] Like other heterodox Presbyterians before them, Moderates described religious belief that was limited to "speculative truths" as mere "historical faith"—that is, "intellectual belief or assent, as distinct from faith that is practically operative on conduct."[47] Any "man of common sense, and common honesty," wrote Oswald, was easily capable of such a faith, but unless a belief had the power to "bend the will" and to reform conduct, it was of no real, practical use: even devils had "historical faith," because they knew and believed, for example, that Christ was the Messiah.[48]

Second, the full meaning of much of revelation was beyond the capacities of human understanding, and it was improper to try to be "wise above what is written."[49] When humans tried to develop a "more precise, abstract, or scientifical conception of the doctrines of religion," the result was usually abstruse, conflicting interpretations of Scripture that led to sectarian strife. The most important truths of Christianity were within anyone's grasp. If a particular passage was obscure, then its precise meaning could not be essential to salvation. Many theologians directed particular attention to such passages, however, not out of a desire for clarity, but because, as Campbell, for example, argued, these uncertain passages could be more easily interpreted to serve these theologians' self-interested ends. The result was that "the Christian world hath gotten many masters and rabbies, fathers and guides" instead of a harmonious agreement on religion.[50] This corruption of faith had begun already in late antiquity. Of course any Protestant author had to account for the decline of Christianity and the rise of the papal church that had made the Reformation necessary, but Moderates tended to follow a distinctive interpretation indebted to a long-standing spiritualist historiography reaching back at least to the early seventeenth century, and which was characterized by the belief that rival sects in the early church began to replace Christ's emphasis on practical holiness of life with competing systems of "speculative" doctrinal beliefs. These systems were little more than pretexts for the secular interests and ambitions of different ecclesiastical factions. The tendency among the early Christians toward abstruse speculation was further stimulated by the inept combination of pagan philosophy with Christian teachings, another common complaint among early modern Protestant authors, not just in Scotland.[51] Thus Robertson lamented the fact that the "presumption of men had added to the simple and instructive doctrines of Christianity the theories of a vain philosophy, that attempted to penetrate into mysteries, and to decide questions which the limited faculties of the human mind are unable to comprehend or to resolve."[52] Robertson was alluding to Colossians 2:8, a passage that was often used in early modern texts to refer to the inappropriate mixture of pagan philosophy with Christian belief. These "over-curious speculations," Robertson said, "were incorporated with the system of religion, and came to be considered as the most essential part of it."[53] Campbell made a similar point, describing the ancient Greeks as "that ingenious, inquisitive, and disputatious people, who were then divided into philosophical sects." They had not

> thoroughly imbibed the spirit of the religion they had so recently been taught, still retaining a tincture of their former sentiments in regard to theology and morals, and so warped from the truth in different ways, would soon disagree among themselves, concerning the doctrine of that gospel which they had received. Each would exercise his ingenuity in giving such a turn to the dictates of revelation as would make them appear conformable to his favourite opinions, and would conciliate both, where they appeared to clash.[54]

Medieval scholasticism was often described as being built on such a corrupt and incoherent intellectual synthesis of Christian religion and classical pagan thought. As Robertson wrote, for example, it was not until the fifteenth and sixteenth centuries that "the human mind felt its own strength, broke the fetters of authority by which it had been so long restrained, and venturing to move in a larger sphere, pushed its inquiries into every subject, with great boldness, and surprising success."[55] Only then did the absurdity of medieval scholasticism become apparent. The intellectual revival of the Renaissance not only liberated secular learning; it also allowed Christianity to be purified and returned to its original foundation, by stripping out the philosophy that had been mixed with it. The Reformation marked the beginning of that process, though Robertson, and other Moderates, believed that it was not complete by the time they were writing: the insistence among their orthodox opponents on doctrinal truth was a relic of the papal church and its scholastic thought.

The reason for the Moderates' reluctance to uphold the doctrinal standard of the Westminster Confession was not a secular indifference toward religious doctrine, but, rather, a belief that genuine piety was defined in nondoctrinal terms, and that religion had been corrupted by an overemphasis on doctrinal standards that were founded on human speculation, not divine authority. The main casualty of abstruse doctrinal controversies was charity, the sincere love of God and of fellow human beings. Charity, Moderates believed, was "the end of all religion" and its proper essence.[56] But it was also the foundation of secular virtue, because it was the primary motive for sincere benevolence and unselfish affection toward others. Morality and piety were thus intimately related to each other, as they had been in the writings of heterodox Presbyterians earlier in the century; salvation was to be achieved through moral reform and regeneration. "Sanctity and virtue," wrote Robertson, "alone can render man acceptable to the great author of order and of excellence";[57] for Blair, Christianity was by its very nature practical and moral, piety being "joined with charity, faith with good works, devotion with morality."[58] The key question was how the moral reform that led to justification was to be brought about. It could not be by purely individual effort: saying so would be tantamount to a "papist" belief in the efficacy of good works for salvation, and would contradict the principle of the indispensability of divine grace. Moderates seem therefore to have conceived salvation as a cooperative enterprise, in that the struggles of the sinner for redemption were necessary to merit it, but they were not sufficient, because they had to be supported by divine grace to be successful.

Since justification required moral regeneration and reform, and justification could not be achieved without divine assistance either, it followed that genuine moral reform was also impossible without divine support. Moderates were of course closely involved in the secular enlightened learning of their time, and sympathetic to it. They considered moral philosophy, even when not supplemented by divine revelation, a valuable and useful discipline, but the Moderates also stressed the *practical* insufficiency of this moral philosophy for bringing about the virtuous behavior that was the end of all moral teaching. Some kind of divine support was always necessary. Blair suggested that some people thought that becoming a moral person did not require any religious belief at all, because a preference for morality was, in some sense, a natural feature of humankind. These scoffers at religion, however, failed to realize that the natural principles of virtue were generally too weak to make us act virtuously with any consistency. Our actual behavior was often corrupt, for no matter how natural virtue was, it was also subject to many pressures and temptations in temporal life, and did not invariably prevail. Philosophical argument was of very little use in solving this problem, because "refined reasonings concerning the nature of the human condition, and the improvement which philosophy teaches us to make of every event, . . . may perhaps contribute to soothe [the mind] . . ., when slightly touched with sorrow," but these reflections availed little when it was "torn with any sore distress"; compared "with a direct promise from the word of God," they were "cold and feeble."[59]

A particular problem was that virtue was not invariably rewarded, or vice punished in this life. Sometimes the wicked prospered, increasing the temptation to abandon virtue for the sake of narrowly selfish motives. Some support for virtue was offered by the prospect of divine retribution in an afterlife, when the injustices of the temporal state would be redressed. However, Blair, like heterodox Presbyterians earlier in the century, believed that there was no firm, natural knowledge of the immortality of the soul and the existence of an afterlife. Skepticism about a reasonable belief in the afterlife was characteristic of Moderates more generally, and one of the main areas of disagreement with orthodox thinkers, who were far more willing to defend a natural, reasonable religion that included knowledge of the immortality of the soul. For Blair, as for his fellow Moderates, any reliable knowledge of the afterlife depended on an act of divine revelation. Although there were some arguments "which reason affords in behalf of future rewards to the righteous,"[60] these fell short of certainty. There were some signs that virtue was "a chief object of his [God's] care. In the constitution of human nature, a foundation is laid, for comfort to the righteous, and for internal punishment to the wicked,"[61] which was why virtue was attended by pleasures that were far superior to the crude delights of immoral conduct. As early as 1739 Blair had written that "the benign and social affections . . . always contribute to the tranquility of the mind, by their own force and nature: even when they are unsuccessful, they suffuse the mind with a pleasure far purer than anything that ever flows from private and more selfish delights."[62] Moreover, virtue might often be disappointed, but the imperfect distribution of happiness in this life was a strong hint that humankind's current existence was only "the beginning, not the whole of things; the opening only of a more extensive plan, whose consummation reaches into a future world."[63] "Can we believe," Blair asks rhetorically, "that under the government of the Supreme Being, those apparent disorders [in the moral world] shall not be rectified at last?"[64] Finally, the belief in a future state had existed "throughout all ages, and among all nations."[65] It did not spring from "the refinements of science, or the speculations of philosophy; but from a deeper and stronger root, the natural sentiments of the human heart,"[66] and was therefore common to barbarous and civilized societies alike. It was theoretically possible that this belief had no foundation in truth at all, and had been instilled by God just to restrain humankind from evil. But that would be to "suppose, that a principle of delusion was interwoven with the nature of man," and that "his [man's] Creator was reduced to the necessity of impressing his heart with a falsehood, in order to make him answer the purposes of his being,"[67] something Blair considers improbable.

And yet, all these arguments for the afterlife from natural reason and sentiments did not amount to certitude. The general belief in an afterlife might still be "owing to inclination and desire, more than evidence," and perhaps the belief that God would want the injustices suffered by the virtuous to be redressed exaggerated the importance humankind had "in the system of the universe."[68] It was therefore all the more important that God had revealed the existence of an afterlife directly, thereby giving "full authority to all that reason had suggested," and placing "this capital truth beyond the reach of suspicion or distrust."[69]

Similar to earlier heterodox Presbyterians, Blair also believed that the threat of divine punishment had important beneficial effects for humankind, even when the motive behind an outwardly moral action was no more than fear of consequences in the afterlife. The "bulk of mankind," as Blair thought, might not be truly virtuous, but at least the fear of God restrained them from harming others. A society that was, by and large, at peace because the multitude feared the revenge of God in life after death might not be the best imaginable, but it was preferable to one in which no such restraint existed. This was the reason why "all legislators have supposed"[70] the immortality of the soul, though only Christian societies enjoyed the advantage of having proper evidence for the truth of this belief. Even more important was the role that the prospect of an afterlife played in the "culture of the mind," by which individuals became moral characters and thereby earned their salvation. The afterlife was an educational tool, a support that allowed virtuous dispositions to develop and gain in strength, and to ripen into habit, against the competing temptations of corrupt, worldly desires. It was important that the prospect of the afterlife was not so clear and overwhelming as to remove all need for effort on the part of the individual. Blair and other Moderates struck a delicate balance between an emphasis on the insufficiency of human powers to achieve moral regeneration and salvation, and the need to avoid implying the complete passivity of the individual in this process. Individual effort was a necessary, but not sufficient, condition of salvation. In a sermon on "Our Imperfect Knowledge of a Future State," Blair had emphasized the obscurity of the afterlife, because, although its existence was known, its nature was so unclear that its prospect did not automatically counterbalance the influence of worldly desires. There might be short phases of mystical contemplation during which humans could approach some idea of the future state, but

> such efforts of the mind are rare, and cannot be long supported.
> When the spirit of meditation subsides, this lively sense of a future
> state decays; and though the general belief of it remain, yet when
> they return to the ordinary business and cares of life, good men
> themselves seem to rejoin the multitude, and to re-assume the same
> hopes, and fears, and interests, which influence the rest of the
> world.[71]

There was thus plenty of room, and need, for struggles on the part of the individual against "the world," and opportunity to merit the eventual reward in the afterlife.[72] In fact, Blair believed that truly moral action depended precisely on the obscurity of a future state, which meant that its prospect was incapable of influencing human actions directly, through the force of overriding hope or fear. Truly moral action had to be the spontaneous, unforced expression of a virtuous character to be formed in this life. "His [man's] preparation for a better world required a gradual purification, carried on by steps of progressive improvement."[73] If "man" enjoyed full knowledge now of the situation awaiting him in the afterlife, this would defeat the whole purpose of temporal life, of "calling forth all his active power, by giving full scope to his moral disposition, and bringing to light his whole character."[74] None of the temptations of this life would be difficult to overcome if they were compared to the true potential pleasures and horrors of the afterlife. Continual exercise and labor were the means by which moral character had to be formed and improved in this life. In the course of their lives, humans were faced with a series of trials, which offered them opportunities to reaffirm and strengthen any existing dispositions they might have toward virtue. "Hence it became proper that difficulty and temptation should arise in the course of his duty."[75] We were, as Blair described elsewhere, "trained up for heaven."[76] The purpose of this moral formation was to produce constant, regular habits of virtuous action. Of course, it was possible in principle for bad habits to be formed, too, but Blair seems to have considered it more likely that individuals would be led astray not by confirmed evil dispositions, but by "dissipation," the inability to resist the many distracting temptations of "the world." "Dissipation is a more frequent cause of their ruin, than determined impiety. It is not so much because they have adopted bad principles, as because they have never attended to principles of any kind, that their lives are so full of incoherence and disorder."[77]

A constant, virtuous character, on the other hand, was the product of "culture." As in the case of the earlier heterodox thinkers discussed above, "culture" was an incremental process and depended on the formation of habit, which was built up through repeated exercises and trials; every time an individual passed such a trial by choosing virtue over vice, his or her internal disposition toward virtue was reinforced and made a little firmer. It was not enough to realize intellectually the superiority of virtue over vice, the reality of an afterlife, or the existence of a divine providence if these truths were not reflected and affirmed repeatedly in conduct. Labor occupies an important place in Blair's view of moral culture. Labor (or industry) transformed the agent's character and thereby contributed to his or her salvation in the afterlife. It was not single good actions that deserved a reward, but the labor that a person devoted toward improvement over long period of time, and the consistency of that labor.[78]

Although knowledge of the afterlife therefore did not determine a person to seek salvation, it could help to nudge him or her toward it, by drawing attention to the fact that self-interest did not really contradict virtue in the long run. Christians, therefore, who had been informed of this truth in Scripture, enjoyed certain advantages in obtaining salvation. But, like other Moderates,[79] Blair also believed that there was no need to be a Christian to be eligible for salvation. Although salvation depended on divine assistance, Scripture was only one possible channel through which it could be granted. Immediate divine intervention, on behalf of one particular individual, was also possible, as took place in the case of the pagan Roman centurion Cornelius. Cornelius was ignorant of the truths of Christian revelation, but he was a "devout man, and one that feared God with all his house, which gave much alms to the people, and prayed to God always." He worshipped God "according to his measure of religious knowledge,"[80] which was limited to the principles of natural, reasonable religion. His sincerity was rewarded when an angel was sent to him from heaven to inform him about those religious truths of which he had been unaware. Thus God "rewarded the amiable dispositions which rose in the heart of this good man [Cornelius]. But he saw that they were yet imperfect, while he remained unenlightened by the principles of the Christian religion," and therefore resolved to "remove this obstruction to his rising graces, and to bring him to the full knowledge of that God, whom he sought to honour."[81] Unlike Scripture, the revelation vouchsafed to Cornelius was directed at a particular individual, not disseminated by human means, orally and in written form. In both cases, however, the "rising graces" of an individual faced obstructions that could be removed only with some kind of divine help.

Moderatism and "Common-Sense" Philosophy

Some Moderates from the 1760s onward are considered members of a distinct "school" of "common-sense philosophy." Its adherents are usually identified by their criticism of the extreme epistemological skepticism that seemed to them a necessary consequence of David Hume's philosophical system. The most notable member of this "school" of common-sense philosophy is generally agreed to be Thomas Reid, who was first a minister, then taught at King's College in Aberdeen from 1751, and later became Adam Smith's successor in the chair of moral philosophy at the University of Glasgow in 1764. Other, less well-known figures included in the same group are George Campbell, principal at Marischal College and known for his critique of Hume's argument against belief in miracles; the clergyman James Oswald;

and the philosopher James Beattie, who taught at Marischal College, and whom David Hume described as that "bigotted silly Fellow."[82] The term "common-sense philosophy" was used during the lifetime of these thinkers, though the extent to which they really constituted a coherent and distinct "school" is debatable, as Paul Wood has shown.[83] Reid, for example, disliked the suggestion that he and these other thinkers formed such a school. The intellectual relationship of the "common-sense" philosophers to Moderates like Blair or Robertson is difficult to characterize. In some matters, such as the nature of human volition, the views of thinkers such as Reid or Beattie are distinct from those of Blair and other Moderate Presbyterians before the 1760s, as will be shown later.[84] However, there are also important similarities between "common-sense" philosophers and the heterodox Presbyterians associated with the Rankenian club earlier in the century, as well as the Edinburgh-based Moderates who emerged in the 1750s. For, much like the Rankenians, Hutcheson, or Blair, common-sense philosophers were skeptical of the value of "speculative" reasoning, though they did not consider it worthless. They did not believe in the need for a standard of doctrinal ortho- doxy, but thought of Christianity as a "practical" moral religion; they also accorded a central role to "moral culture" as the means to obtain the virtue and genuine piety that would procure salvation; and they also believed that this moral culture required divine assistance of some kind to be achieved, because natural religion and reason were not enough for it. Although the distinctive arguments of Reid, Oswald, and Beattie should not be neglected,[85] they also exemplify the broader shift from doctrine to conduct that was a more widespread feature of eighteenth-century Presbyterianism.

In several respects the common-sense philosophers and the heterodox Presbyterians of the earlier part of the eighteenth century were directly connected. The Rankenian club member George Turnbull had taught Thomas Reid at Aberdeen in the 1720s, and later David Fordyce, who had attended Francis Hutcheson's lectures at the University of Glasgow in the 1730s, was a regent at Marischal College in Aberdeen from 1742 until his death in a shipwreck in 1751, on his return from a tour of Continental Europe. Both Turnbull and Fordyce thought there was an order and harmony in nature that indicated the providential government of the world by a just and benevolent deity. Francis Hutcheson, Blair, and Lord Kames also held a providentialist view of creation. There was more than sufficient evidence that this world was not the product of chance, but that it was ruled by a benevolent creator, although many aspects of this belief might be mysterious and beyond the reach of human understanding.

Providentialism of this kind had been challenged by Hume in Section 11 of his *Enquiry concerning Human Understanding* of 1748, "Of a particular Providence and of a Future State," in which he had argued that it was impossible to prove the wisdom and goodness of the deity from the characteristics of the universe. There was in this world such a mixture of good and evil that it was impossible to infer either the goodness or the omnipotence of the creator. Even the idea of a God as a "first cause" of the world could not be proved from reason or experience. Our belief in cause and effect, Hume said, rested on our experience of a constant conjunction between two types of events. That experience was the only grounds for assuming some sort of connection between the two. Yet the world was one of a kind, at least as far as humans knew. They could not, therefore, compare it with any other, and of course they had not witnessed the creation of any other. Reid had been aiming to provide a more robust and systematic defense of the kind of providentialism that had been typical of, for example, Turnbull, by showing that divine providence, however mysterious it might often be, offered the best possible explanation for many features of the created world. Reid thought of causation in terms of a constant conjunction between two events, very much like Hume had done. There was nothing inherent in material nature, Reid said, that could explain the effect of one thing on another, and "when we ascribe power to things inanimate as causes we mean nothing more than a constant conjunction by the laws or rules of nature which experience discovers."[86] Yet there was a crucial distinction between Reid's notion of constant conjunction and Hume's. For Hume, the repeated experience of constant conjunctions strengthened the "vivacity" of the belief in them, and their vivacity, not some principle of reason, was the only basis for the belief in causation. Reid agreed that the belief in causation did not rest on rational conviction, but "vivacity" was not enough to explain human confidence that the same conjunction that had been observed in the past would continue to operate in the future. The only possible explanation for this trust which humans had in the regularity of these causal connections had to be an instinct, placed in them by God, as a guide in temporal life, to expect the continuation of the same patterns that had been observed in natural phenomena in the past.[87] This trust could not be the product of some kind of ratiocination, because "children and ideots" have this belief as soon as they know that fire will burn them.[88] James Beattie offered another, similar, if perhaps less sophisticated, defense of providentialism. "Some," Beattie wrote, in an obvious allusion to Hume, "have urged that there are in the universe many marks of irregularity and want of design, as well as regularity and wisdom,"[89] but even if that were true it would not follow that there was no just and all-powerful Creator. There was enough "wonderful contrivance" in the world to prove these attributes of the deity, and it was absurd to argue that things could have been better. Rather, the imperfections that did exist could often be shown to reflect the "Divine goodness and wisdom."[90] Moreover, our knowledge of the workings of creation was clearly incomplete, and "a most wise and beneficent dispensation" may appear "to a captious mind and fallible judgement" to be the opposite.[91] It was also argued by James Oswald that the phenomena of nature bore full testimony to the moral character of its author.[92]

Although the "common-sense" philosophers believed that there was sufficient evidence for the existence of a divine providence, even without the assistance of divine revelation, they were as skeptical as Blair or Robertson of the possibility of natural knowledge of the immortality of the soul. Only Christianity confirmed the existence of an afterlife, in which rewards and punishments would be distributed and divine justice be complete. Christianity therefore offered the best support for the moral culture that was the means of obtaining virtue and salvation alike. Like earlier Moderates, common-sense philosophers were not arguing that acting out of fear of punishment in the afterlife was itself meritorious, but rather that knowledge of the afterlife, which was granted by revelation, was a particularly useful instrument in the process of moral education. Like Turnbull and Fordyce, and authors such as Blair or Kames, "common-sense" philosophers generally believed that natural reason was insufficient to demonstrate the existence of a future state. Reid, Beattie, and Oswald all believed that humans were always dependent on some act of revelation for their knowledge of it. This, they wrote, was evident from the shortcomings of pagan natural religion and morality. The "notions of the ancient philosophers, with regard to the nature of the soul," according to Reid, were not "much more refined than those of the vulgar," nor were they formed in any other way.[93] In some of his lectures on the nature and duration of the soul, Reid considered the strength of the arguments for natural knowledge of a future state. Similar to Blair, he pointed out that the belief in a future state had been near universal: "even most of the more barbarous Nations have been perswaded that there is a future life," in which the good will be happy and the wicked will suffer the just punishment for their deeds.[94] The origins of this notion predated the emergence of any sophisticated forms of argument so that it was clear they could not be founded on "any refined Notions {or subtile reasoning} concerning the Soul."[95] The expectation of a system of divine justice after death was a natural response to the wise order that was observed in this world, and which indicated the existence of an all-powerful and benevolent creator. That order extended to moral affairs, for the exercise of the virtues of justice, generosity, and humanity was generally attended by feelings of pleasure and satisfaction, while "every vice brings its own punishments along with it, or is followed by it sooner or later."[96] However, "it cannot be denied that there are instances, {both} of successful Villanies which are not punished as they deserve in this World, & of virtuous Actions for which men Suffer {or are not rewarded}." It was thereby that humans were "led to think that Justice compleats that work in another State (which we evidently see begun here) of an universal Retribution according to the Merit and Demerit of Persons."[97]

There were other grounds for assuming the continued existence of the soul after the death of the body. They included the fact that the mind was a simple substance that could not perish as the result of a disaggregation into its constituent parts,[98] that the powers of the soul to improve continually in virtue and knowledge were not exhausted at the end of life,[99] and that the tendency in nature was for animals to pass through a succession of stages, of which temporal life was probably only one.[100] And yet "it must be acknowledged that [all] the Arguments that Philosophy suggests upon this head are not of such Strength but that they may leave some doubt even in the Minds of wise and thinking Men,"[101] and "full assurance of a future & immortal state of Existence" had therefore to be given to humankind "by a Revelation from heaven."[102] Oswald also had commented that it would be foolish to assert that there could be no future state. Without revelation, however, there was nothing in the present state that could inform humans of this afterlife with complete authority. In fact, "until that great light [that is Christ] appeared, the true light who enlighteneth every man, the nations did, in spite of all their improvements in philosophy and the fine arts, proceed from one degree of barbarism to another, till they were plunged in the grossest idolatry, and the most abominable vices."[103] Beattie also argued that the "character of the Supreme Being, and the nature and destination of man, must be very imperfectly known to those who have received no positive information concerning the reality of a future state, and its connection with the present. Now this is a point on which all the evidences collected by human reason, while unaided by divine light, amount to nothing higher than probable conjecture."[104] Infidels thought that natural reason provided them with all they needed to know, but if there had been no divine revelation, they would still be practicing idolatry and performing sacrifices and other rites established by human law. Even Socrates, the wisest of all ancient philosophers, preached conformity to the religion established by the human legislator. He was well aware, however, that "all ancient philosophy was very incomplete" as a "system of natural religion and moral duty." Thus, Beattie declared, revelation

> seems to be necessary to give such evidence of another life, and such intelligences concerning it, as may vindicate the divine goodness and wisdom with respect to the constitution of the present; and such as may also prove a comfort to good men, and a restraint on the passions of the wicked; and such, moreover, as may serve for a solemn intima-tion to all men, that their behaviour in this state of trial is to them a matter of infinite importance. That this last consideration strengthens morality, or promotes at least the peace of society, and consequently, the happiness of mankind, seems to be admitted by the enemies, as well as by the friends of religion. Else how can we account for that favourite notion of the infidel, that religion was contrived, and is patronised by politicians, in order to overawe the world, and make the passions of men more manageable.[105]

Insofar as arguments from natural reason were used to defend religious beliefs such as the immortality of the soul and the existence of an afterlife, these were not "accompanied with evidence or authority sufficient to raise the attention, or convince the understanding of any, except perhaps of a few speculative men,"[106] such as Socrates or Zeno, whose ideas on the afterlife were not only absurd, but so contrived and complex they were of little use in persuading the common people to act morally.[107] Hence, revelation, Beattie believed, was necessary to make the whole of human duty "not only *known*, but *obvious to all capacities.*"[108] Much as Archibald Campbell, Turnbull, or Blair before them, therefore, philosophers like Reid, Oswald, or Beattie believed that the teachings of the Gospel were not only more accurate than the speculations of pagan thinkers, but far more effectual in bringing about the moral reform that was the essence of genuine Christianity. The Christian revelation, wrote Oswald, addressed "every spring of the human mind, the moral sense in particular, with an energy and force superior to that of the most sublime poets and philosophers."[109]

The prospect of an afterlife, even after it had been revealed, was never so powerful and distinct that every effort on the part of the individual sinner was made superfluous and virtue turned into a matter of purely "mercenary" self-interest, as Shaftesbury had feared.[110] Oswald argued that there was a fundamental difference between the rewards and punishments of the after-life, and considerations of self-interest in this life, because "the interest and honours of this life are near at hand, and full in view, and operate so forcibly, and in a manner so mechanical and necessary, that, strictly speaking, the good actions produced by such motives are no virtues; and, however beneficial in their effects, do not intitle him who performs them to praise or reward from God or man." It was quite different with the "glory and happiness of another life," which were "out of sight and at a distance" and derived "all their power in determining the will, not from any blind impulses or sense or imagination, but from the free and frequent, and often the long and painful exertion of our nobler powers, such exertions to wit, as are deemed rational and manly; and discover that greatness of mind, and grandeur of character, which make one a proper object of esteem and love with God and men."[111] Reid thought that external factors, including divine support, might encourage the moral education of the individual, but they did not detract from the liberty of the moral agent.

> The Moral Character of a Man must chiefly depend upon himself and on that account is imputable to him. The fixed Purposes he has formed with regard to the Conduct of Life. The Ends he Pursues and the Habits he has acquired of restraining his passions and Appetites, and of prosecuting with steadiness and industry the End he proposes in Life must constitute his Moral Character But it cannot be denied that there are various things that are external to us, & which therefore are not alltogether in our Power that may have a considerable influence upon our Morals.[112]

For Reid, virtue and salvation were the result of a form of cooperation between the individual and God: "as our industry is not the less necessary in providing for Subsistence though we ask it of God and depend on him for it,

So neither is our industry and best endeavours less necessary in acquiring true Wisdom and Virtue though we ask these things of God and depend upon his Divine Aid."[113]

Moral reform and salvation were still an achievement of the individual sinner, for nobody would merit eternal life without struggling for it. However, this struggle on the part of the individual was never sufficient, unless it received divine assistance. The knowledge of the afterlife was far more effective at encouraging the process of moral culture than any human argument. Yet the moral reform that was the essence of Christianity, and the salvation that followed from it, did not depend on knowledge of the afterlife. This knowledge was merely practically useful, not absolutely necessary for the moral culture that was the essence of justification. Although some form of divine support was always needed, this might be granted directly by God, by means of some revelation to the individual, and not necessarily through the text of Scripture.

It has been suggested that Moderates were, in some sense, more "enlightened" than their orthodox opponents because they were more optimistic about the capacities of natural, unassisted human reason, but it is evident that Moderates were not distinguished by a greater confidence in the powers of human reason, believing that neither morality, nor salvation, was possible without divine grace. More orthodox Calvinists in the 1750s, on the other hand, were not distinguished by particular hostility to human reason as a standard of argument. In some respects the orthodox were even more "rationalist" than the Moderates. What really differentiated the orthodox from their Moderate opponents was their theological view of the conditions of salvation. They were concerned above all to defend the necessity of a standard of doctrinal truth for salvation. The disagreements between Moderates and orthodox manifested themselves in a series of controversies during the 1750s. They are the subject of the following chapter.

4. Orthodoxy

The divisions between Moderates and orthodox over church patronage were accompanied by several other controversies. In his 1753 satire, the *Ecclesiastical Characteristics,* John Witherspoon criticized and lampooned the Moderates on various grounds, not just for their support of lay patrons. Two years later, in 1755–56, orthodox clergymen tried to have Lord Kames and David Hume censured by the General Assembly for their philosophical beliefs. The campaign against them came to nothing, as the Moderate Party within the Assembly prevented the original motion from being put to a vote, and then succeeded in watering it down until it was no more than a vague, anodyne declaration against irreligion, without reference to either Hume or Kames.[1] Another controversy erupted soon afterward, over the drama *Douglas,* which had been written by the Moderate minister John Home, and which was first performed in Edinburgh in 1756. This led to a quarrel between Moderate and orthodox authors about the permissibility of a public stage, the orthodox accusing the theater of encouraging immorality, and the Moderates defending the harmlessness of plays, even pointing out their potential to contribute to the moral education of their audiences.[2]

Controversies such as these were reflective of wider intellectual disagreements. There were three particularly significant areas of debate that separated the two factions: first, natural religion; second, the need for an orthodox doctrinal standard in religion; and third, the role of the passions and affections in human conduct. In contradiction to what is commonly assumed, orthodox Calvinist theorists were in fact generally far more confident of the capacity of human reason to arrive at various religious truths, including the existence of an afterlife, without assistance from revelation than the Moderates were. Indeed, one of their main objections to Hume and Kames in 1755–56 was that these two philosophers were undermining natural religion. The orthodox also believed that sincerity of belief was not enough for salvation The content of the belief mattered, too, and a standard of true, orthodox doctrine was essential for salvation to be possible. And finally, the orthodox argued that moral action required the passions and affections to be subordinated to the understanding, which had to be informed by the correct beliefs.

Moderates, on the other hand, tended to be more skeptical about the possibility of a natural religion; they did not consider having a single doctrinal standard essential for faith; and they also regarded the passions and affections as the true springs of all conduct, including our virtuous actions. Although they believed that reason and understanding were important, and that false ideas could certainly lead us astray, the general ends toward which our actions were directed, and our motives for performing them, were founded on pre-rational dispositions. These might be called passions, affections, or sentiments, but the terminology used was often fluid. Moral action, like piety, was not a matter of "the head"—that is, of correct beliefs in the understanding—but of having certain dispositions in "the heart." The concern of the Moderates was with inculcating these right dispositions, not with establishing "speculative" truths that would inform the understanding without necessarily improving our conduct, which was the real measure of virtue and piety alike.

The views of the Moderates and the orthodox on each of these three questions were linked. The orthodox position on doctrinal truth made it necessary for them to defend a strong belief in natural religion, and it was also closely tied to their emphasis on reason and understanding in human action. In contrast, the Moderates' relative skepticism about the possibility of a natural religion was connected with their emphasis on the "practical" and nondoctrinal rather than the "speculative" nature of Christianity, and with the belief in passions and affections as the proper springs of all human actions, including those that were morally good and pious. There were of course differences in nuance within the orthodox and the Moderate Party, neither of which was ever anything but a loose association between individuals who were broadly like-minded. Yet it is possible to identify on each side a shared set of beliefs in the three areas of natural religion, doctrine, and the importance of the passions and affections for moral actions.

The Defense of Natural Religion

The orthodox Calvinist opponents of the Moderates were staunch defenders of natural religion, an aspect of their thought that has been neglected, perhaps because traditional Calvinists are often expected to be skeptical about the value of human reason in general, let alone any kind of natural, reasonable religion. Thus, Calvinist orthodoxy is commonly associated with a firm belief in the depravity of human nature since original sin. However, similar to orthodox Calvinists such as John Erskine writing earlier in the century, figures such as Witherspoon in the 1750s were far more concerned than is often realized to defend the viability of a natural religion. In fact, their particular theological beliefs on the justification and salvation of sinners required them to do so. Moderates, on the other hand, are sometimes credited with a desire to substitute a natural religion, founded on reason, for traditional Calvinist beliefs.[3] This seems all the more plausible because a preference for natural religion is often thought to be characteristic of the kind of compromise between secular reason and Christian revelation that is thought to have characterized the "religious Enlightenment" the Moderates represented. Yet Moderates, like their heterodox predecessors earlier in the century, were, if anything, more skeptical than the orthodox about the viability of a natural religion. The positions of Moderates and the orthodox on natural religion, are, essentially, the reverse of what they are usually thought to be.[4]

The divisions between the orthodox and Moderates over natural religion became especially apparent in the publications that appeared around the time of the attempt to have David Hume and Lord Kames censured by the General Assembly of the Presbyterian Kirk for infidelity. The campaign against the two philosophers had begun with the anonymous publication of a pamphlet, *An Analysis of the Moral and Religious Sentiments contained in the Writings of Sopho and David Hume, Esq.,* which was almost certainly by a minor orthodox clergyman, the Reverend John Bonar of Cockpen. "Sopho" was a nickname for Kames, whose *Essays on the Principles of Morality and Natural Religion* had been published anonymously a few years previously, in 1751, though the identity of the author was widely known. Hume's thought had, by that time, been the subject of debate and of much criticism for more than a decade. Although his first work, the *Treatise of Human Nature* (1739–40), had also appeared anonymously, Hume's authorship was no secret, and its controversial doctrines had been responsible for his failure to be elected to the Edinburgh chair of moral philosophy in 1745. Hume later complained that his *Treatise* had fallen "dead-born from the press,"[5] a statement that is often interpreted to mean that his book was largely ignored, even by those conservative, orthodox figures like Bonar who were most likely to oppose it.[6] Yet John Bonar clearly knew the *Treatise*, even describing it as the "compleat system" of Hume's philosophy. He did not quote from it in his pamphlet, not, as Bonar explained, because he did not know it, but because Hume had never "thought fit to own" his first work, and it therefore seemed wrong to use it as evidence against him.[7] In any case, there was little need to draw on the *Treatise*, since Hume's two *Enquiries*, which came out in 1748 and 1751, respectively, and the first volume of his *History of Great Britain* (1754) were more than sufficient to substantiate Bonar's accusations.

The works of Hume and Kames had caused offense for several reasons,[8] but one of the most important—and one that has received little attention— was their skepticism concerning natural religion. John Bonar, for example, summarized some of Kames's main offending arguments as follows: "The powers of reason can give us no satisfying evidence of the being of a God"; "The perfections of God are either such as we cannot prove, or cannot comprehend"; and "It is whimsical and absurd to pretend that the material world is subject to the providence of God."[9] Another example of this type of orthodox literature is the 1753 *Estimate of the Profit and Loss of Religion* by the clergyman George Anderson, who had originally coined the nickname "Sopho" for Lord Kames. A substantial part of Anderson's *Estimate* was devoted to defending natural religion against the doubts of Lord Kames. Although the Moderates' position on natural religion was much less extreme than that of Hume, there was at least an intellectual affinity between their skepticism and that of Kames.

Kames had argued that the usefulness of human reason as a guide to religious truth was limited. He even cited Hume's argument from Section XI of the *Enquiry concerning Human Understanding* about the futility of attempts to demonstrate philosophically the existence and attributes of God, or the creation of the world by God, in which Hume, according to Kames, proposed that "we have no foundation for ascribing any attribute to the Deity, but what is perfectly commensurate with the imperfection of the world."[10] It was therefore impossible to use the world as evidence for, say, the benevolence or omnipotence of God, since the nature of events in this world was mixed, "partly good and partly evil."[11] The argument that the world had to have a cause and that only an all-powerful deity could be that cause did not stand up to scrutiny, because our reasoning from effects to causes assumed that we had experience of other causal relationships of this kind. The world, however, was unique. We had not been present at its beginning and had not witnessed the creation of other worlds. Therefore, the existence of this world was no reason to argue that it must have been created by a God.[12] And, conceded Kames, "supposing reason to be our only guide in these matters, which is supposed by this philosopher [Hume] in his argument, I cannot help feeling his reasoning to be just."[13]

Reason was, however, not "our only guide." We could depend on other, non-rational "principles implanted in our nature"—namely, "sense" and "feeling."[14] The power, wisdom, and benevolence of God were "intuitively certain,"[15] because the deity had "not left us to collect his existence from abstract or uncertain arguments, but has made us feel, that he exists."[16] Reason did not contradict these conclusions of sense and feeling; it could even help to support them. But we were not directed to those truths or persuaded of them by reason.[17] The deity was "too grand an object, to be comprehended, in any perfect manner, by the human mind,"[18] which was incapable even of demonstrating the most basic attribute of the deity, its unity. Indeed this was "what, of all, we can have the least certainty about, by the light of nature,"[19] for there was no logical inconsistency in assuming the existence of two or more supreme beings, "whose essence and actions are so regulated by the nature and essence of the beings themselves, as to be altogether concordant and harmonious."[20] We had no conception of the wisdom and power of God, which "are so far beyond the reach of our comprehension, that they may justly be called *infinite.*"[21] Although we were conscious that the world was not "governed by chance or blind fatality," as "Epicureans" like the Roman poet-philosopher Lucretius had maintained in his *De Rerum Natura,* and we were determined "by a principle in our nature, to attribute such effects to some intelligent and designing cause"—namely, God[22]—that principle was a feeling; it was not rational. Rational argument indeed would never suffice to persuade us of this truth, "because our reasonings upon this subject, must, at best, be abstruse, and beyond the comprehension of the bulk of mankind."[23] Reason had some uses. It could give "its aid, to lead us to the knowledge of the Deity. It enlarges our views of final causes, and of the prudence of wisdom and goodness." Yet on the whole it was "not so mighty an affair, as philosophers vainly pretend," because it afforded "very little aid, in making original discoveries." The conclusion from "beautiful and orderly effects to a designing cause" was thus entirely a matter of "sense and feeling," and of an "internal light," not rational conviction.[24]

Similar to Blair's skepticism of the value of human reasoning on religious matters,[25] Kames's also extended to the belief that was the most important for morality: the immortality of the soul and the existence of a future state. Hume, famously, denied the possibility of natural knowledge of the immortality of the soul, because there was no means of knowing the substance of anything, whether this was the human soul or a material body, since "neither by considering the first origin of ideas, nor by means of a definition are we able to arrive at any satisfactory notion of substance."[26] And that, he said, "seems to me a sufficient reason for abandoning utterly that dispute concerning the materiality and immateriality of the soul, and makes me absolutely condemn even the question itself."[27] In his essay on the immortality of the soul, which was withheld from publication until after his death, Hume again argued that it was futile to try to arrive at a notion of the soul and its afterlife by means of philosophical reasoning, ending the essay with a statement (which may or may not have been ironical) that mankind owed the knowledge of the immortality of the soul entirely to divine revelation.[28]

Kames, too, wrote that reason was incapable of proving the immortality of the soul and the existence of an afterlife. When James Boswell, for example, commented that "it was hard that we were not allowed to have any notion of what kind of existence we shall have," Kames replied that "there was an impenetrable veil between us and our future state and being sensible of this, he never attempted to think on the subject, knowing it to be in vain."[29] There is no philosophical argument for the immortality of the soul in the first edition of Kames's 1751 *Essays on the Principles of Morality and Natural Religion,* and not even a discussion of the substance of the soul. The third edition of Kames's *Essays* in 1779 did include a chapter on "Matter and Spirit," in which Kames contradicted the common argument, that matter was inert, and only the soul was active. Matter was active, too, but at the same time Kames also argued that human nature included a spirit, adding, however, that its immortality was not known to unaided reason. "That the latter [spirit] can subsist independent of the former, is a fact for which we are indebted to Revelation, being far beyond the reach of human investigation."[30]

Like Blair, other Moderate clergymen were similarly doubtful about the capacity of unassisted, natural reason to find out and prove certain religious truths such as the immortality of the soul and the existence of a future state in which rewards and punishments would be meted out.[31] Blair's friend John Logan wrote, for example, that, on the one hand, the "light of nature affords us many discoveries, and the religion of nature suggests many obligations to virtue. The heathens reasoned well concerning the existence of a supreme Cause; from the things which are seen, they inferred his eternal Power and Godhead, and gave many excellent lessons for the conduct of human life."[32] These heathen thinkers' reasoning, however, fell short of endowing these moral rules with the binding force of laws, or the "authority of uncontroverted truth."[33] In a passage that appears to echo the skepticism of Kames and even Hume, Logan stated that there was no conclusive evidence in the natural world for the "wisdom and goodness" of the Creator. Although there was "order and beauty" in creation, there were also "irregularities and evils of the moral world," which did not seem compatible with the idea of a just and benevolent deity. Moreover, and crucially, among pagans, the "immortality of the soul," the basis of any coherent moral theory, "was rather the object of their wishes, than of their firm belief." In these circumstances, the "sense of moral good and evil, amidst the universal degeneracy and depravity of manners, was in danger of being altogether lost."[34] The "wisest of the ancient philosophers" recognized that arguments from natural reason were no effective support for virtue, and concluded that some form of immediate "revelation of the Divine will,"[35] which they lacked, was needed to establish morality on a robust foundation.

Another Moderate who shared these skeptical attitudes about natural religion was the clergyman and historian William Robertson. His views on religious matters are difficult to establish because his surviving religious writings are limited to a very small number of sermons.[36] But Robertson was also one of the most prominent and prolific historians of his age. His histories are a rich source of evidence for his views on the natural knowledge of the immortality of the soul and its connection with morality, particularly if they are read in conjunction with the sermon Robertson gave to the Scottish Society for the Propagation of Christian Knowledge in 1755, on the "Situation of the World at the Time of Christ's Appearance." From these texts it is clear that Robertson shared the doubts of figures like Blair and Logan about the capacity of unassisted reason to demonstrate the immortality of the soul and the existence of an afterlife. In his 1755 sermon, Robertson wrote that the "doctrine of future rewards and punishments . . . hath been, and must ever be, the chief foundation of virtuous obedience."[37] One could not expect to find "pure and undefiled virtue, among those people who were destitute of the instructions, the promises, and assistance of divine revelation. Unenlightened reason often errs: Unassisted virtue always deviates from the right path."[38]

The limitations of natural religion were particularly evident, Robertson believed, from the history of pagan societies, because they offered case studies of communities that had, in some cases, achieved very high levels of refinement and sophistication, but by definition did not enjoy the benefits of Christian revelation. Robertson wrote about several heathen civilizations. He argued, for example, that in the small city-states of pre-Roman classical antiquity the shortcomings of natural religion were to some extent compensated by their political institutions. These states were "unbroken by the refinements of luxury, and animated with the noblest of human passions, struggled for liberty,"[39] having been founded by wise lawgivers who understood human nature. Moreover, these states were small, and "the conduct of every citizen" was therefore "subjected to the eye of the magistrate; and the nature of the government obliged him, to inspect their manners with severity. The smallest crimes could not escape observation."[40] Such human supports of virtue, however, were "temporary and precarious,"[41] and those states that did not perish from internal strife eventually succumbed to the onslaught of Roman imperial expansion, with the result that "the alliance betwixt morals and government was now broken," as the "petty states" of early antiquity were absorbed into the enormous Roman empire.[42] Pagan religion could never quite fill the gap left by the collapse of the virtuous city-states because it lacked the certainty concerning the afterlife that would have been needed to have a beneficial effect on public morality. Instead, pagan religion was a form of superstition, which "far from giving any aid to virtue, seems not to have had the least connection with it. No repentance of past crimes, no future amendment of conduct, are ever prescribed by it, as proper means of appeasing the offended deities."[43] Whenever pagan religion was used to support the practice of virtue, Robertson believed, it could do so only with the help of superstition and deceit, because the real threats of punishment in the afterlife were unknown. Robertson quoted the Greek geographer Strabo, who had said that the "thunder of Jupiter, the aegis of Minerva, the trident of Neptune" were "fables, which the legislators who formed the political constitution of states employ[ed] as bugbears to overawe the credulous and simple."[44] These fables might serve to keep the vulgar and unlearned in order, but they could not, in the long run, satisfy the educated and intellectually more accomplished elites.

It is worth pausing here, briefly, to consider the common characteriza-tion of Robertson and other "Moderate" clergymen as "Christian Stoics," who recognized an affinity between Christianity and Stoic philosophy and tried to produce a synthesis of the two.[45] Certainly, Robertson, like many of his contemporaries, admired the Stoics. He even began a translation, which he never completed, of Marcus Aurelius's *Meditations*.[46] It would, however, be a mistake to believe that the positive references to classical antiquity indicate a desire to merge pagan philosophy with Christian thought. The "splendid actions among the heathens" of classical antiquity, Robertson wrote, had been "justly celebrated by Christians," yet this was "in order to rouze the zeal and emulation of a degenerate age"—namely, his own.[47] The point Robertson was making was that if even heathens, who only had the inferior resources of natural reason to draw upon, were capable of such remarkable acts of virtue, how shameful was it if Christians who enjoyed the advantages of the Gospel could not do the same, let alone exceed the standards set by the best of the ancients. Stoicism was the most noble system of philosophy that natural, unassisted reason was capable of, but it was not equal to Christianity, or suit-able for supplementing it.

The shortcomings of paganism were not limited to the societies of European classical antiquity. They occurred in all non-Christian civilizations that had reached a certain level of refinement by natural means, but were not aware of the superior truths of the Gospel. Thus, Robertson drew explicit parallels between pagan classical antiquity and the Hindu civilization of ancient India. There the Brahmins "had established a system of morals, founded on principles the most generous and dignified which *unassisted reason is capable of discovering* [my italics]."[48] But the religious foundations of their morality were deficient because they were ignorant of the Gospel. For "so unable are the limited powers of the human mind to form an adequate idea of the perfections and operations of the Supreme Being, that in all the theories concerning them, of the most eminent philosophers in the most enlightened nations we find a lamentable mixture of ignorance and error,"[49] because they are destitute of "superior guidance."[50] As in ancient Greece, the purpose of religion in Hindu civilization was to be a prop for morality. And since the vulgar and unlearned, in India as much as in ancient Greece, did not have the ability or leisure to engage in the same subtle and refined speculations as the Brahmins and the philosophers, respectively, the common people "were to be kept in order by delusion, and allowed to do what is right, or deterred from venturing upon what is wrong by the hope of those imaginary rewards which superstition promises, and the dread of those punishments, which it threatens."[51] The pagan civilizations of pre-Columbian South and Mesoamerica suffered from the same defects. The Incas of Peru, for example, practiced a rudimentary form of natural religion that had been introduced by the founders of Inca civilization, Manco Capac and Mama Ocollo, when the Peruvian population was still in a state of savagery. It was a form of natural religion because in it the mind was "employed in contemplating the order and beneficence that really exist in nature,"[52] but it was still based on a very limited understanding of the natural order.[53] And like the Greek elites or the Brahmins, the rulers of the Peruvians could not rely on natural religion alone to uphold discipline within society, so that they were forced to resort to superstition. Hence, the family of the ruler was held to be sacred and of divine descent, and all crimes were "punished capitally" because they were "not considered as transgressions of human laws, but as insults offered to the Deity."[54] The "dread of punishment, which they were taught to consider an unavoidable vengeance inflicted by offended Heaven, withheld them from evil."[55] Again, ignorance of the Christian doctrine of the afterlife leads politicians to invent superstitious beliefs as a second-rate expedient for restraining their subjects from crime. Natural religion, Robertson believed, offered no robust foundation for a moral theory.[56]

It may seem paradoxical that orthodox Presbyterians were far more vigorous defenders of natural, reasonable religion than an "enlightened" philosopher such as Kames or the Moderates. The orthodox believed, however, that natural morality required a system of natural religion, including knowledge of a future state, because humans had to be able to realize the sinfulness of their own nature. Otherwise they would not feel compelled to seek out the remedies offered by the Gospel for their corruption. Above all, they had to recognize their inability to adhere perfectly to the rules of morality, and their liability for divine punishment, unless they obtained God's pardon. Without natural religion and the belief in the immortality of the soul, however, this natural morality was incomplete, because there was no clear system of sanctions attached to morality in this life, in which humans often "disobey the law of God . . . with safety."[57] Vice might be accompanied by some disadvantages, especially in the long run, but these disadvantages did not qualify as proper punishments, because they did not always follow from an immoral action, and insofar as they did occur, they were part of the normal, natural course of events, not inflicted by an angry deity in such a way that they were recognizable as a form of chastisement. Natural religion supplied that defect by providing "plain presages" of punishments "in the world to come,"[58] which were, in principle, known to all humans, Christians and infidels alike. Anderson thought, for example, that all the heathen philosophers of classical antiquity, with the exception of the Epicureans, entertained some notion of the immortality of the soul and a divine judgment in an afterlife. "For time beyond tradition, all the ancient world believed, that the soul survived the body, and was immortal."[59] Witherspoon, too, had declared that the belief in a "future state of rewards and punishments has been as universal as the belief of a Deity, and seems inseparable from it, and therefore must be considered as the sanction of the moral law."[60] In his student dissertation on *The Immortality of the Mind* (1739) he had explained that we did not know the true essences of things— that is, their inner nature—on which their external, sensible qualities depended. It was possible, however, to form some limited conclusions about the substance of the soul from external qualities. "Since therefore the qualities of the mind, that is, thought and reasoning, and spontaneous acts, seem entirely opposed to the known qualities of matter, it is possible to conclude, that the human mind is something utterly different from the [material] body."[61] Unlike the soul, all physical bodies were composed of innumerable small material particles. Even "the best and most refined material objects are nothing but pieces of matter, which are assembled in different ways."[62] The connections between these material particles could be dissolved, leading to the disintegration of the material body they formed. The soul, however, could not be subdivided into smaller elements. It was a simple, indivisible substance that could not perish as a result of a disaggregation of parts. Within the ordinary course of nature, therefore, the soul was immortal. It could perish only as a result of complete annihilation, "and as this exceeds the powers of any natural causes whatsoever, it is possible to affirm that the human mind is by its nature immortal."[63]

Judgment in the afterlife, Witherspoon believed, was necessary to account for the fact that the distribution of external good fortune in this world often seemed unfair: "Frequently we see everything turning out well for the most criminal of all people, while the good are weighed down by countless evils."[64] If there were no life after death, these injustices in temporal life would mean either that God was not a wise and just deity, or that he was incapable of governing the world through his providence. As a source for

Witherspoon's own ideas, his dissertation of 1739 should be treated with caution, since it was a student exercise and it is not certain how much was composed by Witherspoon himself. Whether or not Witherspoon was the main author, it is clear that he adhered to this view of the soul in later life. In his *Lectures on Moral Philosophy* he wrote that knowledge of an afterlife did not require any kind of divine revelation, Scriptural or other.[65] Although we could not "at present form any complete or adequate idea of a spirit," it was clear that mind or intelligence must be a substance altogether distinct from matter. "Matter as such and universally, is inert and divisible; thought or intelligence, active and uncompounded."[66] Again, he related the argument for the immortality of the soul to a kind of theodicy: "If you deprive a good man of the hope of future happiness, his state seems very undesirable. On the contrary, sometimes the worst of men enjoy prosperity and success to a great degree, nor do they seem to have much remorse, as to be an adequate punishment for their crimes."[67]

Morality had to rest on a natural religion that included a belief in divine providence, some kind of theodicy, and an afterlife with appropriate rewards and sanctions. This natural religion was necessary for leading everyone, infidels especially, to a recognition of their dependence on the saving doctrines of the Gospel. The means of obtaining this pardon were known only from revelation, not natural reason, because "pardon," Anderson explained, "is an act of absolute sovereignty."[68] There was no rational necessity for God to forgive anybody their violations of natural morality, which was identical to the original Law of Works given to humankind in the Garden of Eden. "And though those who admit natural religion might justly conclude, that unto the supreme Being belonged mercy and forgiveness of sins; yet, they must be at a loss to know, how this forgiveness of sins was to be sued for, and upon what terms it was to be obtained."[69] Witherspoon argued similarly that humans had to be capable of knowing the complete duties of natural morality without the aid of revelation. Otherwise, those humans who were not Christian could plead ignorance of the Law of Works as an excuse for their actions. The universal consciousness of guilt led humankind to seek a further remedy—namely, the Gospel—and especially the merit of Christ's death on the cross, which had to be known and believed sincerely in order to effect the justification of the sinner. Witherspoon's defense of natural religion was therefore closely tied to his theological views on the means of obtaining salvation.

The Defense of Doctrine

Witherspoon subscribed to an orthodox federal theology, as it was set out in the Westminster Confession, according to which humans would have been able to merit eternal life in the state of innocence by the strict observance of the Law of Works given to Adam by God. Following original sin, the Law of Works remained in force, but humans were incapable of fulfilling it perfectly. The guilt of Adam and Eve was transmitted to all their posterity. In addition, humans were liable to commit many particular sins for which they could be justly punished by God. The only hope for salvation lay not in humans' actions, but in their faith in Christ: "no man, whatever be his character, or whatever be his hope, shall enter into rest, unless he be reconciled to God, through Jesus Christ . . . all mankind are by nature in a state of guilt and condemnation."[70] Christ's role in justification was not that of a moral teacher, who was on the same level as "mortal reformers,"[71] any of whom might offer the means for redemption from the effects of original sin. Yet that was what was implied by "nominal Christians" (by which he meant the Moderates), who offered an "unnatural mixture" of "modern philosophy with ancient Christianity" and "softened, concealed, or denied" the fundamental doctrines of the Gospel.[72] Access to salvation, however, was granted exclusively through Christ. In one long footnote Witherspoon criticized those, like the Moderates, who wanted to replace doctrinal truth with charity as the foundation of Christian faith. It was the "fashionable language of the age, to give large encomiums upon charity," when the real intention was to remove the distinction between truth and falsehood in doctrinal matters, in a way that reduced the importance of Christ for salvation and thus came close to Socinian and Arian ideas.[73]

A common objection to the emphasis on the knowledge of Christ's sacrifice, according to Witherspoon, was that it would exclude those who had never heard of his name from any hope of gaining salvation, so that, in effect, the efficacy of Christ's death did not extend to those who were ignorant of him. Yet it was a sufficient sign of divine mercy that God had not allowed all of humankind to perish "in a state of sin and misery."[74] Nobody was entitled to the chance of salvation, though Witherspoon suggests that those who earnestly sought it would be rewarded with divine assistance. One objection to the strong emphasis on the mediatory role of Christ and the absolute need for knowledge of and belief in Christ and the merit of his sacrifice on the cross, rather than virtuous actions, was that it might encourage a superficial faith, based on an excessive reliance on the acceptance of the truth of particular doctrinal propositions, while neglecting the practical conduct expected of a Christian believer. It was the extreme implications of "solfideism," the belief in salvation by faith alone and not by works, that had helped to stimulate many of the religious revival movements from the seventeenth century onward, whose members wanted to replace superficial belief in doctrine with a "true," spiritual Christianity based on charity. Witherspoon was of course not opposed to "holiness of life," but he argued that such holiness of life was the necessary fruit of the sincere belief in the merit of Christ's death on the cross: sinners were not justified by achieving holiness of life; they achieved holiness of life by being justified. Thus, it was legitimate to assume that a profligate person who professed to be Christian could not be a sincere believer, but in order to be saved it was not enough to act morally. In any case, nobody was capable of acting perfectly morally at all times, so faith in Christ was necessary to secure forgiveness for particular sins, even in the case of sincere believers. The key point Witherspoon was concerned to make was that Christian faith always depended on the recognition of particular *truths,* especially the significance of the sacrifice of Christ on the cross for humankind, rather than certain forms of conduct, even if certain forms of conduct were necessarily associated with the acceptance of the key truths of Christian religion.

Witherspoon's view was characteristic of orthodox Calvinism in the mid-eighteenth century. The clergyman Robert Walker, a colleague and friend of Hugh Blair's at St. Giles Church in Edinburgh, is another example of this orthodox view. Walker believed that all humans were conceived in sin: they were sinners from the moment of birth, regardless of their particular actions. This was evidenced by the fact that all humans were mortal. Death, according to Walker, was a punishment, and this punishment presupposed guilt, because God, who was perfectly just, would not have imposed this punishment on humankind for no reason.[75] Human nature was fallen because of the guilt inherited from the protoplasts. Of course humans were guilty of particular sins, too, because of their corrupt nature, but they were guilty even before they had committed any particular sins. When humankind was created it was placed under a law by God, which was broken by Adam and Eve, and they and all their descendants were punished for their transgression by their expulsion from paradise and by the introduction of death into the world.

From then on, humans became incapable of observing perfectly the law imposed on them in the state of innocence, and any lapse was enough to justify a person's eternal damnation.[76]

The law of the state of innocence was known to humans on the basis of their natural reason, but they also realized their inability to follow its precepts at all times and their liability for the punishment that would follow from it. The only hope for salvation was the Gospel of Christ. By believing in Christ and the merit of Christ's death on the cross, the believer was not freed from the obligations of the original law. He or she would not even become capable of perfect obedience to that law, for even sincere believers committed sins occasionally, though it had to be assumed that they were less likely to sin than unbelievers. Believers' faults would not disappear, but they would be pardoned and overlooked because of their faith in Christ.[77]

Walker's sermon made it clear that knowledge of and belief in Christ was essential to salvation. Arriving at this belief required divine grace, but it did not transform the nature of the believer in such a way that the original law became superfluous. Even after grace had been received, there was a constant struggle between spirit and flesh, and it was always uncertain which would prevail. Lapses were always possible, and the righteous man fell seven times every day, and rose again.[78] Walker described the condition of the regenerate person as a delicate balance between "spirit" and "flesh," which could be upset any instant, if the spirit was momentarily weak. He also characterized this conflict as one between the senses and reason, or the "earthly tabernacle" and "its immortal inhabitant."[79] Consequently, believers should guard against anything that might "inflame your passions" and strengthen the power of the senses as opposed to that of reason and understanding.

Importantly, Walker, like Witherspoon, believed faith to be a matter of convincing the *understanding*, and of overcoming the passions and controlling them. One of the main differences between orthodox clergymen like Witherspoon or Walker, and their Moderate contemporaries, was that the latter considered faith to be a matter of cultivating charity—that is, the sincere love of God and one's fellow human beings, which was also the foundation of the true social virtues. Such love was, essentially, a passion or affection, and the disagreement between Moderates and orthodox over the role of doctrine and conduct in salvation therefore also reflected differences over the proper role of the intellect and the passions or affections in human nature.

Reason, Sentiment, and the Will

Blair, for example, argued that although reason and the understanding were important, they were only instruments of the feelings and dispositions that were the true motive forces behind our conduct. It was such non-rational powers of human nature that determined the kinds of ends toward which our actions were directed. Hume made this point bluntly when he declared that reason was the slave of the passions, and ought to be nothing else,[80] but Blair believed, too, that "arguments may convince the understanding, when they cannot conquer the passions."[81] Being virtuous depended on having the right kinds of feelings or sentiments, and on balancing or replacing bad desires with good ones. Morality, like religion, was very much a matter of the "heart" rather than the "head." Just as piety was not a matter of holding the correct doctrinal opinions, so too was virtue not the product of ideas in the intellect. False ideas in the understanding could be detrimental to practical morality, because they might mislead us about the nature of a particular end or the best means of achieving it. But moral judgment itself was founded on feeling and "sense," rather than ratiocination, and the motivation for acting morally depended on desires and sentiments rather than the conclusions of the intellect, which did not have the power to motivate conduct. More important for morality than a "speculative" understanding of its foundations was "practical" knowledge about the means of improving human nature by reforming those dispositions that were corrupted.

Kames also thought that we could not depend on our reason as a guide in moral matters. God had instead wisely endowed us with a variety of feelings and passions that inclined us toward virtuous behavior, prior to any reasoning about the rights and wrongs, or even the consequences of a particular action. We followed these passions without regard to our self-interest. Although morality was often compatible with or even furthered the interests of the agent, self-interest was not the motive of the action, and although we might derive pleasure from the gratification of our social affections, even this pleasure was not the original motive for our action, either. It might reinforce our desire to perform it, but we would have acted in the same way if our action had not been accompanied by this feeling. Our motive was a "direct impulse arising from the appetite or affection, which, as I have said, operates blindly, and in the way of instinct, without any view to consequences."[82] We were, for example, Kames said, drawn to "objects of distress"—that is, the sufferings of others, which might be thought painful and unpleasant to witness. Yet God, in his wisdom, had equipped us with a desire to succor our fellow humans in times of need.[83]

Not every passion, of course, drew humans toward performing moral actions. Some passions were corrupt and the cause of vicious conduct. There was a need for an additional principle that was capable of distinguishing between good and evil actions and restraining humans from committing the latter. That principle, Kames believed, was the moral sense, which approved or disapproved of our actions depending on their moral quality and resisted tendencies toward immoral actions, even though it might fail to prevent them. Some actions were not only disapproved by the moral sense, but also contrary to a natural sense of duty, which imposed a much stricter obligation on us than the moral sense alone. The actions included were those "directed against others, by which they are hurt or prejudged in their persons, in their fame, or in their goods," and were "the objects of a peculiar feeling. They are perceived and felt not only as *unfit* to be done, but as absolutely *wrong* to be done, and what, at any rate, we *ought* not to do."[84] The reason why these actions were a duty rather than just meriting approbation was that they concerned justice, which was far more necessary "to the support of society" than virtues such as "benevolence and generosity," though the latter were "more beautiful, and more attractive of love and esteem, than justice."[85] Justice was more limited than virtue, but it was also more essential to human life. Like the moral sense, our sense of justice was a "direct feeling." It was our conscience, which was the "voice of God within us which commands our strictest obedience, just as much as when his will is declared by express reve-lation."[86] Whenever we violated our conscience, we were filled with a dread of merited punishment so strong that "every unusual accident, every extraor-dinary misfortune is considered as a punishment purposely inflicted for the crime committed."[87] That feeling turned "into a law what without it can only be considered as a rational measure, and a prudential rule of action."[88] Our sense of duty ensured that the rules of justice, which were essential to the continued existence of human society, were, by and large, preserved.

Similarly, Blair believed that virtue depended on the operation of the affections, sentiments, and passions of human nature. In his 1739 student dissertation he argued that even a superficial examination of our nature informed us that we were naturally and necessarily impelled to approve of honesty and benevolence, and to feel revulsion at moral turpitude.[89] Our reaction to moral good and evil was analogous to our perception of aesthetic beauty, which was spontaneous and involuntary; its principles were rooted in our nature and were prior to any conclusions of the understanding, let alone abstract philosophical reflection. We were by nature endowed with a faculty of conscience, which was capable of making judgments on moral questions. The judgments of this conscience were reinforced by certain passions or affections, which were also part of human nature. Humans were, for example, endowed with a natural affection of benevolence, a desire to do good to others that might often be weak and obscured by competing affections, but there could be no doubt about its presence in human nature. Performing acts of benevolence alone satisfied this desire. The result was a particular pleasure that further strengthened our desire to behave virtuously. The pleasures associated with such moral actions were more refined than, and superior to, all selfish, immoral pleasures, and the effect of the constant exercise of virtue was to achieve the greatest possible personal happiness in this life: "Nothing contributes more to a happy life than the benign and social affections, which lead us to further the well-being of others. They always contribute to the tranquility of the mind, by their own force and nature: even when they are unsuccessful, they suffuse the mind with a pleasure far purer than anything that ever flows from private and more selfish delights."[90] We derived far greater joy, Blair believed, from doing good to others than from following our narrow self-interest. There were of course those who held a false idea of pleasure, but they always suffered more discomfort than pleasure from the pursuit of their corrupt desires. The criminal, for example, who believed he was serving his private interests, was afflicted with continual pangs of conscience and a constant fear of just punishment. And yet, the immoral desires and passions were often firmly rooted in human nature and difficult to eradicate: "the beginnings of virtue," Blair wrote, therefore "are laborious. But, by perseverance its labours diminish, and its pleasures increase."[91] A virtuous character was acquired incrementally and was built up through repeated exercises and trials. Whenever an individual passed such a trial by choosing virtue over vice, his or her habitual disposition toward virtue, it appears, was reinforced and made a little firmer, and as virtue "ripens into confirmed habit, it becomes both smoother in practice, and more complete in its reward."[92] Whether a person could be considered moral or not depended on the stability and constancy of his or her virtuous dispositions, not the occasional performance of a good deed. In a sense, humans had no choice whether to be virtuous or not in any particular situation because their conduct was the necessary expression of their dispositions. They did not have the power to act differently. Yet we were responsible for the dispositions that made up our character, because they were formed in a process of moral culture.

The problem from an orthodox perspective was that Moderates like Blair appeared to downplay the authority of reason and understanding, and the freedom of the human will. The disagreement is illustrated particularly clearly by a passage in Witherspoon's *Ecclesiastical Characteristics*, which was first published in 1753, in the period between the first edition of Kames's *Essays on the Principles of Morality and Natural Religion* and the campaign to have Hume and Kames censured by the General Assembly. In this passage Witherspoon criticizes the Moderates' admiration for a variety of philosophical works—namely, "Leibnitz's Theodicee and his Letters, Shaftsbury's Characteristics, Collins' Enquiry into Human Liberty, all Mr H—n's [Francis Hutcheson's] Pieces, [Matthew Tindal's] Christianity as Old as Creation, D—n's [William Dudgeon's] Best Scheme, and H—e's [David Hume's] Moral Essays."[93] It is not immediately evident what Leibniz, Shaftesbury, Collins, Hutcheson, Tindal, Dudgeon, and Hume should have in common. Several of them, such as Leibniz and Hume, are, if anything, at odds with each other on several matters, including natural religion. Yet, to Witherspoon, the idea that all these authors appeared to share was that the human will was not a "full *natural* or *Physical* power of acting differently," as Leibniz's opponent Samuel Clarke had defined it,[94] but a desire, which determined the ends toward which actions were directed. The question of the nature of human volition was central to eighteenth-century interest in the Leibniz–Clarke correspondence, as is evident from the fact that attached to the very end of the 1717 London edition, which was probably the one used by Witherspoon, were Anthony Collins's "Letters to Dr Clarke concerning Liberty and Necessity" with Clarke's responses, as well as Clarke's "Remarks upon a Book, entitled, A Philosophical Enquiry concerning Human Liberty," in which Clarke criticized Collins's necessitarian interpretation of the human will. In the appendix to this edition were also several passages from Leibniz's *Theodicy* and other writings. Several of these excerpts seemed to imply a necessitarian interpretation of human volition as a kind of desire. In one of them, for example, Leibniz described the will as an "inclination," stating that "we may . . . compare the Soul to a *Force*, which has at one and the same time a *Tendency many ways*, but *acts on That part only* where it finds the Greatest

Ease, or the Least Resistance ... Thus the *Inclinations of the Soul*, tend towards All apparent Goods; And these are the antecedent Volitions: But the Consequent Volition, which is the last Result, determines itself towards That Good which affects us the most strongly."[95]

Matthew Tindal's *Christianity as Old as Creation* is included in Witherspoon's list of authors admired by Moderates, not necessarily, as might perhaps be thought, because Tindal was a deist, although Witherspoon would certainly have objected to that side of his thought, too, but because of his (Tindal's) view that "God had endow'd Man with such a Nature, as makes him *necessarily desire* [my italics] his own Good."[96] And according to William Dudgeon, a tenant farmer and freethinker from Berwickshire who died of consumption at age thirty-seven, the determination that necessarily affects all intelligent beings is a "natural Desire of Good or Happiness."[97] The emphasis, in various ways, of Shaftesbury, Hutcheson, and Hume on the affections and passions of human nature as the springs of action appeared to Witherspoon to exemplify the same necessitarian tendency, which he detected in the thought of his Moderate opponents, and which, only a few years later, he and other orthodox clergymen would be criticizing in the writings of Lord Kames.

Many orthodox worried that the Moderates who thought of the human will as a passion or affection were unable to explain how and why we choose to follow our "good" rather than our "bad" passions. Affections, passions, and sentiments might be capable of motivating actions, but they are unsuitable for discerning between different kinds of action, because feelings are without powers of judgment. All judgments about right and wrong, and, indeed, about anything, are actions of the understanding and involved ratiocination. Terms such as the "*moral sense, impression, sentiment, feeling*, and *the light within*" have no place there.[98] For the

> intellect or understanding ... is exerted in three operations, the first of which is called *apprehension, perception,* or *idea*. These are terms which philosophers, antient and modern, have used to express a single representation of any object, of which we neither affirm or deny any thing, as *man, circle;* all abstract terms, as *manness, rotundity whiteness;* and all *verbs,* without person, number, or time, as *speak, write* &c. The second operation of the intellect is called judgment, *judicium,* and that elegantly enough. By this *propositions* or

enunciations are formed, by adding two of these perceptions or simple ideas together; if they agree, as *man* and *animal,* we judge and pronounce that man is not a tree. The third operation of the *understanding* is called *discursus* or discourse; and by some, *reasoning* or *ratiocination.* By this we gather, or collect, or infer one thing from another . . .[99]

Therefore, Anderson wrote, "I defy SOPHO [Kames] . . . to find in the human understanding a place for sentiment, feeling, and the light-within, distinct from all, or any of the aforementioned operations: for these are the literal and logical acts of the mind, as they have for their objects things *as true.* "[100] By substituting feelings for judgments of the intellect "sensitive" philosophers such as Kames took "morality off the old and solid foundation, to place it upon an internal sensation, to be understood according to everyone's fancy,"[101] for they considered such feelings "not as figurative, but as real and new-discovered faculties of the soul."[102] However, the only way "sensitive philosophers" could account for the full range of different operations of which the mind was capable was to multiply the different types of feeling, each of which was made responsible for a particular mental action: "Feeling is perception, feeling is taste, feeling is knowledge, feeling is a notion, feeling is conscience, and feeling is the light within. Thus there is a feeling of approbation, and a feeling of disapprobation, a feeling of property, a feeling of duty, a feeling of justice, a feeling of merited punishment, a moral feeling, and a metaphysical feeling."[103] In effect, Anderson commented, by calling every operation of the mind a feeling, Hume and Kames ended up explaining nothing: "With SOPHO's leave, a term applied to every thing, signifies nothing; and his feeling, applied to so many things and so contradictory things, signifies very little more."[104]

Witherspoon was equally reluctant to ground moral action in the human passions. Moral principles, he believed, were truths of reason, known by the human intellect. For an individual to be moral, reason had to rule and discipline the passions, which were the immediate cause of sinful actions. Humans were composed of a material body and an immaterial soul or mind, which, for Witherspoon, was a simple, indivisible substance. The mind had different faculties, which "are commonly divided into . . . the understanding, the will, and the affections," though Witherspoon argued that "these are not three qualities wholly distinct, as if they were three different beings, but different

ways of exerting the same simple principle. It is the soul or mind that under-
stands, wills, or is affected with pleasure and pain."[105] The exact relationship
between the three faculties, however, the degree to which any one of them was
dependent on or subordinate to the direction of another, was a matter of some
difficulty. It was possible to imagine a person who joined great intellectual
powers to a corrupt character. It would therefore seem that the moral good
was not "the object of the understanding."[106] But at the same time, the choices
made by the will in favor of one course of action over another appeared to rest
on the conclusions of the understanding. From this, Witherspoon wrote, had
resulted a debate between philosophers like Samuel Clarke "and some others,
[who] make understanding or reason the immediate principle of virtue," and
those like Shaftesbury or Hutcheson, who "make affection the principle of it."
Witherspoon's view was that "perhaps neither the one nor the other is wholly
right. Probably both are necessary."[107] The affections of the mind were also
called passions because they were "often excited by external objects,"[108] and
were, to that extent, "passive." They could exert considerable influence over
the understanding and the will, biasing the former and inclining the latter to a
particular end.

Unlike Blair or Kames, let alone Hume, however, Witherspoon never
equated the will with desire, and he did not consider reason to be a mere
instrument of this will-as-desire. Rather, it was reason that established intellectual truth and moral goodness, independently of the affections or passions:
"truth naturally and necessarily promotes goodness, and falsehood the
contrary."[109] The problem, however, was that the affections, in the current
fallen state of humankind, often interfered with the proper functioning of
the understanding, and prevented it from forming a true and morally good
conclusion. The morally good was not, he believed, considered morally good
because it was the object of a moral affection. Rather, moral goodness was
founded on intellectual, rational truth.

Orthodox fears about the Moderates' naive trust in the guidance of the
affections and passions of human nature are especially apparent from the
controversy over the performance in Edinburgh in 1756 of the play *Douglas*,
which had been written by the Moderate minister John Home. Controversies
over the permissibility of the stage had arisen when, for example, the poet
Allan Ramsay in 1731 completed *The Gentle Shepherd*, a historical-pastoral
play set in the Pentlands after the Restoration of 1660. Staging a play became
even more difficult after the British Parliament passed the Licensing Act of

1737, which required a Royal Patent to present spoken drama. From the 1740s, however, the Licensing Act was regularly circumvented by advertising plays as gratis intervals between pieces in a musical concert, a development that led to the foundation of a permanent theater in 1746 at Canongate Concert Hall, where *Douglas* was first performed.[110] The concerns of the orthodox over theatrical performances reflected their philosophical disagreement with the Moderates over the role of the affections and passions in moral conduct. In 1757 Witherspoon argued that theatrical performances that promoted moral education and piety were imaginable: "I believe it is very possible to write a treatise in the form of a Dialogue, in which the general rules of the Drama are observed, which shall be as holy and serious, as any sermon that was ever preached or printed."[111] The catch, as he recognized, was that such "holy and serious" plays were rather unlikely to enjoy commercial success, because a public theater had to adapt itself to the tastes of its spectators, the majority of which would always be guided by their corrupt passions, as long as human nature persisted in its sinful, post-lapsarian state.[112] Attending plays that were popular would only inflame these passions further: "the chief influence of theatrical representations upon the spectator, is to strengthen the passions by indulgence, for there they are all exhibited in a lively manner, and such as is most fit to communicate the impression."[113] Passions, according to Witherspoon, spread as if by contagion, even if they were not real but only represented on stage or in writing.

The Moderates' belief in the moral usefulness of passions and affections was an example of a much wider culture of sensibility that was prominent in eighteenth-century thought, especially in literature.[114] Similar concerns to those of the orthodox opponents of *Douglas* were expressed by contemporary critics of sentimental novels, such as Samuel Richardson's *Pamela* and *Clarissa*, which involved "stories of alluring and vulnerable young women who either triumph over real or threatened violence and various kinds of temptation (*Pamela*) or become victims of it (*Clarissa*)." Such novels allowed, and indeed encouraged, readers to identify with the main characters and experience their desires and passions, which "many critics at the time found worrisome and questionable," because some "degree of faith in the goodness of human nature was required in order to regard such narratives as morally beneficial."[115] Witherspoon was similarly convinced that the vicarious experience of the passions of characters in a play or novel was more likely to damage than to improve the reader's or spectator's virtue, because *any* stimulation of the passions was bad for morality. Witherspoon's Moderate opponents, however, believed that moral action was founded precisely on the natural, regular operation of sentiments, passions, and affections, and the exercise of a moral sense, not on some dictate of reason or obedience to a law. Although these feelings and senses might of course be corrupted, the cause of sin was the subordination not of reason to the passions, but of good passions to bad passions. Stage plays, however, even commercially successful ones, were not likely to stimulate evil desires, at least in the present age, when society was more refined than in previous, more barbarous centuries. "[A] certain degree of indecency and licentiousness," wrote Adam Ferguson, "once permitted, is now rejected. . . . Plays more pure, and of a better moral tendency are . . . chosen from our antient stock," and "these qualities . . . are expected from every Writer of the present age."[116] Ferguson was also far more optimistic than Witherspoon about the response of a modern audience to the representation of sinful actions on stage. The latter had argued that depicting sinful actions on stage would stimulate the corresponding corrupt passions in members of the audience, because the immediate effect of the representation on stage and a peculiar aesthetic pleasure associated with any exact imitation of nature removed the critical detachment that was necessary for the audience to judge the moral qualities of characters in the play. Such performances were unlikely to improve the state of virtue in the audience. Ferguson replied that it was often impossible not to show immoral actions in plays because "in every story of distress, which is not merely accidental, wicked characters must appear, as well as good ones; for we cannot impute injury and cruelty to any other but the wicked."[117] Spectators were not invariably corrupted by witnessing immoral conduct on stage, in a novel, or in real life. Witherspoon had feared that the representation of wicked characters would seduce the audience into identifying with and then imitating them, but Ferguson was convinced that revulsion in such cases was instinctive, especially in the present, "refined" age. The moral message of the play did not have to be spelled out in the form of an instruction addressed to the intellect, nor was it necessary to banish all portrayal of sin from the play, because the appearance of evil characters by itself "improves the mind, by fostering our aversion to wickedness, in the same degree as the view of amiable characters heightens our love of virtue, by engaging our hearts in its behalf." By these means "a tender and affecting story improves the heart, and strengthens every good disposition."[118] This was the effect of the tragedy *Douglas,* in which, as

Ferguson wrote, "The designs of one person are painted in such colours of hateful depravity, as to become a necessary object of detestation. The mistakes of another awaken our caution, and become a lesson of prudence. The generous and elevated mind of a third, warms and exalts our sentiments; and that person, on whom the chief distress of this story falls, moves to compassion, and proves at last a warning against rash and fatal despair."[119]

The achievement of plays such as *Douglas* was to "convey instruction under the show of amusement."[120] Ferguson admitted that there might be corrupt plays that did not serve to encourage morality. But he also believed that these would not appeal to their audience, especially in a more refined age such as the one in which he was living. "A tragedy, which fails in exciting these emotions, or which would shock our favourable apprehensions of virtue, would soon be rejected with disgust."[121] A "just moral and true representation of nature" was sufficient to "carry the preference with every audience from more splendid and showy performances."[122]

"Common-Sense" Philosophy, Sentiments, and the Will

The trust in the natural sentiments of humankind seemed naive, not just to the orthodox. There were others among the Moderates, broadly defined, who believed that the tendency of Kames or Blair, and, before them, Hutcheson, to downplay the importance of reason and understanding in human action, and conflate the human will and its decisions with the operation of affections and feelings implied a necessitarian interpretation of human conduct. If all our behavior was motivated by desires that had certain determinate ends, and reason and the understanding were only the instruments of these desires, how could humans be said to have the power, in any given situation, to choose freely between various possible courses of action? The need to distinguish more clearly a power of human volition from the affections, passions, and sentiments of human nature was in particular the concern of the Moderates associated with the "common-sense" philosophy.[123]

Thomas Reid, for example, criticized Hutcheson for identifying "desire, aversion, hope, fear, joy, sorrow, all our appetites, passions and affections, as different modifications of the will."[124] He thought that Kames had made the same mistake. Volition, Reid believed, had to be separate from desires or passions, because we were clearly able to act contrary to them. Reason did not determine our will, either, but when reason and passion were in conflict the will had to decide what to do. How the will reached its decision was, to Reid's mind, an otiose and unanswerable question. What mattered was that the will was distinct from both reason and passion, and had the power to choose a course of action independently of them. He refused to address the classic problems presented by the two traditional alternative theories of the freedom of the will, those of "indifference" and "spontaneity." A liberty of indifference appeared to lead to a regress ad infinitum, as it was impossible to explain why a genuinely indifferent will, which was not inclined toward any particular course of action, should choose to do one thing rather than another. A "liberty of spontaneity," on the other hand, seemed to be no kind of liberty at all, because it suggested that the agent could not have acted any differently than he or she did. James Beattie stated, in terms very similar to Reid's, that the controversy over the liberty or necessity of the will was "unprofitable speculation," and announced his intention of confining himself to "plain, practical, and useful truths."[125] The freedom of the human will, its ability to determine itself, and not be determined by "motives, purposes, intentions, or reasons"[126] was a "matter of fact and experience, whereof the human mind is conscious, and which the language and behaviour of mankind in all ages prove that they did, and do, and must acknowledge."[127] It was of course possible for the will to be overwhelmed by the brute impulses of the passions and to follow them blindly without making the effort of a proper deliberation, but even then, volition was never identical to affection or passion. The will might be "determined by motives, purposes, intentions, or reasons," but that determination did not mean the will had no choice, since "it is the will itself, or the self-determining power of the mind, that gives a motive that weight and influence whereby the will is determined: in other words, it depends on ourselves, whether we are to act from one motive or another."[128] Genuine virtue required the exertion of this independent will. Although some affections and passions bore the same name as certain virtues, they were, in fact, separate from them, because all moral virtues were more than a desire to do something morally good; they were "fixed purposes of acting according to a certain rule."[129]

This view of human volition was quite different from the sentimentalism of earlier Moderates like Blair, and from the rationalism of orthodox thinkers like Witherspoon. The differences, however, did not preclude that they had a similar emphasis on the importance of habit and "culture." Both Reid and Beattie, for example, attributed a central role to an incremental "culture of the mind" in the making of a virtuous and godly character. Such a culture was the result of many particular good actions, each of which contributed to a reinforcing of our dispositions toward virtue, and it assumed the presence of "a self motive Power" in the mind "which we call Liberty by the vigorous efforts of which that impetus which is given to the mind by particular Appetites or passions may be opposed and resisted."[130] That was a necessary condition, if we were to be considered free agents at all whose actions could be morally imputed to them.[131] But "culture" was more than these particular exertions of our will that restrained the impulses of our appetites and passions on some occasions. It referred also to the process by which the passions that interfered with our virtuous conduct were brought to "that tone, that degree of Strength which answers best their natural End and purpose,"[132] and this transformation was possible because the natural "Strength of every appetite passion and affection" was not "so fixed by Constitution of our Nature or by other causes which are not in our power as that nothing we can do can either increase or diminish their force."[133] Our "resolution" or "fixed purpose" to be virtuous could therefore be strengthened by repetition and training, to such an extent that it became habitual. Even a habitual action of this kind was still an act of the will, because it had been formed by the continual exercise of that will, in concert with reason and against contrary influences from the passions. There were, Reid said, "acts of the will which are not transient and momentary, which may continue long, and grow into a habit."[134] "By such habits," Reid believed, "men are governed in their opinions and their practice."[135]

That emphasis on "culture" and habit was accompanied by a strong skepticism of "speculative" as opposed to "practical" knowledge. Like the Moderates of the 1750s or the heterodox Presbyterians earlier in the century, the "common-sense philosophers" emphasized the "practical" nature of their teachings, because they were concerned with the reform of conduct, rather than "speculative" ideas in the understanding. Oswald wrote, "Our ablest advocates for religion and virtue judging rather from abstract ideas than from plain facts, have long been of opinion, that the judgment being convinced, the will follows of course; and have accordingly devoted themselves to the study of logic and rhetoric." Yet that was a mistake, because in doing so they neglected "that noble art of touching the springs of the heart, so much practised by the sages of antiquity, and have thereby lost the influence they ought to have on the minds of men; for it is the heart, the heart alone, under just direction, and put into full motion, that has the power to balance the animal affections, and check the blind impulses of the will."[136] Although these thinkers did not deny the value of abstract, theoretical argument, they also believed that, as Reid put it, it was "evidently the intention of our Maker that man should be an active, and not merely a speculative being."[137] This skepticism about the usefulness of "speculative" knowledge is similar to the attitudes of earlier heterodox Presbyterians and Moderates, and it already appears in one of Reid's graduation orations, held in 1756 when he was a regent at King's College in Aberdeen. On this occasion he described the corruption of both philosophy and theology "throughout many centuries" (per Multa Secula) by "questions, that were often subtle, or even beyond human understanding, vain, and irrelevant to human happiness" (Questiones, Subtiles saepe quidem, sed vel supra humanum captum positas vel vanas & nullius prorsus ad humanam faelicitatem Momenti), when philosophy was excluded from common life and languished "in the cells of monks and scholastic theologians" (in Claustris Monachorum & Theologorum Scholasticorum), and was forced to serve no purpose because of the "garrulousness and prurient desire of idle men to argue over things" (ociosorum hominum Garrulitate & pruritia disputandi de rebus).[138] But just as "the more sensible and experienced theologians have taught us to purge and cleanse theology, because they had a low opinion of the theological questions and disputations that were of little relevance to encouraging virtue and Christian piety; so too was it necessary to remove the dirt and rust, which had accumulated in the cloisters throughout the many centuries of darkness."[139] The concentration on useless, speculative questions in philosophy and theology alike was a legacy of the dark ages, following the fall of Rome, the barbarian invasions of the Empire, and the ascendancy of the papal church and scholastic philosophy in western Europe; it was not the means to promote the moral reform that Christianity required of its adherents. Christianity was a practical, moral religion. It was superior to the best systems of philosophy in encouraging virtue and conducting humankind toward salvation. Above all, it made clear that human effort and knowledge, without divine assistance, was necessary, but insufficient for achieving the moral reform that was also the essence of piety.

Conclusion:
Moderates in the Late
Enlightenment

By the early nineteenth century Moderates were sometimes described as a conservative interest group that had lost its intellectual vigor and openmindedness, and was held together primarily by its members' opposition to social and political change.[1] Moderates not only were critical of the French Revolution, but also worked closely with the crown's political manager in Scotland, Henry Dundas, Viscount Melville, who used his far-reaching control over appointments to various posts and offices to secure support for the government. Moreover, in the early 1800s they seemed suspicious of any skeptical or heterodox ideas, far more than had been the case in the mid- and late eighteenth century. In the mid-1750s the Moderate Party had sided with David Hume and Lord Kames against the orthodox clergy, but in 1805 the Moderates resisted the appointment of a professor, John Leslie, on the grounds that he had endorsed Hume's skeptical notion of causation in an obscure note on a scientific work on heat.[2]

The growing conservatism of the Moderates is often traced to the 1790s and believed to be a reaction to the increasing violence of the French Revolution. The revolution had at first been widely welcomed in Britain. Most observers, including the majority of Moderates, had viewed it as a belated, but laudable attempt to follow the example of the Glorious Revolution exactly a century earlier and to transform France into a constitutional monarchy. That perception had, however, been shattered by the increasingly violent turn the revolution took, with the assault of the Parisian sans-culottes on the Tuileries palace in August 1792, the slaughter of the Swiss guards protecting the royal family, the prison massacres in Paris in September of that same year, and, most alarmingly, the execution of the king in January 1793. Thomas Somerville had initially expressed his admiration for the revolution in France, but like other Moderates now regretted his premature enthusiasm.[3] Robertson's family suppressed the centenary sermon he had held in November 1788 on the significance of the Glorious Revolution for the liberties of modern Europe, because parts of it might be seen as dangerously radical in the circumstances of the 1790s.[4] In subsequent years a large number of sermons and commentaries by Moderates appeared that defended the British constitution and its ecclesiastical establishments, and deplored the anarchy, irreligion, and immorality of the French.

The hostility toward the revolution had, however, been a response to particular events, and although the Moderates' support for church patronage and the British constitution was reinforced by the developments in France, it had been present earlier. The intellectual and religious outlook of Moderates in the early nineteenth century was in fact similar to that of Moderates before 1789, which was characterized by skepticism about natural religion, an emphasis on the "practical" nature of Christianity rather than doctrine, and a belief in the importance of revelation and grace in bringing about the moral reform that was the most important characteristic of a genuinely religious person. Although Moderates responded to changing circumstances, there was also strong continuity in their intellectual attitudes and principles.

Religion and the French Revolution

Religion and the importance of an established church for a flourishing society and state were probably the most prominent themes in Moderates' criticisms of the French Revolution. In his *Effects of the French Revolution*, for example, the minister Thomas Somerville explained at length how the overthrow of the religious institutions of France had undermined public morality and order, and led to the extraordinary outbreak of violence of recent years. "It is a maxim," he wrote, "founded in the nature of man, and confirmed by the experience of ages, that, without religion, or the fear and acknowledgement of deity, no civil government can be maintained and supported; and to this maxim, it may be added, that the principles of the Christian religion, rooted in the hearts of a people, must ever be the firmest bond for upholding the authority of the magistrate, and preserving the peace of society."[5] The abolition, in effect, of Catholicism as the established church of France by the revolutionaries was immediately relevant to the debate over the relationship between church and state in Britain, where the status of the established churches had been under pressure from dissenters for some time before the revolution in France. A campaign by dissenters in 1787–1790 to have the Test and Corporation Acts repealed was ultimately unsuccessful, but when repeal was put to the vote in the House of Commons in 1789, it was defeated by only twenty votes.[6] As late as 1790 Thomas Somerville himself had campaigned for a repeal of the Test Acts as they applied to members of the Church of Scotland resident in England.[7] On 27 May 1790 the reform campaign was debated and passed without a vote in the General Assembly, where it enjoyed the support of the Popular Party and an influential group of Moderates, though some Moderates, such as George Hill, had opposed it.[8] By 1793, however, proposals for any kind of disestablishment had been largely set aside, because nearly all Church of Scotland clergymen rallied to the defense of British liberties and blamed the bloodshed in France on the subversion of its religious institutions.

This change of attitude had not been restricted to the Moderates, but extended to their main rival faction in the General Assembly, the Popular Party, which joined the Moderates in praising the British state and warning against the dangers of the French Revolution,[9] despite the fact that the Popular Party had been more critical of the British state than the Moderates, largely because of the continuing system of patronage in ecclesiastical appointments.

Locally, patronage continued to be a cause of popular unrest and disturbances, throughout the wars with France, with at least twenty-one instances of violent intrusion of presentees in the period from 1780 to 1815.[10] Parishes and associations such as the Glasgow Society for the Abolition of Patronage denounced patronage, in terms that were often similar to those used by Hutcheson in his 1735 pamphlet the *Considerations,* describing it as part of a corrupt political machine that used its control over ecclesiastical appointments to bribe and reward the government's supporters, to the detriment of true religion.[11]

In the General Assembly the patronage issue faded into the background from the mid-1780s onward. It had been raised by the Popular Party in 1781, when their hopes for change were kindled by the retirement of William Robertson from the leadership of the Moderate Party,[12] but in 1784 the Moderates secured a clear majority against the abolition of patronage in the General Assembly. Until that time, the instructions of the General Assembly had required its commission each year to protest against the grievance of patronage. This annual protest ceased after 1784, however.[13] When the issue arose again in 1785, the opponents of patronage were defeated once more. Once the French Revolution degenerated into the Terror from 1792, the issue of patronage disappeared largely from debates in the General Assembly, as the excesses of the revolution were widely blamed on the irreligion of the revolutionaries and their subversion of France's religious institutions. However eager the Popular Party may have been to curb the Erastianism of the British state, the perceived consequences of disestablishment in France made its advocacy almost impossible in Britain. The dilemma was particularly acute in the case of the various secession churches, whose relationship to the British state was even more difficult than that of the Popular Party. The overthrow of the ecclesiastical establishment in France had revived their demands for the separation of church and state, but they struggled to square their justifications of this goal with their professions of loyalty to king and Parliament.[14]

The fear of the consequences of religious disestablishment also greatly dampened enthusiasm for political reform, because demands for religious reform were often associated with proposals for various political changes, in various ways. The Popular Party in the 1780s, for example, regarded political reform as the means to abolishing the system of patronage, because patronage, they argued, was part of a corrupt political machine that was used to shore up support for the government. If political corruption were removed, the need for patronage would disappear. In this case, the Popular Party was often aligned with the opposition Whigs in Scotland, who tended to side with the Popular Party in their criticism of patronage,[15] and who also "tended to support the extension of civil liberties in Scotland, such as reform of the electoral system for both Scottish peers and commoners (though not usually to the extent of greatly enlarging the franchise), reform of local government, and various reforms to the legal system."[16] These demands did not disappear in the 1790s, and resurfaced to some extent in the Leslie controversy of 1805. But in the meantime Moderates and orthodox were united in their hostility to the French Revolution. Underlying their beliefs was a shared loyalist commitment to the British constitution. There were also deep concerns over the unbridled nationalist "enthusiasm" that the revolution had unleashed in the French.[17] The reason why the differences between Moderates and orthodox reappeared in 1805 during the so-called Leslie affair is related to particular circumstances, which made it seem safer than before for the Popular Party and Whigs like Stewart to oppose the installation of a government candidate in a university post.

The "Leslie Affair"

The "Leslie affair" began when the chair of mathematics at Edinburgh fell vacant after the incumbent John Playfair had moved to a more prestigious professorship in natural philosophy. One of the first to apply for Playfair's former post was the clergyman Thomas McKnight. At first it seemed that the election would not be a contentious issue. McKnight was considered a competent, if not exceptional candidate. The controversy began, however, when several of the leading Moderates in Edinburgh insisted that McKnight be elected to the chair, but also be allowed to retain his post as minister of the Trinity Church, although McKnight himself was, in fact, willing to relinquish his parish charge, or at least pretended to be so. Until then, the other professors at the university had not opposed McKnight's candidacy, but the prospect of a professor of mathematics who continued to serve as a parish minister elicited strongly worded memoranda to the town council, which was responsible for university appointments, from the professor of moral philosophy, Dugald Stewart, and the previous incumbent, John Playfair. Plural appointments to parishes and university chairs, Playfair wrote, were a "dangerous innovation" that threatened to undermine the independence of the university, although both Blair and Robertson had held university appointments at the same time as being ministers in Edinburgh churches.[18] Stewart complained that plural appointments were part of a systematic policy by Henry Dundas to give all university posts to clergymen, "if clergymen could be found competent to fill them," a policy that tended toward turning the university into an extension of the Edinburgh presbytery.[19] Stewart, Playfair, and others now began to support the candidacy of John Leslie, who was not a clergyman, but a much more distinguished scientist than McKnight, as was evident from Leslie's *Experimental Inquiry into the Nature and Propagation of Heat* (1804), which had won the 1805 Rumford medals of the Royal Society of London.

The main justification of the Moderates to back McKnight was the need to strengthen the role of the established church in public life.[20] But that need probably seemed less urgent in 1805 than it had in the mid-1790s, because by 1805 Napoleon Bonaparte had restored the Catholic Church to a central place in French life, indicating that France had turned its back on the extreme religious experiments of the 1790s, which had begun with the Civil Constitution of the Clergy and culminated in the revolutionary Cult of the Supreme Being. Napoleonic France presented at least as much of a threat to Britain as the previous French republican governments, but it was no longer dangerous as an example of radical de-Christianization. In 1801 Napoleon had concluded a Concordat with the papacy, and in 1804 Pope Pius VII was present at the coronation ceremony in Notre Dame at which Napoleon crowned himself. Although France had not simply returned to the *ancien régime* church, the preeminent position of Catholicism in French public life had been formally acknowledged.[21]

It is probably no coincidence that the Popular Party and opposition Whigs like Dugald Stewart were prepared to resist the Moderates' candidate for the chair of mathematics in 1805, since the rationale for the exercise of government patronage and installing ministers of the established church in university chairs must have seemed much weaker than it had been in the mid-1790s, when religious institutions seemed the most important bulwark against French-style anarchy, irreligion, and violence. Stewart, Playfair, and their associates appear to have sensed an opportunity to break Dundas's system of patronage in Scotland, which served the political interests of the Tory government. Their position was further strengthened when Dundas was forced to resign as First Lord of the Admiralty and from the Privy Council in the spring of 1805 because of fiscal irregularities in the Naval Office.[22] Stewart wrote in a letter in June 1805 to Francis Horner, the "affair of Lord M. [Melville] has, since the date of your letter, assumed a much more serious aspect than it then wore, and I trust that it will terminate in a manner so decisive as to close for ever his political career,—an event which I consider as synonymous with the emancipation and salvation of Scotland."[23]

The Moderates had of course benefited enormously from Dundas's system of patronage, and their opposition to Leslie can be explained, in part, as an attempt to preserve the advantages they had derived from it.[24] But the grounds on which the Moderates challenged Leslie's candidacy were more than a pretext: they mattered, if only because they were intended to persuade the general public and the town council that Leslie was not a fit candidate for a professorial chair.[25] The strategy was to question the soundness of Leslie's religious beliefs, based on note xvi of his *Experimental Inquiry into the Nature and Propagation of Heat,* where Leslie had appeared to endorse Hume's skeptical notion of causation. The copy of a letter by Leslie to a member of the town council, protesting his orthodoxy, failed to satisfy them. Although the Edinburgh clergy did not have the right to appoint professors, the Moderates claimed that the Edinburgh presbytery held the right of *avisamentum,* which entitled them to advise the town council about appointments.[26] The right of *avisamentum,* however, had not been used for some time, and was never used, apparently, in appointments to a chair of mathematics.[27] Also, it was not clear whether the *avisamentum* was only advice, which the town council could ignore, or whether it entailed, in effect, a veto power over professorial appointments. In the event, the town council received the *avisamentum* of the presbytery with respect, but appointed Leslie anyway. The orthodox members of the Edinburgh presbytery were happy to acquiesce in Leslie's election, but the Moderates continued to oppose the appointment. They won a vote in the Edinburgh presbytery to raise the issue of the *avisamentum* before the next higher church court, the Synod of Lothian and Tweedsdale, which eventually passed the matter on to the supreme ecclesiastical body, the General Assembly. Following a bitter debate, the General Assembly voted to dismiss the Moderates' case against Leslie, who then went on to hold the chair of mathematics until 1819, when he succeeded Playfair to the chair of natural philosophy.

During the Leslie controversy the traditional positions of Moderates and orthodox seemed to be almost reversed: Moderates had opposed Leslie's election to the chair of mathematics on the grounds of heterodoxy and philosophical skepticism, while the orthodox clergy had joined forces with several professors at the university, including Stewart and Playfair, to support Leslie's candidacy. Even contemporaries commented on what seemed to be a puzzling *volte face.* A writer in the *Scots Magazine* pointed out "the extreme surprize of the public, who, from ideas previously formed relative to each, would have been led to expect the direct reverse of such an arrangement."[28] Ian D. Clark has argued that the positions of the Moderates and the orthodox were consistent with their earlier beliefs. The Moderates, he wrote, were concerned that Leslie's views undermined "rational religion," whereas the orthodox were in favor of Leslie precisely because he appeared to have downplayed the usefulness of natural reason, and thus allowed the orthodox to insist on the absolute necessity of revelation and grace.[29] There were strong continuities between the eighteenth-century arguments and the early nineteenth-century views of Moderates and orthodox. Yet the distinction between Moderates and orthodox in the early nineteenth century is not one between supporters of a "rational religion," on the one hand, and anti-rationalists, on the other.

Moderatism, Orthodoxy, and Reason

The Moderates' concerns about Leslie's religion were based on a note on the main text of his 1804 *Experimental Inquiry*, in which Leslie praised David Hume as "the first . . . who has treated of causation in a truly philosophic manner" in his "*Essay on Necessary Connexion*," which was a "model of clear and accurate reasoning."[30] All that Hume had done in this essay was to confirm the "unsophisticated sentiments of mankind," which were "in perfect unison with the deductions of logic, and imply nothing more than a *constant and invariable sequence.*"[31]

Ian Clark writes that this statement by Leslie shook the "whole framework of 18th century 'rational' religion . . ., and many of the presuppositions upon which Moderatism had hitherto rested were destroyed."[32] Yet Moderates in the eighteenth or early nineteenth century were not distinguished from the orthodox by a stronger commitment to "rational religion." In fact, although Moderates were not as reluctant as Hume to draw conclusions about the existence and attributes of the deity from natural reason, they often emphasized the limitations and imperfections of natural knowledge on these matters. In some respects even they were more skeptical than the orthodox concerning the possibility of a natural religion.[33] When, during the Leslie controversy, the Moderate John Inglis had warned of the dangers of "false philosophy," which had subverted "the Christian faith in one of the most polished nations of Europe"—namely, France—and "threatened to break down, in our land also, the altars of the Most High!"[34] he had not intended to suggest that reason and philosophy were a sufficient foundation for religious belief, but only that sound philosophy and true revealed faith had to be compatible with each other. False philosophy contradicted Christianity and threatened to undermine it. But true philosophy was no substitute for divine revelation.

An orthodox supporter of Leslie pounced on Inglis's comment and used it to attribute a belief in the sufficiency of reason in religious affairs to the Moderates. Yet this would seem a polemical exaggeration rather than an accurate description of the Moderates' views. The author, an Aberdeen professor named William Brown, commented that Inglis

> has told us that his *party rests the claims of our religious faith on the foundation of sober reason, and sound argument.* This, I must confess, is not a very favourable representation of the creed of the *moderate Interest.* For, if, *by our religious faith,* we understand the *doctrines of Christianity which faith embraces,* it is certain that, . . . their claims extend greatly beyond the sphere, and the attainments of human reason; and revelation, in its very definition, implies discoveries made by God, and supported by this testimony. If, by *religious faith,* we understand that act of the mind by which Christianity is cordially embraced and rendered the standard of sentiment, and conduct, it is equally certain that this can never be accomplished by reason alone, but, according to the doctrine of the gospel, must be effected by the influence, and agency of the holy Spirit, in perfect consistence with our rational nature.[35]

Moderates would not have disagreed with this statement by Brown because the truths of revelation, they thought, were always superior to natural reason. Christianity rested on the former, not the latter.

Nor were the orthodox particularly hostile to reason, even in relation to religious matters. Brown noted the importance and usefulness of "reason, and argument," which were "successfully employed" in the "defence, and . . . illustration" of Christian doctrines, "and accompany both their admission by the understanding, and their influence on the affections and conduct."[36] Orthodox authors, in the early nineteenth century, as before, believed in the importance of natural reason in religious argument. Clark points out that even an Evangelical author such as Thomas Chalmers, for example, writing *On Natural Theology* some years later stated that reason provided at least an inkling of the truth, though it needed to be supplemented by revelation and grace.[37] Daniel Rice has shown that Chalmers incorporated a natural theology derived especially from Beattie into his religious thought.[38]

By the early nineteenth century most Moderates and orthodox would seem to have held not entirely dissimilar views on the place of reason in religious argument, both sides stressing the limitations of reason in religious matters and its insufficiency for salvation, though neither dismissing it entirely. For example, when William Brown defended Leslie he did not embrace the anti-rationalist implications of his position on causation and adopt a consciously fideist position. Instead, he dismissed the entire controversy as a "metaphysical" and "scholastic" squabble over words, similar to the dispute between nominalists and realists during the Middle Ages,[39] and asserted also that Leslie had never intended his brief comment on Hume's notion of causation to be applied to arguments concerning the existence of a deity.[40] Brown never denied the importance of rational religion; rather, he downplayed the threat that Leslie's very brief reference to Hume had presented to it. The disagreement between Moderates and orthodox was not so much over the status of reason in religious affairs[41] as to the precise meaning and implications of Leslie's brief and casual reference to Hume, essentially, whether it was applicable only to the phenomena of the material world, or whether it extended to arguments about the existence and attributes of the deity.

Even the orthodox author A. M. Thomson, who had declared that Leslie had "the right to discard all the ordinary foundations of natural religion, and assert, at the same time, his claim to the character of a sound theist,"[42] did not set out to deny the acceptability of natural religion as such, but only implied that a belief in natural religion was not necessary to be a faithful Christian. There had, Thomson wrote, been many who had questioned the usefulness of natural religion, and yet had been respected Christian theologians. The Dutch Arminian theologian Philip van Limborch, for example, "neither despised nor rejected" the "arguments . . . drawn from the light of nature . . . to prove the existence of God," but "he accounted them extremely feeble, and had recourse to miracles and revelation, as the only grounds of certain conviction."[43] Faustus Socinus had gone even further, declaring that there was "no such thing as a *natural* knowledge of the Supreme being, or in other words, no such thing as natural theology." Revelation was the only secure source of "all our information concerning divine things."[44] Thomson also cited the mid-eighteenth-century Presbyterian clergyman Robert Riccaltoun, an opponent of orthodox Calvinism, whose 1722 satire, the *Politick Disputant*, was directed against James Hadow.[45] According to Thomson, Riccaltoun "did not scruple to express his approbation of those parts of Mr. Hume's writings, in which the foundations of *natural* religion are attacked,"[46] and that a skeptical attitude toward natural religion did not contradict a Christian faith founded on revelation. Consequently, Leslie's statements should not be interpreted as a sign of atheism.

The position of the Moderates in the Leslie affair had anyway not marked a profound change from their former views. Their earlier support for Hume had always been hedged with qualifications, and although they defended him fifty years previously against the attempts of the orthodox to have him censured by the General Assembly, they had never backed him for a university chair. Hugh Blair had expressed his reservations concerning Hume's views, even while defending him from orthodox criticism.[47] Hume's philosophical skepticism had come under attack from several other Moderates earlier, such as Reid, Gerard, and George Campbell. Inglis aligned himself with these thinkers when he criticized Leslie, because he thought they had saved natural religion and a philosophical belief in divine providence from Hume's skeptical doubts.[48]

On the other hand, Leslie's supporters did not simply endorse Hume's skepticism. They appealed to the same philosophers as the Moderates, and especially to Reid, but they interpreted them, and their relationship to Hume, differently, in an effort to downplay the radical implications of Leslie's casual reference.

Hume had written that our idea of causation rested on our experience of a constant conjunction between two types of events. That experience was the only reason for assuming some sort of connection between the two. Hume's skepticism had had significant implications for natural theology, because it became then impossible to argue from the existence of the world to the existence of a divine creator. The world, he stated, was one of a kind, at least as far as humans knew, and they had never experienced the creation of this or any other world, let alone the creation of several worlds. However, it was only the repeated experience of the creation of worlds that would have allowed humans to draw conclusions about the cause of their own.

Hume's most accomplished critic, Reid, accepted several elements of Hume's notion of causation, in that he too thought of causation in terms of a constant conjunction between two events, much as Hume had done. There was nothing, Reid wrote, that was known to be inherent in material nature, and that could explain the effect of one thing on another, so "when we ascribe power to things inanimate as causes we mean nothing more than a constant conjunction by the laws or rules of nature which experience discovers."[49] Hume's and Reid's respective notions of causation could therefore seem quite similar.

There were of course also important differences.[50] For Hume, the repeated experience of constant conjunctions strengthened the "vivacity" of the belief in them. Vivacity, not some principle of reason, was the basis for the belief in causation. Reid, however, thought that vivacity was not enough to explain the human confidence that a conjunction that had been observed in the past would continue to operate in the future. Humans trusted the regularity of such causal connections because of an instinct, which had been placed in them by God, to expect the same patterns of natural phenomena that had been observed in the past to continue in the future.[51] Such trust could not be the product of ratiocination, because even "children and ideots" had this belief as soon as they knew that fire would burn them.[52] The instinctive confidence in the regularity of natural phenomena was evidence of the providential care of God for his creation.

Hume's idea of causation as no more than constant conjunction could, however, be made to look like an earlier, less developed version of Reid's much less controversial doctrine of causation. Leslie himself probably did not believe he was making a provocative statement when he referred to Hume. It is possible that he never read Hume's essay on "necessary connexion," but derived his view of it from Dugald Stewart, whose student he had been in 1786. As Wright has shown, it is likely that Leslie thought he was only endorsing the standard interpretation of Hume's theory of causality accepted by Reid and Stewart.[53] The strategy of Leslie's defenders among the secular professors at the university was to emphasize these similarities between Reid and Hume, and thereby lessen the radical implications of Leslie's reference to Hume's notorious opinion.

Thus, Stewart could argue that Leslie's account of causation coincided almost exactly with his own view of it, which he had advanced in volume one of his *Elements of the Philosophy of the Human Mind* published many years earlier, and which he quoted at length in his defense of Leslie, the *Short Statement of some Important Facts:*

> It seems now to be pretty generally agreed among philosophers, that there is no instance in which we are able to perceive a necessary connection between two successive events; or to comprehend in what manner the one proceeds from the other, as its cause. From experience indeed we learn, that there are many events which are constantly conjoined, so that the one invariably follows the other:

but it is possible, for any thing we know to the contrary, that this connexion, though a constant one, as far as our observation has reached, may not be a necessary connexion; nay, it is possible, that there may be no necessary connexions among any of the phenomena we see: and if there are any such connexions existing, we may rest assured that we shall never be able to discover them.[54]

The question then was whether this doctrine "lead to those sceptical conclusions, concerning the existence of a First Cause, which an author of great ingenuity [Hume] has attempted to deduce from it."[55] Stewart denied that it did, and, like Brown, believed that Leslie had only ever agreed with Hume's notion of causation as it applied to natural philosophy, because it was no more than a continuation of a Baconian program of induction, "which, if it does not explicitly state Mr Hume's doctrine concerning our ignorance of necessary connexions, takes it for granted in every step."[56] According to Stewart, Leslie had done no more than recapitulate an entirely conventional, unobjectionable notion of causation, which was applicable to natural philosophy alone and was not relevant to arguments concerning the existence of a First Cause.

Another example of this kind of argument came from Thomas Brown. Brown, who from 1810 co-occupied the chair of moral philosophy with Stewart, also minimized the differences between Hume and Reid, arguing that Reid had misunderstood Hume's notion of causation, which was, in fact, much closer to his own views than he realized. When Hume expressed his skeptical doubts that made it impossible for him to infer a necessary connection "in the parts of a sequence," Brown thought that it only seemed "to render power a word without meaning."[57] When Reid objected that there were events which occurred in succession, but which were never perceived as cause and effect (such as night and day), Reid, according to Brown, was being imprecise, because he was referring to whole bundles of phenomena, which had to be disaggregated to form clear notions of cause and effect,[58] and all that Hume had done was to show that "we *believe*, rather than *discover*, the relation of cause and effect."[59] That dependence on belief rather than deductive proof was not unusual, for in "every reasoning, however small its number of propositions, there must always be one proposition assumed without proof; and it is not wonderful, therefore, that, in our reasonings concerning matters of fact, Mr. Hume should have been able to point out such a proposition."[60] Hume did not deny "that we have an idea of *power* or of *invariable priority* in sequences:

he denies only that we can perceive or confer it, as a quality inherent in the subjects of a sequence."[61] Hume, however, also offered a solution to this doubt by suggesting that our notion of causation rested on a feeling of a customary connection of ideas. The word "power" therefore was not "considered by him [Hume], as altogether without meaning." Yet that was the belief imputed to him, unfairly, by Reid and "the other philosophers, by whom the doctrine was originally opposed; and this opinion, under the authority of respectable names, has become a sort of traditionary article of faith, and of wonder at the possible extent of human scepticism, so as to preclude even that very slight examination, which alone seems necessary to confute it."[62] Brown concludes, "by an oversight that is altogether unaccountable, Dr. Reid, and the other writers who have considered Mr. Hume's theory, neglect the solution of the doubts, as if it formed no part of the theory, and thus gain an easy triumph over a scepticism, which its author himself had been the first to overthrow."[63]

The Religion of the Moderates, 1793–1805

The Leslie affair has been used as a *terminus ad quem* for the history of the eighteenth-century Moderate Party, as an illustration of the intellectual decline of the Moderate Party and their transformation from a "progressive," broadly "liberal" party of clergymen into a reactionary and conservative force and interest group. In reality, the fundamental attitudes of the Moderates had remained much the same throughout the period from the late 1780s to the early 1800s. When they had criticized the French Revolution, they were engaged in a defense of the British constitution and the system of patronage, which they had always accepted. Many of them had praised the early stages of the revolution, because they had not anticipated the far more sweeping changes that would take place from the early 1790s. When Robertson held his centenary sermon on the anniversary of the Glorious Revolution in 1788, he was only aware of the limited reforms that had occurred in France by that time, which were uncontroversial in Britain generally, and of which he approved wholeheartedly.[64] Also, Moderates were not alone in their concern to defend the British constitution during the 1790s. Their rivals in the Popular Party joined them, regardless of earlier differences over patronage and religious disestablishment. Yet their disagreements over ecclesiastical patronage, and the resentment of the Popular Party at the system of government control orchestrated by Henry Dundas, were probably suppressed only temporarily during the 1790s, in the face of the religious threat from France. It is likely that the religious threat seemed much less significant, once the religious experiments of the 1790s had ceased, and Catholicism had been restored to a preeminent role in French public life by Napoleon in the early 1800s.

On the whole, the outlook of the Moderates changed little in the period from the death of Robertson until 1805. It was in the interests of the Popular Party, however, to suggest that the Moderates had become rigid and narrow-minded, and were mainly interested in the material benefits of Dundas's patronage system. For by the early nineteenth century the reputation of the mid-eighteenth-century Moderates as opponents of extreme, covenanting "enthusiasm" was well established. A successful critique of the early nineteenth-century successors of Blair and Robertson, therefore, had to suggest that the later Moderates were not the same Moderates who had been necessary half a century earlier to restrain the religious fanaticism that was the legacy of seventeenth-century Presbyterianism. This had been, for example, the strategy of an orthodox clergyman such as Brown during the Leslie affair. Brown had first expressed some sympathy for the goals of the mid-eighteenth-century Moderate Party, writing that "there was, perhaps, a period in the history of our Church, when religious opinions, and feelings elevating the mind, and inspiring a vehement ardour of zeal; or the controversy concerning patronage being too violently agitated, it was proper and laudable to adopt, and extend a *moderate spirit* in regard to the questions then commonly discussed." But, he then continued,

> circumstances are, now, greatly altered. Time has operated its natural effects, both in reducing the *fervid spirit* to its proper temperature, and, perhaps, also, in refrigerating the *tepid*. *Moderation* has, now, in regard to ecclesiastical affairs, scarcely any object for its exercise, and must pine away, or sink into lethargic slumber, unless called into action by another prosecution similar to that of Mr Leslie, or employed as a mere *cant-word*, a name of distinction for a party.[65]

According to Brown, therefore, eighteenth-century Moderatism had achieved its goal of toning down the "enthusiasm" of traditional Presbyterianism, and had now lost its original raison d'être as a movement within the Presbyterian Kirk.

The religious principles of Moderates had, however, remained broadly the same. The leader of the Moderate Party in the General Assembly, George Hill, still argued, as had previous Moderates, that "good conduct" was itself the "end of religion,"[66] and, like earlier Moderates, stressed the very limited usefulness of natural religion. The Gospel was a "republication" of natural religion, but not in the sense that Tindal had used that term. For Tindal the Gospel only offered a republication of truths that were already known from natural reason, whereas Hill, like earlier Moderates, argued that the truths of natural religion had to be republished in the Gospel, because they had been corrupted and obscured:

> NATURAL Religion, which consists of the knowledge of God, the obligations, and the hopes that may be deduced from the light of nature, is founded in the constitution of the human mind;—was transmitted by tradition from the first man;—is supposed in Scripture;—and had no original defect.
>
> YET, from the religious history of the Heathen world, it appears, that a republication of Natural Religion was most desirable. The Gospel gives this republication with authority,—with simplicity;—and by establishing a popular mode of instruction, formerly unknown, has produced in every Christian country, an universal diffusion of the principles of Natural Religion.[67]

In another passage Hill again underlined the limitations of human reasoning with regard to natural religion: "The principles of Natural Religion have never existed apart, as a System resting upon deductions of Reason: They were incorporated with much error in the religious systems of the Heathen world: They are delivered pure in the Gospel; and provision is there made for preserving and transmitting them."[68] Within the Popular Party, some change was occurring as evangelicalism grew in strength toward the end of the eighteenth century, and the emphasis on practical holiness of life also became more pronounced than before in the writings of orthodox theologians. Even then, however, the orthodox, as John R. McIntosh has argued, believed that "faith was essentially a matter of knowledge and belief."[69] Good conduct was still only a fruit of the sincere belief in Christ and his sacrifice for human-kind, not the essence of religion itself.

Conclusion: Morality and Salvation

The eighteenth-century Moderates believed that salvation was achieved by means of a moral culture for which divinely revealed truth of some kind was essential. This truth might be vouchsafed directly to an individual, as in the

case of the Roman centurion Cornelius or the Emperor philosopher Marcus
Aurelius, or it might be made known more widely, through the revealed
word of God in Scripture. In either case, however, the end of this revelation
was the reform of conduct, not the communication of doctrinal orthodoxy.
Knowledge of certain truths such as the immortality of the soul might
contribute to achieving moral reform, but what mattered was the reform
itself, however it was brought about, not knowledge of a truth. A significant
reason for this change in emphasis from doctrine to morality was the need
to resolve the difficulties raised by the Protestant emphasis on salvation *sola
fide,* which, it was feared, encouraged a belief that good conduct was no
necessary part of Christian religion. Complaints about the proliferation of
hypocrites and nominal Christians abounded in the many seventeenth-
century spiritualist reform movements throughout Europe, ranging from the
German Pietists to the British Societies for the Reformation of Manners.
Although their complaints cannot be taken literally, they mattered because
they were believed. Hence, one of the key concerns in late seventeenth- and
eighteenth-century religious culture was to explain how practical virtue, or
"holiness of life," could be considered a necessary part of salvation, while
avoiding a "papist" belief in the efficacy of good works. The eighteenth-
century Moderates who had articulated a "religion of morality" were doing
so because of their theological views about the conditions of salvation. They
were trying to steer a middle course between the extremes of an overemphasis on doctrinal orthodoxy on the one hand, and religious "enthusiasm"
on the other, which was characterized by a belief in sudden, dramatic conversions, of a type associated with the revivalist movements that emerged in the
eighteenth century. The Moderates propounded a gradual, incremental
improvement of the individual by means of a moral culture that was a cooperative enterprise, requiring labor and effort on the part of the sinner to be
meritorious, but which could never be achieved fully without divine support
of some kind. In one sense, the Moderates were giving Christian religion a
"secular" focus by emphasizing practical virtue. Yet at the same time they
were also underlining the, as they thought, singular advantages of Christian
revelation over secular philosophy for moral reform in this life. They did not
relativize the importance of Scripture; on the contrary, they elevated it to the
status of a superior moral code, known only to those fortunate enough to
have been the recipients of the Gospel revelation. Natural religion was much
less important in this transition from doctrine to conduct than is sometimes

argued. The skepticism of the Moderates concerning the possibility of a natural religion, in particular, is striking, and contradicts the common view of them as stereotypical "enlightened" clergymen, since, on the whole, they believed that the support natural religion could provide for morality was very weak, especially compared with the assistance offered by Christian revelation. This fact, they said, was evident from the example of pagan societies: their rulers and legislators recognized the social and moral advantages of religion in general, but they lacked the truths of Christian religion, and were thus forced to resort to superstition and priestcraft as means of social control, because natural religion was inadequate for that purpose. These pagan religious beliefs contributed nothing to salvation. Their effectiveness in preserving public order and morality was also greatly inferior to that of Christianity. Orthodox Calvinists in the mid-eighteenth century were much more concerned than the Moderates to defend natural religion. The orthodox never considered natural religion equivalent to Christianity, as deists like Matthew Tindal did, but they thought that without natural religion, non-Christians could have no complete sense of moral obligation, and of their guilt before God, and hence could not be made to realize their complete dependence on the saving truths of Christianity in order to escape damnation. For Moderates, on the other hand, the "moral culture" that led to salvation took place through a series of "trials," which might be forms of suffering or temptation. They were tests of individuals' moral fiber, which allowed them, by means of constant exercise and the formation of virtuous habits, to progress gradually toward a moral character, a development that need not be complete in their lifetime. Those "trials" were also part of a theodicy. They involved hardship and evil, but their existence was compatible with the belief in an all-powerful and benevolent creator, who permitted them as opportunities for humankind's moral education.

The belief that the main purpose of Christianity was moral, and that faith was not about the correct understanding of doctrine, at least not primarily, continued among various British thinkers of the post-Napoleonic and Victorian era. Like the Moderates, they did not necessarily relativize the importance of Scripture. The Bible was still considered superior to all other comparable texts.[70] But it was superior as a repository of moral truth, because the essence of religion was truly good conduct and a pure heart, not the accurate knowledge of crabbed orthodoxies. The Victorian poet and literary critic Matthew Arnold, for example, managed to antagonize some of the most powerful religious groups in Britain, yet he did so, as Stefan Collini has pointed out, "in the hope of rescuing Christianity from the abyss of unbelief, and of securing for the Bible its proper place as the pre-eminent sacred book."[71] The Bible, he believed, was a uniquely powerful educational tool for inculcating the moral message that was the core of real religion; the Church, Arnold wrote, "exists not for the sake of opinion, but for the sake of moral practice."[72] The deeper truth of Scripture had, however, been obscured over the centuries by the growth of superfluous doctrines, which were the product of over-intellectualized speculations. Speculations of this kind had begun soon after the death of the apostles, who had kept alive the "immediate remembrance of Jesus":[73] it was then that Christianity began to be turned into dogmatic, orthodox theology that was addressed to the head, without appealing to the heart. Even a far more clearly Christian (and, by then, Catholic) author like John Henry Newman in his 1854 *Idea of a University* emphasized the role of the Bible as an agent of the kind of "culture" that was the means of educating the mind to its "perfect state."[74] This "culture," in nineteenth- as much as eighteenth-century writings, was often thought to proceed by a series of "trials" that reflected God's providential purposes for humanity. Its purpose was the formation of a sound moral character. As in the writings of the eighteenth-century Moderates, secular self-improvement was part of the economy of salvation.

Notes

1. Winfried Schröder, *Ursprünge des Atheismus. Untersuchungen zur Metaphysik-und Religionskritik des 17. und 18. Jahrhunderts* (Stuttgart-Bad Cannstatt: Frommann-Holzboog, 1998), p. 19; Martin Mulsow, *Moderne aus dem Untergrund: radikale Frühaufklärung in Deutschland 1680–1720* (Hamburg: F. Meiner, 2002), pp. 2–8. Jonathan Israel has argued for the intellectual importance of a radical, secular Enlightenment, first articulated by Spinoza in the Dutch Republic, in a trilogy of works (*Radical Enlightenment: Philosophy and the Making of Modernity, 1650–1750* [Oxford: Oxford University Press, 2001]; *Enlightenment Contested: Philosophy, Modernity, and the Emancipation of Man, 1670–1752* [Oxford: Oxford University Press, 2008]; and *Democratic Enlightenment: Philosophy, Revolution, and Human Rights, 1750–1790* [Oxford: Oxford University Press, 2011]). For a critical assessment of Israel's interpretation, see A. J. LaVopa, "A New Intellectual History? Jonathan Israel's Enlightenment," *Historical Journal* 52 (2009), 717–738. On the importance of a tradition of clandestine, radical literature inspired by Spinoza for the "High Enlightenment," see also the classic work by Margaret C. Jacob, *The Radical Enlightenment: Pantheists, Freemasons and Republicans* (London: George Allen & Unwin, 1981).

2. On the problem of defining "Religious Enlightenment," see, for example, David Sorkin, *The Religious Enlightenment: Protestants, Jews, Catholics from London to Vienna* (Princeton, NJ: Princeton University Press, 2008); Simon Grote, "Religion and Enlightenment," *Journal of the History of Ideas* 75 (2014), 137–160; Jonathan Sheehan, "Enlightenment, Religion, and the Enigma of Secularization: A Review Essay," *American Historical Review* 108 (2003), 1061–1080; Jeffrey Burson, *The Rise and Fall of Theological Enlightenment: Jean-Martin de Prades and Ideological Polarization in*

Eighteenth-Century France (Notre Dame, IN: Notre Dame University Press, 2010), pp. 1–16; Charly Coleman, "Resacralizing the World: The Fate of Secularization in Enlightenment Historiography," *Journal of Modern History* 82 (2010), 368–395.

3. See the contrasting views in J. C. A. Gaskin, *Hume's Philosophy of Religion*, 2nd ed. (Basingstoke: Macmillan, 1988), and Paul Russell, *The Riddle of Hume's Treatise: Skepticism, Naturalism, and Irreligion* (Oxford: Oxford University Press, 2008). On the difficulties of classifying Hume's position on religion, see Alexander Broadie, *A History of Scottish Philosophy* (Edinburgh: Edinburgh University Press, 2009), pp. 192–193.

4. See, for example, the essays in Paul Oslington (ed.), *Adam Smith as Theologian* (New York: Routledge, 2011). In his introduction (pp. 1–16), Oslington argues for the influence of some kind of Calvinism on Smith, but also points out Smith's own reticence concerning his religious beliefs. Oslington appears to imply that Smith might have been influenced by Calvinist religion without fully believing in it. Smith must have lectured on natural theology at the University of Glasgow, but no notes of these lectures survive (see I. S. Ross, *The Life of Adam Smith* [Oxford: Clarendon Press, 1995], pp. 116–119). Nicholas Phillipson points out that Smith as a professor in Glasgow "tried to break with the custom of beginning each lecture with prayer but had not been allowed to do so." However, the fact that Smith did not continue Hutcheson's practice of Sunday discourses is perhaps not that remarkable, since Smith, unlike Hutcheson, had no university degree in divinity (Phillipson, *Adam Smith: An Enlightened Life* [London: Allen Lane, 2010], p. 132). For an attempt to prove the "providentialist" nature of Smith's philosophy, see R. A. Kleer, "Final Causes in Adam Smith's *Theory of Moral Sentiments*," *Journal for the History of Philosophy* 33 (1995), 275–300.

5. On the publishing history of Blair's sermons, see Ann Matheson, "Hugh Blair's Sermons," in Stephen W. Brown and Warren McDougall (eds.), *The Edinburgh History of the Book in Scotland*, vol. 2: *Enlightenment and Expansion* (Edinburgh: Edinburgh University Press, 2012), pp. 471–475.

6. Ernst Cassirer, *The Philosophy of the Enlightenment*, trans. Fritz. C. A. Koelln and James P. Pettegrove (Boston: Beacon Press, 1966), p. 169.

7. Blair Worden, "The Question of Secularization," in Alan Houston and S. Pincus (eds.), *A Nation Transformed* (Cambridge: Cambridge University Press, 2001), p. 39. For a discussion of the increasing emphasis on conduct in seventeenth- and eighteenth-century Calvinist Geneva, see Helena Rosenblatt, *Rousseau and Geneva: From the* First Discourse *to the* Social

Contract, *1749–1762* (Cambridge: Cambridge University Press, 1997), pp. 11–17.

8. Charles Taylor, *A Secular Age* (Cambridge, MA: Belknap Press, 2007), p. 266.

9. Simon Blackbourn, "Morality without God," *Prospect*, April 2011, pp. 2–3.

10. An example of this approach in the case of Enlightenment England is Brian Young, *Religion and Enlightenment in Eighteenth-Century England: Theological Debate from Locke to Burke* (Oxford: Clarendon Press, 1998). See also Isabel Rivers, *Reason, Grace, and Sentiment: A Study of the Language of Religion and Ethics in England, 1660–1780*, vol. 1: *Whichcote to Wesley* (Cambridge: Cambridge University Press, 1991), and Brian Young, *Reason, Grace, and Sentiment*, vol. 2: *Shaftesbury to Hume* (Cambridge: Cambridge University Press, 2000). J. G. A. Pocock has drawn attention to the importance of ecclesiastical history for understanding the religious dimensions of Enlightenment thought (see, for example, his *Barbarism and Religion*, vol. 5: *Religion: The First Triumph* [Cambridge: Cambridge University Press, 2010]). An older study, originally published in 1976, of the relationship between religion and Enlightenment in England is John Redwood, *Reason, Ridicule and Religion: The Age of Enlightenment in England, 1660–1750* (London: Thames and Hudson, 1996). On the importance more generally of integrating religion and theology into intellectual history, see, for example, John Coffey and Alister Chapman, "Introduction: Intellectual History and the Return of Religion," in Alister Chapman, John Coffey, and Brad S. Gregory (eds.), *Seeing Things Their Way: Intellectual History and the Return of Religion* (Notre Dame, IN: Notre Dame University Press, 2009), pp. 1–23.

11. Roy Porter, *Enlightenment: Britain and the Creation of the Modern World* (London: Penguin, 2000), p. 100.

12. Jonathan Israel, *Democratic Enlightenment: Philosophy, Revolution, and Human Rights, 1750–1790* (Oxford: Oxford University Press, 2011), p. 11.

13. Israel, *Democratic Enlightenment*, p. 11.

14. Israel, *Democratic Enlightenment*, pp. 14–15.

15. David Sorkin, *The Religious Enlightenment* (Princeton, NJ: Princeton University Press, 2008), p. 13.

16. Taylor, *A Secular Age*, ch. 6.

17. Sorkin, *The Religious Enlightenment*, pp. 19–21.

18. Winfried Schröder, "Natürliche Religion und Religionskritik in der deutschen Frühaufklärung," in Hans-Erich Bödeker (ed.), *Strukturen der*

deutschen Frühaufklärung (Göttingen: Vandenhoeck & Rupprecht, 2008), pp. 147–164.

19. Peter Gay, *The Enlightenment: The Rise of Modern Paganism* (New York: W. W. Norton, 1995).

20. James Moore and Michael Silverthorne, "Introduction," in Marcus Aurelius, *The Meditations of the Emperor Marcus Aurelius,* ed. James Moore and Michael Silverthorne, trans. Francis Hutcheson and James Moor (Indianapolis: Liberty Fund, 2008), p. xxiii. Note that James Moor, the classical scholar and contemporary of Hutcheson, is not to be confused with James Moore, the modern scholar of the Scottish Enlightenment.

21. Richard B. Sher, *Church and University in the Scottish Enlightenment* (Edinburgh: Edinburgh University Press, 1985), p. 177. Recently, Jonathan Yeager has argued that one of the opponents of these "Moderate literati" was also a "Christian Stoic" (see Jonathan Yeager, *Enlightened Evangelicalism: The Life and Thought of John Erskine* [Oxford: Oxford University Press, 2011]).

22. See William Robertson, "Translation of Book II of Marcus Aurelius, Meditations, 1742," in Robertson, *Miscellaneous Works and Commentaries,* ed. J. Smitten (London: Routledge/Thoemmes, 1996), pp. 15–23.

23. See, for example, Thomas Ahnert, "Francis Hutcheson and the Heathen Moralists," *Journal of Scottish Philosophy* 8 (2010), 51–62.

24. J. Hoppit, *A Land of Liberty: England, 1689–1727* (Oxford: Oxford University Press, 2000), p. 223. See also D. W. R. Bahlman, *The Moral Revolution of 1688* (New Haven: Yale University Press, 1957). The first meeting of the Edinburgh Society is recorded in *Register of the Resolutions and Proceedings of a Society for Reformation of Manners* (Edinburgh University Library, MS La III.339).

25. W. R. Ward, *The Protestant Evangelical Awakening* (Cambridge: Cambridge University Press, 1992); on Pietism in particular, see Thomas Ahnert, *Religion and the Origins of the German Enlightenment: Faith and the Reform of Learning in the Thought of Christian Thomasius* (Rochester, NY: Rochester University Press, 2006), ch. 1.

26. See, for example, Augustine, *The City of God against the Pagans,* ed. R. W. Dyson (Cambridge: Cambridge University Press, 1998), pp. 924–925.

27. On the association of charity with secular virtue in eighteenth-century thought, see, for example, Donald Greene, "Latitudinarianism and Sensibility: The Genealogy of the 'Man of Feeling' Reconsidered," *Modern Philology* 75/2 (1977), 161.

28. Brian Young, "Enlightenment Political Thought and the Cambridge School," *Historical Journal* 52 (2009), 240. On the moral and political thought of Jansenists, see Nannerl Keohane, *Philosophy and the State in France: The Renaissance to Enlightenment* (Princeton, NJ: Princeton University Press, 1980), and, more recently, Michael Moriarty, *Disguised Vices: Theories of Virtue in Early Modern French Thought* (Oxford: Oxford University Press, 2011). On the affinity between Jansenist Augustinianism and Epicureanism, see Jean Lafond, "Augustinisme et Épicurisme au XVIIe Siècle," in *L'Homme et son Image: Morales et literature de Montaigne à Mandeville* (Paris: Honoré Champion, 1996), pp. 347–458; Pierre Force, *Self-Interest before Adam Smith: A Genealogy of Economic Science* (Cambridge: Cambridge University Press, 2003), especially pp. 48–63; John Robertson, *The Case for the Enlightenment: Scotland and Naples, 1680–1760* (Cambridge: Cambridge University Press, 2005), pp. 127–130. See also the classic work by A. O. Hirschman, *The Passions and the Interests: Political Arguments for Capitalism before Its Triumph*, 2nd ed. (Princeton, NJ: Princeton University Press, 1997).

29. Robertson, *The Case for the Enlightenment*, pp. 121–148.

30. Moriarty, *Disguised Vices*, p. 249.

31. From Marischal College (1736), and King's College in Aberdeen (1737). See Isabel Rivers, "Doddridge, Philip (1702–1751)," *Oxford Dictionary of National Biography* (Oxford: Oxford University Press, 2004); Philip Doddridge, *Some Remarkable Passages in the Life of the Honourable Col. James Gardiner, who was slain at the Battle of Preston-Pans, September 21, 1745* (London, 1747).

32. Doddridge, *Some Remarkable Passages*, p. 30.

33. Doddridge, *Some Remarkable Passages*, pp. 30–35.

34. Ned C. Landsman, "Evangelists and Their Hearers: Popular Interpretation of Revivalist Preaching in Eighteenth-Century Scotland," *Journal of British Studies* 28 (1989), 120–149.

35. John Locke, *An Essay concerning Human Understanding*, ed. P. H. Nidditch (Oxford: Clarendon Press, 1975), bk. 4, ch. 19, "Of Enthusiasm." On "enlightened" hostility to enthusiasm, see J. G. A. Pocock, "Enthusiasm: The Antiself of Enlightenment," in Lawrence E. Klein and A. J. LaVopa (eds.), *Enthusiasm and Enlightenment in Europe, 1650–1850* (San Marino, CA: Huntington Library, 1998), pp. 7–28.

36. On the importance of "culture" and *cultura* in early-modern thought, see Joseph Niedermann, *Kultur: Werden und Wandlungen des Begriffs und seiner*

Ersatzbegriffe von Cicero bis Herder (Florence: Bibliopolis, 1941), as well as the important study by Sorana Corneanu, *Regimens of the Mind: Boyle, Locke, and the Early Modern* Cultura Animi *Tradition* (Chicago: University of Chicago Press, 2011). On Samuel Pufendorf's use of the term, see Tim Hochstrasser, *Natural Law Theories in the Early Enlightenment* (Cambridge: Cambridge University Press, 2000), pp. 95–106.

37. Corneanu, *Regimens of the Mind*, p. 50. See also Cicero, *Tusculan Disputations* II.13: "just as a field, however good the ground, cannot be productive without cultivation, so the soul cannot be productive without teaching. So true it is that the one without the other is ineffective. Now the cultivation of the soul is philosophy" (Cicero, *Tusculan Disputations*, trans. J. E. King. The Loeb Classical Library [London: William Heinemann, 1927], II.13, p. 159).

38. Corneanu, *Regimens of the Mind*, p. 19.

39. On the importance of practical morality in eighteenth-century philosophy, see Colin Heydt, "Practical Ethics," in J. Harris (ed.), *The Oxford Handbook of British Philosophy in the Eighteenth Century* (Oxford: Oxford University Press, 2013), ch. 16.

40. David Hume, *A Treatise of Human Nature*, ed. L. A. Selby-Bigge and P. Nidditch (Oxford: Oxford University Press, 1978), II.ii.3, p. 415.

41. Hugh Blair, "Sermon X. On Devotion," in *Sermons* (Edinburgh, 1777), p. 274.

42. M. A. Stewart, "Hume's Intellectual Development, 1711–1752," in M. Frasca-Spada and P. Kail (eds.), *Impressions of Hume* (Oxford: Clarendon Press, 2005), p. 12. See also Gordon Graham, "The Ambition of Scottish Philosophy," *The Monist* 90 (2007), 154–169.

43. Robertson, *The Case for the Enlightenment*, p. 8.

44. J. G. A. Pocock, "Introduction," in *Barbarism and Religion*, vol. 1: *The Enlightenments of Edward Gibbon, 1737–1764* (Cambridge: Cambridge University Press, 1999), pp. 1–10.

45. See above, p. 4.

46. Paul Giles, "Enlightenment Historiography and Cultural Civil Wars," in S. Manning and F. Cogliano (eds.), *The Atlantic Enlightenment* (Aldershot: Ashgate, 2008), p. 22.

47. On the question of "character" in Scottish Enlightenment moral thought, see Susan Manning and Thomas Ahnert, "Introduction: Character, Self, and Sociability in the Scottish Enlightenment," in Thomas Ahnert and Susan Manning (eds.), *Character, Self, and Sociability in the Scottish Enlightenment*

(New York: Palgrave, 2011), pp. 1–30. See also Susan Manning, *Poetics of Character: Transatlantic Encounters* (Cambridge: Cambridge University Press, 2013). On "character" in Victorian thought, see Stefan Collini, "The Idea of 'Character' in Victorian Political Thought," *Transactions of the Royal Historical Society* 35 (1985), 29–50.

1. PRESBYTERIANISM IN SCOTLAND AFTER 1690

1. Tim Harris, *Revolution: The Great Crisis of the British Monarchy, 1685–1720* (London: Penguin, 2007), p. 376.

2. Harris, *Revolution*, p. 415. On the effects of the Glorious Revolution on the University of Edinburgh, see Nicholas Phillipson, "The Making of an Enlightened University," pp. 53–58, in Robert D. Anderson, Michael Lynch, and Nicholas Phillipson, *The University of Edinburgh: An Illustrated History* (Edinburgh: Edinburgh University Press, 2003), pp. 51–101.

3. Colin Kidd, "Religious Realignment between Restoration and Union," in J. Robertson (ed.), *A Union for Empire: Political Thought and the Union of 1707* (Cambridge: Cambridge University Press, 1995), p. 158. See also Colin Kidd, *Union and Unionisms: Political Thought in Scotland, 1500–2000* (Cambridge: Cambridge University Press, 2008), ch. 6. For a discussion of the tensions between crown and Presbyterian church in the immediate aftermath of the Glorious Revolution, see Alasdair Raffe, "Presbyterianism, Secularization, and Scottish Politics after the Revolution of 1688–90," *Historical Journal* 53 (2010), 317–337. On those Episcopalians who supported William and Mary, see Tristram Clarke, "The Williamite Episcopalians and the Glorious Revolution in Scotland," *Records of the Scottish Church History Society* 24 (1990), 33–51.

4. Harris, *Revolution*, p. 415.

5. Alasdair Raffe, "Presbyterians and Episcopalians: The Formation of Confessional Cultures in Scotland, 1660–1715," *English Historical Review* 125, no. 514 (2010), 571.

6. Raffe, "Presbyterians and Episcopalians." See also Clare Jackson, *Restoration Scotland, 1660–1690: Royalist Politics, Religion and Ideas* (Woodbridge: Boydell Press, 2003), pp. 109–110.

7. On early modern debates over "universal monarchy," see Franz Bosbach, *Monarchia Universalis: ein politischer Leitbegriff der frühen Neuzeit* (Göttingen: Vandenhoeck & Ruprecht, 1988).

8. C. A. Whatley, *The Scots and the Union* (Edinburgh: Edinburgh University Press, 2007), p. 2–4; Kidd, "Religious Realignment," p. 146.

9. Paul Kleber Monod, *Jacobitism and the English People, 1688–1788* (Cambridge: Cambridge University Press, 1989); Allan MacInnes, "Jacobitism in Scotland: Episodic Cause or National Movement?" *Scottish Historical Review* 86 (2007), 225–252.

10. On this issue, see especially Colin Kidd, "Conditional Britons: The Scots Covenanting Tradition and the Eighteenth-Century British State," *English Historical Review* 117, no. 474 (2002), 1147–1176.

11. A. L. Drummond and J. Bulloch, *The Scottish Church, 1688–1843: The Age of the Moderates* (Edinburgh: Saint Andrew Press, 1973), chs. 11 and 12.

12. See, for example, the "Act against the Atheistical Opinion of the Deists, and for establishing the Confession of Faith," in General Assembly of the Church of Scotland, *Acts of the General Assembly of the Church of Scotland, 1638–1842* (Edinburgh, 1843), p. 253, as well as the "Act anent Preaching or Disseminating Erroneous Doctrine," ibid., p. 329.

13. M. Hunter, " 'Aikenhead the Atheist': The Context and Consequences of Articulate Irreligion in the Late Seventeenth Century," in M. Hunter and D. Wootton (eds.), *Atheism from the Reformation to the Enlightenment* (Oxford: Clarendon Press, 1992), pp. 221–254. On the intellectual origins of Aikenhead's description of the Bible as "Ezra's Fables," see Noel Malcolm, "Hobbes, Ezra, and the Bible: The History of a Subversive Idea," in N. Malcolm, *Aspects of Hobbes* (Oxford: Clarendon Press, 2002), pp. 383–431.

14. See T. B. Howell (ed.), *A Complete Collection of State Trials and Proceedings for High Treason and other Crimes and Misdemeanours from the earliest period to the present time*, vol. 13 (London, 1812), columns 917–938.

15. On deism and its definition, see F. Beiser, *The Sovereignty of Reason: The Defense of Rationality in the Early English Enlightenment* (Princeton, NJ: Princeton University Press, 1996); Jeffrey Wigelsworth, *Deism in Enlightenment England: Theology, Politics and Newtonian Public Science* (Manchester: Manchester University Press, 2009); Wayne Hudson, *The English Deists: Studies in Early Enlightenment* (London: Pickering and Chatto, 2009); Wayne Hudson, *Enlightenment and Modernity: The English Deists and Reform* (London: Pickering and Chatto, 2009).

16. General Assembly of the Church of Scotland, *Acts of the General Assembly of the Church of Scotland, 1638–1842*, 4 January 1696, p. 253.

17. Mungo Craig, *A Satyr against Atheistical Deism with the genuine character of a deist. To which is Prefixt, an account of Mr. Aikenhead's notions, who is now in prison for the same damnable apostacy* (Edinburgh, 1696), p. 14.

18. "Nec ulla Philosophia Moralis, Firma, stabilis, & naturae humanae conjuncta esse potest, nisi cujus Fundamenta non tantum in Numinis Existentia & Providentia, verum etiam in Animae Immortalitatis, & Vitae futurae Praemiis & Poenis ponantur." W. Law, *Theses Philosophicae* (Edinburgh, 1705), §XXII.

19. Michael Graham, *The Blasphemies of Thomas Aikenhead: Boundaries of Belief on the Eve of the Enlightenment* (Edinburgh: Edinburgh University Press, 2008), p. 90.

20. See M. A. Stewart, "Halyburton, Thomas (1674–1712)," *Oxford Dictionary of National Biography* (Oxford: Oxford University Press, 2004).

21. W. Ward, *Early Evangelicalism: A Global Intellectual History, 1670–1789* (Cambridge: Cambridge University Press, 2006), p. 54. See also G. D. Henderson, *Mystics of the North-East* (Aberdeen: The Spalding Club, 1934), p. 36.

22. See Raffe, "Presbyterians and Episcopalians," pp. 580–583.

23. I. Rivers, "Scougal's *The life of God in the soul of man:* The Fortunes of a Book, 1676–1830," in R. Savage (ed.), *Philosophy and Religion in Enlightenment Britain: New Case Studies* (Oxford: Oxford University Press, 2012), pp. 41–45.

24. Henry Scougal, *The Life of God in the Soul of Man: or, the Nature and Excellency of the Christian Religion. With the Methods of Attaining the Happiness it proposes; Also an Account of the Beginnings and Advances of a Spiritual Life*, 4th ed., with a preface by Gilbert Burnet (London, 1702), p. 29.

25. Scougal, *Life of God*, p. 33.

26. Scougal, *Life of God*, p. 16.

27. Scougal, *Life of God*, p. 32.

28. Scougal, *Life of God*, p. 10.

29. Scougal, *Life of God*, p. 10.

30. Scougal, *Life of God*, p. 9.

31. Scougal, *Life of God*, p. 12.

32. Scougal, *Life of God*, p. 12.

33. Scougal, *Life of God*, p. 12.

34. Scougal, *Life of God*, p. 64.

35. Scougal, *Life of God*, p. 64.

36. On the changes in the Scottish church around 1690, see R. Buick Knox, "Establishment and Toleration during the Reigns of William, Mary and Anne," *Records of the Scottish Church History Society* 23 (1989), and Harris, *Revolution*, ch. 9.

37. George Garden, *Comparative Theology or, The True and Solid Grounds of Pure and Peacable Theology* (Edinburgh, 1707), pp. 11–12.

38. Garden, *Comparative Theology*, p. 19.

39. Garden, *Comparative Theology*, p. 20.

40. Garden, *Comparative Theology*, p. 81.

41. Garden, *Comparative Theology*, p. 81.

42. Garden, *Comparative Theology*, p. 82.

43. Raffe, "Presbyterians and Episcopalians," p. 571.

44. John Cockburn, *Right Notions of God and Religion, together, with two Discourses for the better Conduct of the Sincere and for Correcting some prevailing Errors* (London, 1708), p. 256.

45. Cockburn, *Right Notions*, p. 260.

46. Cockburn, *Right Notions*, p. 258.

47. Garden, *Comparative Theology*, p. 51.

48. "Act concerning Probationers, and settling Ministers, with Questions to be proposed to and Engagements to be taken of them," in General Assembly of the Church of Scotland, *Acts of the General Assembly*, 22 May 1711, p. 456.

49. Ian McBride, "The School of Virtue: Francis Hutcheson, Irish Presbyterians and the Scottish Enlightenment," in Robert Eccleshall, D. George Boyce, and Vincent Geoghegan (eds.), *Political Thought in Ireland since the Seventeenth Century* (London, 1992), p. 80; Ian McBride, *Scripture Politics: Ulster Presbyterian and Irish Radicalism in the Late Eighteenth Century* (Oxford: Clarendon Press, 1998), pp. 28–29.

50. Brian Young, *Religion and Enlightenment in Eighteenth-Century Britain* (Oxford: Clarendon Press, 1998), pp. 45–80.

51. On these contacts, see Esther Mijers, *"News from the Republick of Letters": Scottish Students, Charles Mackie and the United Provinces, 1650–1750* (Leiden: Brill, 2012), ch. 3.

52. Anselm Schubert, *Das Ende der Sünde. Anthropologie und Erbsünde zwischen Reformation und Aufklärung*, vol. 84: *Forschungen zur Kirchen- und Dogmengeschichte*, ed. A. M. Ritter and R. Kaufmann (Göttingen: Vandenhoeck & Rupprecht, 2002), pp. 128–133. On Cocceius's federal theology, see Willem J. van Asselt, *The Federal Theology of Johannes Cocceius (1603–1669)* (Leiden: Brill, 2001).

53. Thomas Halyburton, *The great concern of salvation: in three parts; viz. I. A discovery of man's natural state. II. Man's recovery by faith in Christ. III. The Christian's duty, with respect to both personal and family religion* (Edinburgh, 1722), p. 44.

54. Halyburton, *The great concern of salvation*, p. 32.

55. Halyburton, *The great concern of salvation*, pp. 39–40.

56. Halyburton, *The great concern of salvation*, p. 232.

57. Halyburton, *The great concern of salvation*, p. 173.

58. Halyburton, *The great concern of salvation*, p. 171.

59. David Lachman, *The Marrow Controversy, 1718–1723: An Historical and Theological Analysis* (Edinburgh: Rutherford House, 1988), p. 199. See also Giancarlo Carabelli, *Hume e la Retorica dell' Ideologia* (Florence: La Nuova Italia Editrice, 1972), pp. 164–174.

60. "Act concerning a Book, entitled, The Marrow of Modern Divinity," in General Assembly of the Church of Scotland, *Acts of the General Assembly of the Church of Scotland, 1638–1842*, p. 535.

61. Anne Skoczylas, *Mr. Simson's Knotty Case: Divinity, Politics, and Due Process in Early Eighteenth-Century Scotland*, McGill-Queen's Studies in the History of Ideas (Montreal: McGill–Queen's University Press, 2001); Anne Skoczylas, "The Regulation of Academic Society in Early Eighteenth-Century Scotland: The Tribulations of Two Divinity Professors," *Scottish Historical Review* 83 (2004), 171–195.

62. "Act for maintaining the Purity of Doctrine of this Church, and determining the Process, Mr James Webster against Mr John Simson," in General Assembly of the Church of Scotland, *Acts of the General Assembly*, 14 May 1717, p. 518.

63. Anne Skoczylas, "Simson, John (1667–1740)," *Oxford Dictionary of National Biography* (Oxford: Oxford University Press, 2004).

64. John Simson and James Webster, *The Case of Mr John Simson* (Glasgow, 1715), pp. 76–77.

65. Simson and Webster, *The Case of Mr John Simson*, p. 29.

66. Simson and Webster, *The Case of Mr John Simson*, p. 30.

67. Simson and Webster, *The Case of Mr John Simson*, pp. 116, 22.

68. Simson and Webster, *The Case of Mr John Simson*, p. 48.

69. Simson and Webster, *The Case of Mr John Simson*, p. 23.

70. Simson and Webster, *The Case of Mr John Simson*, p. 63.

2. CONDUCT AND DOCTRINE

1. Matthew Tindal, *Christianity as Old as the Creation: or, the Gospel, a Republication of the Religion of Nature*, vol. 1 (London, 1730), p. 21.

2. Henry Scougal, *The Life of God in the Soul of Man: or, the Nature and Excellency of the Christian Religion* (Edinburgh, 1739). On the editions of

Scougal's work in the eighteenth century, see I. Rivers, "Scougal's *The life of God in the soul of man:* The Fortunes of a Book, 1676–1830," in R. Savage (ed.), *Philosophy and Religion in Enlightenment Britain: New Case Studies* (Oxford: Oxford University Press, 2012), pp. 41–45.

3. M. Batty, "Campbell, Archibald (1691–1756)," *Oxford Dictionary of National Biography* (Oxford: Oxford University Press, 2004).

4. Archibald Campbell, *An Enquiry into the Original of Moral Virtue* (Edinburgh, 1733), x–xii.

5. Committee for Purity of Doctrine and Archibald Campbell, *The Report of the Committee for Purity of Doctrine, at Edinburgh, March 16, 1736, and Professor Campbell's Remarks upon it* (Edinburgh, 1736).

6. M. A. Stewart, "Principal Wishart (1692–1753) and the Controversies of His Day," *Records of the Scottish Church History Society* 30 (2000), 64.

7. Anon. [George Wallace], "Memoirs of Dr Wallace of Edinburgh," *Scots Magazine* 33 (July 1771), 341. George Wallace was Robert Wallace's son. See also M. A. Stewart, "Berkeley and the Rankenian Club," *Hermathena* 139 (1985), 25–45, and G. E. Davie, "Berkeley's Impact on Scottish Philosophers," *Philosophy* 40 (1965), 222–234.

8. On Robert Molesworth, see Caroline Robbins, *The Eighteenth-Century Commonwealthman* (Indianapolis: Liberty Fund, 1987), ch. 4.

9. Ian McBride, "The School of Virtue: Francis Hutcheson, Irish Presbyterians and the Scottish Enlightenment," in Robert Eccleshall, D. George Boyce, and Vincent Geoghegan, *Political Thought in Ireland since the Seventeenth Century* (London: Routledge, 1993), p. 80; Ian McBride, *Scripture Politics: Ulster Presbyterian and Irish Radicalism in the Late Eighteenth Century* (Oxford: Clarendon Press, 1998), pp. 28–29.

10. John Abernethy, *Religious Obedience founded upon Personal Persuasion: A Sermon Preach'd at Belfast the 9th of December 1719* (Belfast, 1720), p. 14. On Abernethy's religious views, see Richard B. Barlow, "The Career of John Abernethy (1680–1740): Father of Non-Subscription in Ireland and Defender of Religious Liberty," *Harvard Theological Review* 78, 3/4 (1985), 399–419.

11. William Hamilton, *The Truth and Excellency of the Christian Religion* (Edinburgh, 1732). For examples of contemporaries' views on Hamilton's religious beliefs, see also Henry Sefton, " 'Neu-lights and Preachers Legall': Some Observations on the Beginnings of Moderatism in the Church of Scotland," in Norman MacDougall (ed.), *Church, Politics and Society: Scotland, 1408–1929* (Edinburgh: John Donald, 1983), pp. 188–190.

12. See William Wishart, *Answers for William Wishart, Principal of the College of Edinburgh, to the Charge exhibited against him before the Rev. Synod of Lothian and Tweeddale* (Edinburgh, 1738).

13. Anon., *A Vindication of Mr Hutcheson from the Calumnious Aspersions of a Late Pamphlet. By Several of his Scholars.* (s.l., 1738).

14. The frustration of the Glasgow Presbytery is palpable in their account of events, *The Remarks of the Committee of the Presbytery of Glasgow, upon Mr. Leechman's Sermon on Prayer, with his Replies thereunto &c., to which is prefix'd Historical Account of the whole Proceedings of the said Presbytery and their Committee; and of the Synod of Glasgow in that Affair* (Edinburgh, 1744).

15. Abernethy, *Religious Obedience founded upon Personal Persuasion*, p. 19.

16. George Turnbull, *A Philosophical Enquiry concerning the Connexion betwixt the Doctrines and Miracles of Jesus Christ. In a Letter to a Friend* (London, 1731), p. 27.

17. Robert Wallace, "A little treatise against imposing creeds or confessions of faith," Edinburgh University Library Special Collections, MS: La II.620 (19), 3r.

18. Wallace, "A little treatise against imposing creeds or confessions of faith," 3r.

19. William Wishart, "*Charity the end of Commandment; or Universal Love the Design of Christianity*. A Sermon preached at the Old-Jewry, April 19, 1731," 2nd ed., in Wishart, *Discourses on Several Subjects* (London, 1753), p. 222.

20. Quoted in M. A. Stewart, "George Turnbull and Educational Reform," in J. J. Carter and Joan M. Pittock (eds.), *Aberdeen and the Enlightenment* (Aberdeen: Aberdeen University Press, 1987), p. 96.

21. Wallace, "A little treatise against imposing creeds or confessions of faith," 5v. See also his "The End of Ecclesiastical Splendour in the Church and of Regal or Monarchicall Authority in the State in all the Christian Nations in Europe," Edinburgh University Library Special Collections, MS La. II.620 (15), in which he comments on the corruption of the church in late antiquity.

22. Wallace, "A little treatise against imposing creeds or confessions of faith," 7r. Other, less famous clergymen with similar views include Charles Telfer, William Armstrong, and Patrick Cuming. See Sefton, " 'Neu-lights and preachers legall,' " pp. 191–192.

23. Wishart, "*Charity,*" p. 129.

24. Wishart, "*Charity,*" p. 136.

25. Letter from William Wishart to Viscount Molesworth, 13 October 1722, p. 91, reproduced in Stewart, "Principal Wishart (1692–1753) and the Controversies of His Day."

26. Wallace, "A little treatise against imposing creeds or confessions of faith," 7r.

27. William Hamilton, *The Truth and Excellency of the Christian Religion* (Edinburgh, 1732).

28. Archibald Campbell, *The Necessity of Revelation: or an Enquiry into the Extent of Human Powers with Respect to Matters of Religion; Especially those two fundamental Articles, the Being of God, and the Immortality of the Soul* (London, 1739), pp. 50–51.

29. Turnbull, *A Philosophical Enquiry concerning the Connexion betwixt the Doctrines and Miracles of Jesus Christ*, p. 2.

30. John Abernethy, "Sermon VI: Of Justification by Faith," in *Sermons on Various Subjects*, vol. 1 (London, 1748), pp. 132–133.

31. Campbell, *The Necessity of Revelation*, p. 51.

32. William Wishart, "An Essay on the Indispensible Necessity of a Holy and Good life to the Happiness of Heaven," in *Discourses on Several Subjects*, p. 14.

33. Wishart, "*Charity,*" p. 133.

34. Turnbull, *Principles of Moral and Christian Philosophy*, vol. 2, ed. A. Broadie, (Indianapolis: Liberty Fund, 2005), p. 742.

35. Turnbull, *Principles of Moral and Christian Philosophy*.

36. Jennifer Herdt, *Putting on Virtue: The Legacy of the Splendid Vices* (Chicago: University of Chicago Press, 2008), p. 25.

37. Herdt, *Putting on Virtue*, p. 249.

38. Campbell, *The Necessity of Revelation*, p. 157. On Campbell's moral philosophy, see Anne Skoczylas, "Archibald Campbell's *Enquiry into the Original of Moral Virtue*, Presbyterian Orthodoxy, and the Scottish Enlightenment," *Scottish Historical Review* 87 (2008), 68–100; Christian Maurer, "Archibald Campbell's Views of Self-Cultivation and Self-Denial in Context," *Journal of Scottish Philosophy* 10 (2012), 13–27; and Luigi Turco, "Sympathy and Moral Sense: 1725–1740," *British Journal for the History of Philosophy* 7 (1999), 79–101.

39. Campbell, *The Necessity of Revelation*, p. 10. For Robert Wallace's similar view, see his sermon *The Regard due to Divine Revelation, and to Pretences to it, considered. A Sermon preached before the Provincial Synod of Dumfreis, at their Meeting in October 1729. On 1 Thess. V. 20, 21. With a Preface containing some Remarks on a BOOK lately publish'd, Entitled, Christianity as Old as Creation*, 2nd ed. (London, 1733), p. xxix. See also George Turnbull, *Christianity neither false nor useless, tho' not as old as the Creation: or, an Essay to prove the Usefulness, Truth, and Excellency of the Christian Religion; and to*

vindicate Dr Clarke's Discourse concerning the Evidences of Natural and Revealed Religion, from the Inconsistencies with which it is charged by the Author of Christianity as old as the Creation (London, 1732), v.

40. Turnbull, *Christianity,* p. 43.

41. William Leechman, "Sermon VI. The Wisdom of God in the Gospel Revelation," in William Leechman, *Sermons,* vol. 1 (London, 1789), p. 269.

42. Leechman, "Sermon VI," p. 272.

43. Leechman, "Sermon VI," p. 274.

44. Campbell, *The Necessity of Revelation,* p. 66.

45. Archibald Campbell, *An Enquiry into the Original of Moral Virtue,* 2nd ed. (Edinburgh, 1733), xxvi. Campbell here is quoting from a response by the church father Origen to his pagan critic Celsus, but it is clear that Campbell is in agreement with Origen.

46. Turnbull, *A Philosophical Enquiry,* p. 56.

47. Turnbull, *A Philosophical Enquiry,* p. 41.

48. Ian Maclean, "Heterodoxy in Natural Philosophy and Medicine: Pietro Pomponazzi, Guglielmo Gratarolo, Girolamo Cardano," in Ian Maclean and John Brooke (eds.), *Heterodoxy in Early Modern Science and Religion* (Oxford: Clarendon Press, 2005), pp. 1–29. See also Pietro Pomponazzi, *Tractatus de Immortalitate Animae,* ed. and trans. Gianfranco Morra (Bologna: Nanni & Fiammenghi, 1954), p. 232: "Mihi namque videtur quod nullae rationes naturales adduci possunt cogentes animam esse immortalem."

49. Nicholas Davidson, " 'Le plus beau et le plus mechant esprit que ie aye cogneu': Science and Religion in the Writings of Giulio Cesare Vanini, 1585–1619," in Maclean and Brooke (eds.), *Heterodoxy,* pp. 59–80.

50. John Locke, *An Essay concerning Human Understanding,* ed. P. H. Nidditch (Oxford: Clarendon Press, 1975), bk. 4, ch. 3, §6.

51. David Hume, *Essays Moral, Political and Literary,* ed. E. F. Miller (Indianapolis: Liberty Fund, 1987), p. 591.

52. For an example of this type of argument, see the work of the Scotsman Andrew Baxter, *An enquiry into the nature of the human soul; wherein the immateriality of the soul is evinced from the principles of reason and philosophy* (London, 1733).

53. See the discussion of William Law above, pp. 20–21.

54. John Locke, *Two Treatises of Government,* ed. P. Laslett (Cambridge: Cambridge University Press, 1988), bk. 2, ch. 2, §9, p. 272.

55. Locke, *Two Treatises of Government*, bk. 2, ch. 2, §7, p. 271.

56. Samuel Pufendorf, *On the Duty of Man and Citizen*, ed. J. Tully, trans. M. Silverthorne (Cambridge: Cambridge University Press, 1991), bk. 2, ch. 5, p. 134.

57. On this issue in German and Scottish natural jurisprudence, see Thomas Ahnert, "Pleasure, Pain and Punishment in the Early Enlightenment: German and Scottish Debates," *Jahrbuch für Recht und Ethik* 12 (2004), 173–187, and T. Ahnert, "Epicureanism and the Transformation of Natural Law in the Early German Enlightenment," in N. Leddy and A. Lifschitz (eds.), *Epicurus in the Enlightenment*, Studies on Voltaire and the Eighteenth Century (Oxford: Voltaire Foundation, 2009), pp. 53–68. In the 1684 edition of his *De Jure Naturae et Gentium*, Pufendorf, in response to Richard Cumberland's *De Legibus Naturae*, began to emphasize the existence of certain natural rewards and punishments (see Jon Parkin, *Science, Religion and Politics in Restoration England: Richard Cumberland's* De Legibus Naturae [Woodbridge, Suffolk: Boydell & Brewer, 1999], p. 211).

58. Letter to Bierling (1713), quoted in Patrick Riley, *Leibniz's Universal Jurisprudence: Justice as the Charity of the Wise* (Cambridge, MA: Harvard University Press, 1996), p. 68.

59. John Erskine, "The Law of Nature sufficiently Promulgated to Heathens" (1741), in Erskine, *Theological Dissertations* (London, 1765), p. 204.

60. Erskine, "The Law of Nature," p. 206.

61. Erskine, "The Law of Nature," p. 237.

62. See George Turnbull's comments in J. G. Heineccius and George Turnbull, *A Methodical System of Universal Law, with Supplements and a Discourse by George Turnbull*, ed. Thomas Ahnert and Peter Schröder (Indianapolis: Liberty Fund, 2008), p. 201.

63. See below, chapter 4

64. William King, *De Origine Mali* (Dublin, 1702). On contemporary reactions to the publication of King's *De Origine*, see Philip O'Regan, *Archbishop William King of Dublin (1650–1729) and the Constitution in Church and State* (Dublin: Four Courts Press, 2000), pp. 131–133.

65. George Turnbull, *The Principles of Moral and Christian Philosophy*, vol. 1, ed. A. Broadie (Indianapolis: Liberty Fund, 2005), p. 12.

66. Turnbull, *The Principles of Moral and Christian Philosophy*, vol. 1, pp. 396–397.

67. John Erskine, "The Nature of Christian Faith," in Erskine, *Theological Dissertations*, p. 148.

68. James Harris, "Religion in Hutcheson's Moral Philosophy," *Journal for the History of Philosophy* 46 (2008), 205–222. For literature on the epistemological status of judgements made by the "moral sense," see, for example, D. D. Raphael, *The Moral Sense* (London: Oxford University Press, 1947), pp. 15–46; Kenneth Winkler, "Hutcheson's Alleged Realism," *Journal of the History of Philosophy* 23 (1985), 179–194; David Fate Norton, "Hutcheson's Moral Realism," *Journal of the History of Philosophy* 23 (1985), 397–418; and, more recently, Peter J. Kail, "Hutcheson's Moral Sense: Skepticism, Realism, and Secondary Qualities," *History of Philosophy Quarterly* 18 (2001), 57–77. Daniel Carey has argued that Hutcheson's moral sense theory was a—not entirely successful—attempt to anchor morality in a foundation that was immune to the challenge of moral relativism and "diversity" across different cultures, but this may be exaggerating the extent to which moral diversity, rather than moral motivation and education, is Hutcheson's main concern (Daniel Carey, *Locke, Shaftesbury, and Hutcheson: Contesting Diversity in the Enlightenment and Beyond* [Cambridge: Cambridge University Press, 2006], pp. 150–199).

69. See Bernard Mandeville, *The Fable of the Bees*, 2 vols., ed. F. B. Kaye (Indianapolis: Liberty Fund, 1988), e.g. pp. 41–57 ("An Enquiry into the Origin of Moral Virtue"). On Mandeville's moral theory, see E. J. Hundert, *The Enlightenment's* Fable: *Bernard Mandeville and the Discovery of Society* (Cambridge: Cambridge University Press, 1994).

70. The first edition of Hutcheson's *Inquiry into the Original of Our Ideas of Beauty and Virtue* referred to Shaftesbury on the title page, although the reference disappeared in subsequent editions. See Wolfgang Leidhold's textual note on the title page in Francis Hutcheson, *An Inquiry into the Original of Our Ideas of Beauty and Virtue*, ed. W. Leidhold, 2nd ed. (Indianapolis: Liberty Fund, 2008), p. 199.

71. See Simon Grote, "Hutcheson's Divergence from Shaftesbury," *Journal of Scottish Philosophy* 4 (2006), 159–172.

72. John Clarke of Hull, author of, for example, *The Foundation of Morality in Theory and Practice Considered* (York, 1726), which was a response to Hutcheson's *Inquiry*, should not be confused with Samuel Clarke's younger brother, the mathematician and clergyman John Clarke.

73. Gilbert Burnet and Francis Hutcheson, *Letters between the late Mr. Gilbert Burnet and Mr. Hutchinson, concerning the true Foundation of Virtue or Moral Goodness. Formerly published in the London Journal* (London, 1735); John Balguy, *The Foundation of Moral Goodness: or a Further Inquiry into the*

Original of our Idea of Virtue (London, 1728), for example, pp. 13–14; William Wollaston, *The Religion of Nature delineated* (London, 1722), "Sect. I. Of Moral Good and Evil."

74. See the introduction by Thomas Mautner in Francis Hutcheson, *On Human Nature. Reflections on our common system of morality. On the social nature of man,* ed. T. Mautner (Cambridge: Cambridge University Press, 1993), pp. 38, 41–42. See also Luigi Turco, "La prima Inquiry morale di Francis Hutcheson," *Rivista Critica di Storia della Filosofia* 23 (1968), 39–60, 297–329.

75. Ian McBride, "The School of Virtue: Francis Hutcheson, Irish Presbyterians and the Scottish Enlightenment," in Robert Eccleshall, D. George Boyce, and Vincent Geoghegan (eds.), *Political Thought in Ireland since the Seventeenth Century* (London: Palgrave, 1992), p. 80. See also James Moore, "Presbyterianism and the Right of Private Judgement: Church Government in Ireland and Scotland in the Age of Francis Hutcheson," in R. Savage (ed.), *Philosophy and Religion in Enlightenment Britain* (Oxford: Oxford University Press, 2012), pp. 141–168. Knud Haakonssen has discussed Hutcheson's extensive idea of toleration, which, according to Hutcheson, did not contradict the magistrate's care of religious affairs (Haakonssen, "Natural Rights or Political Prudence? Francis Hutcheson on Toleration," *Proceedings of the British Academy* 186 [2013], 183–200).

76. W. R. Scott, *Francis Hutcheson: His Life, Teaching and Position in the History of Philosophy* (Cambridge: Cambridge University Press, 1900), p. 85.

77. Francis Hutcheson, *Inquiry into the Original of Our Ideas of Beauty and Virtue,* ed. Wolfgang Leidhold, 2nd ed. (Indianapolis: Liberty Fund, 2008), p. 12. On this aspect of Hutcheson's thought, see Wolfgang Leidhold, *Ethik und Politik bei Francis Hutcheson* (Freiburg: Karl Alber, 1985), pp. 122–123.

78. Hutcheson, *Inquiry,* p. 102.

79. Hutcheson, *Inquiry,* p. 112.

80. Gilbert Burnet and Francis Hutcheson, *Letters between the late Mr. Gilbert Burnet and Mr. Hutcheson concerning the True Foundation of Virtue or Moral Goodness. Formerly published in the London Journal* (London, 1735), p. 18.

81. Burnet and Hutcheson, *Letters,* p. 28.

82. Francis Hutcheson, *Essay on the Nature and Conduct of the Passions and Affections,* ed. A. Garrett (Indianapolis: Liberty Fund, 2002), p. 4.

83. Francis Hutcheson, *A System of Moral Philosophy,* vol. 1 (Glasgow, 1755), p. 24.

84. Hutcheson, *An Essay on the Nature and Conduct of our Passions and Affections*, p. 24.

85. Hutcheson, *System*, vol. 1, p. 27.

86. Hutcheson, *Inquiry*, p. 177.

87. Samuel Pufendorf, *The Political Writings of Samuel Pufendorf*, ed. C. L. Carr, trans. M. Seidler (New York: Oxford University Press, 1994), p. 155.

88. See above, p. 46.

89. Hutcheson, *System*, vol. 1, p. 172.

90. Hutcheson, *System*, vol. 1, p. 173.

91. Hutcheson, *System*, vol. 1, p. 181.

92. William King, *De Origine Mali* (Dublin, 1702); Hutcheson sent King a copy of the *Inquiry* (see Hutcheson, *Essay on the Nature and Conduct*, p. 44, footnote).

93. Hutcheson, *System*, vol. 1, p. 182.

94. Hutcheson, *System*, vol. 1, p. 182.

95. Hutcheson, *System*, vol. 1, p. 226.

96. Hutcheson, *System*, vol. 1, p. 45.

97. Hutcheson, *System*, vol. 1, p. 46.

98. For a discussion of these aspects of Campbell's thought, see Maurer, "Archibald Campbell's Views."

99. Hutcheson, *Inquiry*, p. 122.

100. Hutcheson, *System*, vol. 1, p. 43.

101. Hutcheson, *System*, vol. 1, p. 43.

102. Hutcheson, *System*, vol. 1, p. 43.

103. Hutcheson, *An Essay on the Nature and Conduct of our Passions and Affections*, p. 72.

104. Hutcheson, *System*, vol. 1, pp. 78–79.

105. Hutcheson, *System*, vol. 1, p. 77.

106. Hutcheson, *System*, vol. 1, p. 192.

107. Hutcheson, *System*, vol. 1, p. 29.

108. Hutcheson, *System*, vol. 1, p. 37.

109. Hutcheson, *System*, vol. 1, p. 37.

110. Hutcheson, *System*, vol. 1, p. 128.

111. Hutcheson, *System*, vol. 1, p. 131.

112. Hutcheson, *System*, vol. 1, pp. 203–204.

113. Herdt, *Putting on Virtue*, p. 25.

114. Hutcheson, *Inquiry*, pp. 178–179. See also Hutcheson, *An Essay on the Conduct of the Passions and Affections*, p. 29.

115. A. A. Cooper, Third Earl of Shaftesbury, "An Inquiry concerning Virtue or Merit," in A. A. Cooper, Third Earl of Shaftesbury, *Characteristicks of Men, Manners, Opinions, Times,* ed. L. Klein (Cambridge: Cambridge University Press, 1999), p. 185.

116. Hutcheson, *System,* vol. 1, p. 202.

117. On Hutcheson's theodicy in the *System,* see James Moore, "Hutcheson's Theodicy: The Argument and the Contexts of *A System of Moral Philosophy,*" in P. Wood (ed.), *The Scottish Enlightenment: Essays in Reinterpretation* (Rochester, NY: Rochester University Press, 2000), pp. 239–266.

118. Hutcheson, *System,* vol. 1, p. 200.

119. Hutcheson, *System,* vol. 1, p. 200.

120. Hutcheson, *System,* vol. 1, p. 200, note. See Baxter, *An enquiry into the nature of the human soul.*

121. Hutcheson, *Metaphysicae Synopsis; Ontologiam et Pneumatologiam Complectens* (Glasgow, 1742), pp. 31–32. A modern edition and translation of the *Synopsis* is included in Francis Hutcheson, *Logic, Metaphysics, and the Natural Sociability of Mankind,* ed. and trans. James Moore and Michael Silverthorne (Indianapolis: Liberty Fund, 2006), though the text there follows the 1744 edition of the *Synopsis,* which differs slightly from the 1742 version used here.

122. Francis Hutcheson, *Logicae Compendium. Praefixa est Dissertatio de Philosophiae Origine ejusque inventoribus aut excultoribus praecipuis* (Glasgow, 1738), pp. 4–5.

123. Hutcheson is sometimes described as a "Christian Stoic." See, for example, James Moore and Michael Silverthorne, "Introduction," in Marcus Aurelius, *The meditations of the Emperor Marcus Aurelius Antoninus,* ed. James Moore and Michael Silverthorne, trans. Francis Hutcheson and James Moor (Indianapolis: Liberty Fund, 2008), p. xxiii. As Christopher Brooke points out, however, Hutcheson "did . . . remain somewhat cagey about his affinities to the Stoics . . ., and he rarely endorsed their views explicitly." According to Brooke, "that may very well reflect a strategy of prudence with respect to his overwhelmingly Presbyterian environment" (see Christopher Brooke, *Philosophic Pride: Stoicism and Political Thought from Lipsius to Rousseau* [Princeton, NJ: Princeton University Press, 2012], p. 162). Yet Hutcheson may not have identified himself as a Stoic simply because he had serious reservations about Stoicism as a pagan philosophical system (Thomas Ahnert, "Francis Hutcheson and the Heathen Moralists," *Journal of Scottish Philosophy* 8 [2010], 51–62).

124. Francis Hutcheson, *Philosophiae Moralis Institutio Compendiaria, with A Short Introduction to Moral Philosophy*, ed. Luigi Turco (Indianapolis: Liberty Fund, 2007), p. 5.

125. Marcus Aurelius, *The meditations of the Emperor Marcus Aurelius Antoninus*, pp. 145–146, footnote. The statement could in principle be by Hutcheson's collaborator, James Moor, but it is fair to assume that his views would have been consistent with Hutcheson's. Again, Moor the eighteenth-century translator must not be confused with Moore, the twenty-first-century editor of Hutcheson's and Moor's translation.

126. Introduction to Marcus Aurelius, *The meditations of the Emperor Marcus Aurelius Antoninius*, p. 22.

127. Anon., *A Vindication of Mr Hutcheson from the Calumnious Aspersions of a Late Pamphlet. By Several of his Scholars* (s.l., 1738), p. 15.

128. Hutcheson, *Inquiry*, p. 12.

3. MODERATISM

1. See, for example, Isabel Rivers, *Reason, Grace and Sentiment: A Study of the Language of Religion and Ethics in England*, vol. 1: *Theological Debate from Locke to Burke* (Oxford: Clarendon Press, 1998), pp. 36–37. The term was also used with reference to certain Presbyterians by James II and VII in the 1687 Declaration of Indulgence (see Henry Sefton, " 'Neu-Lights and Preachers Legall': Some Observations on the Beginnings of Moderatism in the Church of Scotland," in Norman MacDougall (ed.), *Church, Politics and Society: Scotland, 1408–1929* (Edinburgh: John Donald, 1983), p. 186.

2. Samuel Johnson, *A Dictionary of the English Language*, 2nd ed., vol. 2 (London, 1755–56), s.v. "Moderate."

3. John Witherspoon, *Ecclesiastical Characteristics, or, the Arcana of Church Policy. Being an Humble Attempt to open up the Mystery of Moderation* (Edinburgh, 1753), e.g., pp. 7, 13.

4. See above, p. 19.

5. "Historians tend to use the term Moderatism in a cavalier fashion to describe two distinct but overlapping trends, the first a more polite, ecumenical outlook, the other a position on ecclesiastical polity and the related patronage question" (Colin Kidd, "Subscription, the Scottish Enlightenment and the Moderate Interpretation of History," *Journal of Ecclesiastical History* 55 [2005], 503, fn. 6). For a discussion of intellectual similarities between Moderates and orthodox, see Friedhelm Voges,

"Moderate and Evangelical Thinking in the Later Eighteenth Century: Differences and Shared Attitudes," *Records of the Scottish Church History Society* 22 (1985), 141–157.

6. Ian D. Clark, "From Protest to Reaction: The Moderate Regime in the Church of Scotland, 1752–1805," in N. T. Phillipson and Rosalind Mitchison (eds.), *Scotland in the Age of Improvement,* 2nd ed. (Edinburgh: Edinburgh University Press, 1996), p. 204: "The Moderates did, however inarticulately, grasp the fact that a secular society was emerging"; see also William Ferguson, *Scotland 1689 to the Present* (Edinburgh: Oliver & Boyd, 1978), p. 226: "Robertson was a realist. He knew that the trend of the age was secular, that the powers of the church had been curtailed, and that no good would come from theocratic delusions."

7. Richard B. Sher, *Church and University in the Scottish Settlement* (Edinburgh: Edinburgh University Press, 1985), pp. 153–154.

8. Sher, *Church and University,* p. 154.

9. M. A. Stewart, *The Kirk and the Infidel,* 2nd ed. (Lancaster: Lancaster University Press, 2001), p. 19. Stewart's pamphlet is the most detailed and illuminating account of Hume's failed candidacy.

10. Hugh Blair, *Observations upon a Pamphlet, entitled, An Analysis of the Moral and Religious Sentiments contained in the Writings of Sopho, and David Hume, Esq; &c* (Edinburgh, 1755), p. 22.

11. Adam Smith to William Cullen, November 1751, in Adam Smith, *Correspondence of Adam Smith,* ed. E. C. Mossner and Ian Simpson Ross (Indianapolis: Liberty Fund, 1987), pp. 5–6.

12. Sher, *Church and University,* p. 51.

13. Francis Hutcheson, *Considerations on Patronages: Addressed to the Gentlemen of Scotland* (London, 1735), p. 11.

14. Hutcheson, *Considerations,* p. 5.

15. William Ferguson, *Scotland 1689 to the Present* (Edinburgh: Oliver & Boyd, 1978), p. 13.

16. Hutcheson, *Considerations,* p. 7. Richard Sher and Alexander Murdoch have argued that Hutcheson greatly exaggerated the number of parishes under the control of the Crown (see Richard Sher and Alexander Murdoch, "Patronage and Party in the Church of Scotland, 1750–1800," in Norman MacDougall (ed.), *Church, Politics and Society,* p. 208.

17. Hutcheson, *Considerations,* p. 8.

18. Hutcheson, *Considerations,* p. 20.

19. Hutcheson, *Considerations,* pp. 13–14.

20. Similar fears were expressed by Robert Wallace; see Henry R. Sefton, "Rev. Robert Wallace: An Early Moderate," *Records of the Scottish Church History Society* 16 (1966), 6.

21. Hutcheson, *Considerations,* p. 19.

22. See, for example, Anon., *The Case of the Patrons of the Churches in Scotland, considered with Regard to the Bill now depending in the Honourable House of Commons* (Edinburgh, 1735).

23. This is pointed out by Sher, *Church and University,* p. 48. See also I. D. Clark, "From Protest to Reaction: The Moderate Regime in the Church of Scotland, 1752–1805," in Phillipson and Mitchison (eds.), *Scotland in the Age of Improvement,* p. 204.

24. See below, pp. 89–93.

25. James Oswald, *Letters concerning the Present State of the Church of Scotland, and the consequent Danger to Religion and Learning, from the Arbitrary and Unconstitutional Exercise of the Law of Patronage* (Edinburgh, 1767), p. 19.

26. Oswald, *Letters concerning the Present State of the Church of Scotland,* p. 11.

27. Sher, *Church and University,* p. 49.

28. Nathaniel Morren (ed.), *Annals of the General Assembly of the Church of Scotland from the Origin of the Relief in 1752 to the Rejection of the Overture on Schism in 1766* (Edinburgh: John Johnstone, 1840), p. 334.

29. Anon. [John Hyndman], *A Just View of the Constitution of the Church of Scotland, and of the Proceedings of the last General Assembly in relation to the Deposition of Mr Gillespie* (Edinburgh, 1753), p. 5.

30. William Robertson et al., "Reasons of Dissent from judgment and resolution of the Commission, March 11, 1752, resolving to inflict no censure on the Presbytery of Dunfermline for their disobedience in relation to the settlement of Inverkeithing," in Nathaniel Morren (ed.), *Annals of the General Assembly of the Church of Scotland, from the final secession in 1739, to the Origin of the Relief in 1752* (Edinburgh: John Johnstone, 1838), pp. 231–242.

31. Morren (ed.), *Annals of the General Assembly of the Church of Scotland from the Origin of the Relief in 1752 to the Rejection of the Overture on Schism in 1766,* pp. 1–2.

32. Oswald, *Letters concerning the Present State of the Church of Scotland,* p. 10.

33. Nathaniel Morren (ed.), *Annals of the General Assembly of the Church of Scotland, from the final secession in 1739, to the Origin of the Relief in 1752* (Edinburgh: John Johnstone, 1838), p. 233.

34. Morren (ed.), *Annals of the General Assembly of the Church of Scotland, from the final secession in 1739, to the Origin of the Relief in 1752*, pp. 231–232.

35. John Witherspoon, *The History of a Corporation of Servants* (Glasgow, 1765), p. 47.

36. Clark, "From Protest to Reaction," p. 210. Ferguson also points out that Robertson "carefully dissociated himself, and as far as possible his party, from political management" (Ferguson, *Scotland 1689 to the Present*, p. 226).

37. James Finlayson, "A Short Account of the Life and Character of Hugh Blair," pp. 504–505, in Hugh Blair, *Sermons*, vol. 5 (London, 1801), pp. 491–516. For a modern study of Hugh Blair, see Robert M. Schmitz, *Hugh Blair* (New York: King's Crown Press, 1948).

38. George Campbell, *The Spirit of the Gospel neither a Spirit of Superstition nor of Enthusiasm: A Sermon preached before the Synod of Aberdeen, April 9, 1771* (Edinburgh, 1771), p. 16.

39. James Oswald, *The Divine Efficacy of the Gospel-Dispensation. A sermon, preached before the Society in Scotland for Propagating Christian Knowledge, at their anniversary meeting, in the High Church of Edinburgh, on Friday, June 8, 1770* (Edinburgh, 1770), p. 15.

40. Henry Home, Lord Kames, *Loose Hints upon Education, chiefly concerning the Culture of the Heart* (Edinburgh, 1781), pp. 176–177.

41. Henry Home, Lord Kames, *Loose Hints upon Education*, p. 178.

42. Henry Home, Lord Kames, *Loose Hints upon Education*, pp. 178–179.

43. Henry Home, Lord Kames, *Loose Hints upon Education*, p. 176.

44. Alexander Gerard, *Sermons*, vol. 2 (London, 1782), p. 161.

45. Gerard, *Sermons*, vol. 2, p. 160.

46. Quoted in Jeffrey M. Suderman, *Orthodoxy and Enlightenment: George Campbell in the Eighteenth Century* (Montreal: McGill–Queen's University Press, 2001), p. 205.

47. See s.v. "historical, *a. (n.)*" in the *Oxford English Dictionary*, 2nd ed.

48. Oswald, *The Divine Efficacy of the Gospel Dispensation*, p. 26. See also George Campbell, *Spirit of the Gospel*, p. 3, where he quotes James 2:19: "*The devils believe, and tremble.*"

49. Gerard, *Sermons*, vol. 2, p. 163.

50. Campbell, *Spirit of the Gospel*, p. 43.

51. Thomas Ahnert, *Religion and the Origins of the German Enlightenment: Faith and the Reform of Learning in the Thought of Christian Thomasius* (Rochester, NY: Rochester University Press, 2006), ch. 4.

52. William Robertson, *The History of the Reign of the Emperor Charles V,* vol. 1 (London, 1769), p. 74.

53. Robertson, *The History of the Reign of the Emperor Charles V,* vol. 1, p. 74.

54. Campbell, *Spirit of the Gospel,* p. 44.

55. William Robertson, *The History of Scotland,* vol. 1 (London, 1759), p. 118.

56. Campbell, *Spirit of the Gospel,* p. 51.

57. Robertson, *The History of the Reign of the Emperor Charles V,* vol. 1, p. 74.

58. Hugh Blair, "Sermon I. Of the Union of Piety and Morality," *Sermons,* vol. 1 (Edinburgh, 1777), p. 3.

59. Hugh Blair, "Sermon XV. On the Importance of Religious Knowledge to Mankind," in *Sermons,* vol. 2 (London, 1780), pp. 446–447.

60. Hugh Blair, "Sermon XV. On the Motives to Constancy in Virtue," in Blair, *Sermons,* vol. 1 (Edinburgh, 1777), p. 455.

61. Blair, "Sermon XV. On the Motives to Constancy in Virtue," pp. 456–457.

62. "Nihil est enim quod plus ad vitam beatam valet, quam benigni & sociales Affectus, qui nos ad aliorum bonum promovendum ducunt. Alunt semper aliquid vi sua atque natura, quod tranquillet animos: quin etiam cum successu destituuntur, jucunditate attamen magis pura, animos perfundunt, quam quae ex privatis & contractioribus oblectamentis unquam profluit" (Hugh Blair, *Dissertatio Philosophica Inauguralis, De Fundamentis et Obligatione Legis Naturae* [Edinburgh, 1739], p. 5).

63. Blair, "Sermon XV. On the Motives to Constancy in Virtue," p. 457.

64. Blair, "Sermon XV. On the Motives to Constancy in Virtue," p. 458.

65. Blair, "Sermon XV. On the Motives to Constancy in Virtue," p. 461.

66. Blair, "Sermon XV. On the Motives to Constancy in Virtue," p. 461.

67. Blair, "Sermon XV. On the Motives to Constancy in Virtue," p. 463.

68. Blair, "Sermon XV. On the Motives to Constancy in Virtue," p. 464.

69. Blair, "Sermon XV. On the Motives to Constancy in Virtue," p. 464.

70. Blair, "Sermon XV. On the Motives to Constancy in Virtue," p. 464.

71. Hugh Blair, "Sermon IV. On our Imperfect Knowledge of a Future State," in Hugh Blair, *Sermons,* vol. 1 (Edinburgh, 1777), p. 87.

72. The following section is based on Thomas Ahnert, "The Moral Education of Mankind: Character and Religious Moderatism in the Sermons of Hugh Blair," in Thomas Ahnert and Susan Manning (eds.), *Character, Self, and Sociability in the Scottish Enlightenment* (New York: Palgrave, 2011), pp. 76–78.

73. Blair, "Sermon IV. On our Imperfect Knowledge," p. 96.

74. Blair, "Sermon IV. On our Imperfect Knowledge," p. 96.

75. Blair, "Sermon IV. On our Imperfect Knowledge," p. 96.

76. Hugh Blair, "Sermon IX. On Religious Retirement," in *Sermons*, vol. 1, p. 235.

77. Blair, "Sermon IX. On Religious Retirement," pp. 260–261.

78. On this type of "work ethic" as part of an economy of salvation, see A. J. LaVopa, "The Not-So Prodigal Son: James Boswell and the Scottish Enlightenment," in Ahnert and Manning (eds.), *Character, Self, and Sociability in the Scottish Enlightenment*, pp. 90–93.

79. See, e.g., Henry Home, Lord Kames, *Loose Hints upon Education*, p. 176.

80. Hugh Blair, "On the Union of Piety and Morality," in Blair, *Sermons*, vol. 1, p. 2.

81. Blair, "On the Union of Piety and Morality," p. 22.

82. David Hume, *The Letters of David Hume*, vol. 2, ed. J. Y. T. Greig (Oxford: Oxford University Press, 2011), p. 301.

83. See Paul Wood, "The Scottish Philosophy: Thomas Reid and the Common Sense School," in J. A. Harris and Aaron Garrett (eds.), *Oxford History of Scottish Philosophy*, vol. 2: *Scottish Philosophy in the Age of Enlightenment* (Oxford: Oxford University Press, forthcoming).

84. See below, pp. 118–121.

85. See below, pp. 118–121. The continuities between moral sense theorists like Hutcheson and later "common-sense" philosophers have been stressed by David Fate Norton—e.g., in ch. 4 of his *David Hume: Common-Sense Moralist, Sceptical Metaphysician* (Princeton, NJ: Princeton University Press, 1982). Norton's interest, however, was not in their shared nondoctrinal view of religion, but in their opposition to Hume's skepticism in metaphysical questions. Yet moral-sense theorists had doubts about the limitations of unassisted human reason, too. Although these doubts were not as extreme as Hume's, they were similar in some respects. "Common-sense" philosophers were also very critical of the belief of figures such as Hutcheson or Kames in sentiments as the foundation of human action, as will be shown below.

86. Quoted in Alexander Campbell Fraser, *Thomas Reid* (Edinburgh: Oliphant, Anderson & Ferrier, 1898), pp. 122–123. See also M. A. Stewart, "Rational Religion and Common Sense," in Joseph Houston (ed.), *Thomas Reid: Context, Influence, Significance* (Edinburgh: Dunedin Academic Press, 2004), pp. 123–160.

87. Thomas Reid, *An Inquiry into the Human Mind on the Principles of Common Sense*, ed. Derek R. Brookes (University Park: Pennsylvania State University Press, 1997), 6.24, p. 197.

88. Reid, *Inquiry into the Human Mind*, 6.24, p. 196.

89. James Beattie, *Selected Philosophical Writings*, ed. J. A. Harris (Exeter: Imprint Academic, 2004), pp. 92–93. On Beattie, see Nicholas Phillipson, "James Beattie and the Defence of Common Sense," in Bernhard Fabian (ed.), *Festschrift für Rainer Gruenter* (Heidelberg: Winter, 1978), pp. 145–154.

90. Beattie, *Selected Philosophical Writings*, p. 93.

91. Beattie, *Selected Philosophical Writings*, p. 93.

92. James Oswald, *An Appeal to Common Sense in Behalf of Religion*, vol. 2 (Edinburgh, 1772), p. 290.

93. Reid, *Inquiry into the Human Mind*, p. 205.

94. Thomas Reid, "Three Lectures on the Nature and Duration of the Soul," in Thomas Reid, *Essays on the Intellectual Powers of Man*, ed. D. R. Brookes and K. Haakonssen (Edinburgh: Edinburgh University Press, 2002), p. 620.

95. Reid, "Three Lectures," p. 621.

96. Reid, "Three Lectures," p. 621.

97. Reid, "Three Lectures," p. 622.

98. Reid, "Three Lectures," p. 625.

99. Reid, "Three Lectures," p. 626.

100. Reid, "Three Lectures," p. 627.

101. Reid, "Three Lectures," p. 629.

102. Reid, "Three Lectures," p. 630.

103. Oswald, *The Divine Efficacy of the Gospel Dispensation*, p. 4.

104. James Beattie, *Evidences of the Christian Religion; Briefly and plainly stated*, vol. 1 (Edinburgh, 1786), pp. 16–17.

105. Beattie, *Evidences*, vol. 1, pp. 17–19.

106. Beattie, *Evidences*, vol. 1, p. 25.

107. Beattie, *Evidences*, vol. 1, p. 22–23.

108. Beattie, *Evidences*, vol. 1, p. 22.

109. Oswald, *An Appeal to Common Sense*, pp. 301–302.

110. A. A. Cooper, Third Earl of Shaftesbury, "An Inquiry concerning Virtue or Merit," in A. A. Cooper, Third Earl of Shaftesbury, *Characteristicks of Men, Manners, Opinions, Times*, ed. L. Klein (Cambridge: Cambridge University Press, 1999), p. 185.

111. Oswald, *An Appeal to Common Sense*, pp. 303–304.

112. Thomas Reid, *Thomas Reid on Logic, Rhetoric and the Fine Arts: Papers on the Culture of the Mind*, ed. A. Broadie (Edinburgh: Edinburgh University Press, 2005), p. 89. For an overview of Reid's moral thought, see Knud

Haakonssen, *Natural Law and Moral Philosophy: From Grotius to the Scottish Enlightenment* (Cambridge: Cambridge University Press, 1996), ch. 6.

113. Reid, *Logic, Rhetoric and the Fine Arts,* pp. 89–90.

4. ORTHODOXY

1. See Richard Sher, *Church and University in the Scottish Enlightenment: The Moderate Literati of Edinburgh* (Edinburgh: Edinburgh University Press, 1985), p. 72.

2. Sher, *Church and University in the Scottish Enlightenment,* pp. 74–83; Thomas Ahnert, "Clergymen as Polite Philosophers: *Douglas* and the Conflict between Moderates and Orthodox in the Scottish Enlightenment," *Intellectual History Review* 18 (2008), 375–383; Ralph Mclean, "Introduction," in John Home, *Douglas: John Home's* Douglas: *A Tragedy, with Contemporary Commentaries,* ed. Ralph Mclean (Glasgow: Humming Earth, 2010), pp. ix–xix.

3. James A. Harris, "Answering Bayle's Question: Religious Belief in the Moral Philosophy of the Scottish Enlightenment," *Oxford Studies in Early Modern Philosophy* 1 (2003), 229–254.

4. On Moderates' skepticism about natural religion, see Thomas Ahnert, "The Soul, Natural Religion and Moral Philosophy in the Scottish Enlightenment," *Eighteenth-Century Thought* 2 (2004), 233–253. Daniel W. Howe has pointed out that Witherspoon was far from hostile to reason. Thus Witherspoon, Howe writes, believed that "it was not necessary to adopt the laxity of the Moderates in order to take account of secular moral philosophy" (Daniel W. Howe, "John Witherspoon and the Transatlantic Enlightenment," Susan Manning and Frank Cogliano [eds.], *The Atlantic Enlightenment* [Aldershot: Ashgate, 2008], p. 70; see also Ned C. Landsman, "Witherspoon and the Problem of Provincial Identity," in R. Sher and J. Smitten [eds.], *Scotland and America in the Age of Enlightenment* [Edinburgh: Edinburgh University Press, 1990], 29–45).

5. David Hume, "My Own Life," in David Hume, *Essays Moral, Political and Literary,* ed. E. F. Miller (Indianapolis, Liberty Fund, 1987), p. xxxiv.

6. This conventional interpretation of Hume's statement has been questioned, convincingly, by Stephen Buckle. See his *Hume's Enlightenment Tract* (Oxford: Oxford University Press, 2001), pp. 7–12.

7. Anon. [John Bonar], *An Analysis of the Moral and Religious Sentiments contained in the Writings of Sopho and David Hume, Esq.* (Edinburgh, 1755), p. 26.

8. Sher, *Church and University in the Scottish Enlightenment*, pp. 66–67.

9. Anon. [Bonar], *An Analysis*, pp. 10, 12.

10. Henry Home, Lord Kames, *Essays on the Principles of Morality and Natural Religion, in two parts* (Edinburgh, 1751), p. 354. Although Kames implies that he is quoting Hume, he is, in fact, paraphrasing slightly: see David Hume, *Philosophical Essays concerning Human Understanding* (London, 1748), p. 215.

11. Kames, *Essays*, p. 353.

12. Kames, *Essays*, pp. 354–355. Again, Kames is not quoting Hume exactly, but splicing several distinct passages together and altering them slightly: see Hume, *Philosophical Essays*, pp. 221–223.

13. Kames, *Essays*, p. 355.

14. Kames, *Essays*, p. 357.

15. Kames, *Essays*, p. 360.

16. Kames, *Essays*, p. 386.

17. Kames, *Essays*, p. 360.

18. Kames, *Essays*, p. 350.

19. Kames, *Essays*, p. 350.

20. Kames, *Essays*, pp. 350–351.

21. Kames, *Essays*, p. 352.

22. Kames, *Essays*, p. 342.

23. Kames, *Essays*, p. 348.

24. Kames, *Essays*, pp. 339–340.

25. See above, p. 83.

26. David Hume, *A Treatise of Human Nature*, ed. L. A. Selby-Bigge and P. Nidditch (Oxford: Oxford University Press, 1978), I.iv.v, p. 234.

27. Hume, *A Treatise of Human Nature*, I.iv.v, p. 234.

28. Hume, *Essays Moral, Political and Literary*, p. 598. On Hume's religious views, see J. C. A. Gaskin, *Hume's Philosophy of Religion* (Basingstoke: Macmillan, 1988). Paul Russell has argued forcefully for Hume's atheism (see his *The Riddle of Hume's Treatise: Skepticism, Naturalism, and Irreligion* [New York: Oxford University Press, 2008]). See also Thomas Holden, *Spectres of False Divinity: Hume's Moral Atheism* (Oxford: Oxford University Press, 2010). According to Holden, Hume believes there can be no relation of "sympathy" between God and humans, and therefore, also, no moral relationship of the kind that characterizes human society. That seems true, but it is not clear that proving this absence of a sympathetic relationship between God and humans was Hume's main concern.

29. Quoted in Roy Porter, *Flesh in the Age of Reason* (London: Allen Lane, 2003), p. 107. On Kames's natural religion, see I. S. Ross, "The Natural Theology of Lord Kames," in P. Wood (ed.), *The Scottish Enlightenment* (Rochester, NY: University of Rochester Press, 2000), pp. 335–351.

30. Henry Home, Lord Kames, *Essays on the Principles of Morality and Natural Religion*, 3rd ed. (Edinburgh, 1779), p. 287.

31. On Moderates' skepticism concerning natural knowledge of the immortality of the soul, see Thomas Ahnert, "The Soul, Natural Religion and Moral Philosophy in the Scottish Enlightenment," *Eighteenth-Century Thought* 2 (2004), 233–253.

32. John Logan, "Sermon 1," in *Sermons*, vol. 2 (Edinburgh, 1791), pp. 99–100.

33. Logan, "Sermon 1," p. 100.

34. Logan, "Sermon 1," p. 101.

35. Logan, "Sermon 1," p. 101.

36. William Robertson's only published sermon was *The Situation of the World at the Time of Christ's Appearance, and its Connexion with the Success of his Religion Considered. A Sermon preached before the Society in Scotland for Propagating Christian Knowledge* (Edinburgh, 1755). Another sermon from 1788, on the centenary of the Glorious Revolution, survived in manuscript form, as did notes for a fast day sermon in 1778 on the American Revolution (William Robertson, *Miscellaneous Works and Commentaries*, ed. Jeffrey Smitten [London: Routledge/Thoemmes, 1996], pp. 139–142, 175–187).

37. Robertson, *The Situation of the World at the Time of Christ's Appearance*, p. 22.

38. Robertson, *The Situation of the World at the Time of Christ's Appearance*, pp. 15–16.

39. Robertson, *The Situation of the World at the Time of Christ's Appearance*, p. 16.

40. Robertson, *The Situation of the World at the Time of Christ's Appearance*, p. 17.

41. Robertson, *The Situation of the World at the Time of Christ's Appearance*, p. 17.

42. Robertson, *The Situation of the World at the Time of Christ's Appearance*, p. 18.

43. Robertson, *The Situation of the World at the Time of Christ's Appearance*, pp. 23–24.

44. William Robertson, *An Historical Disquisition concerning the Knowledge which the Ancients had of India; and the Progress of Trade with that Country prior to the Discovery of the Passage to it by the Cape of Good Hope* (London, 1791), p. 333.

See Strabo, *The Geography of Strabo,* vol. 1, trans. Horace Leonard Jones (London: William Heinemann, 1917), 1.2.8, pp. 69–71.

45. Sher, *Church and University in the Scottish Enlightenment,* p. 177.

46. S. J. Brown, "William Robertson (1721–1793) and the Scottish Enlightenment," in S. J. Brown (ed.), *William Robertson and the Expansion of Empire* (Cambridge: Cambridge University Press, 1997), pp. 8–9.

47. Robertson, *The Situation of the World,* p. 17.

48. Robertson, *Historical Disquisition,* p. 299.

49. Robertson, *Historical Disquisition,* p. 330.

50. Robertson, *Historical Disquisition,* p. 331.

51. Robertson, *Historical Disquisition,* p. 332.

52. William Robertson, *The History of America,* vol. 3 (Dublin, 1777), bk. 7, p. 163.

53. Robertson, *The History of America,* vol. 3, bk. 7, p. 164.

54. Robertson, *The History of America,* vol. 3, bk. 7, p. 162.

55. Robertson, *The History of America,* vol. 3, bk. 7, p. 163.

56. Nicholas Phillipson has argued that Robertson believed that the natural development of human societies everywhere reflected a divine providential plan, yet that interpretation does not seem plausible, since Robertson thought that the progress of societies that did not enjoy the benefits of the Gospel was necessarily limited and defective. Non-Christian civilizations, according to Robertson, were always going to be inferior to Christian societies in key respects (Nicholas Phillipson, "Providence and Progress: An Introduction to the Historical Thought of William Robertson," in S. J. Brown [ed.], *William Robertson and the Expansion of Empire* [Cambridge: Cambridge University Press, 1997], pp. 74–91). Stewart Brown has suggested that Robertson drew parallels between Hindu civilization and that of eighteenth-century Britain. However, this seems to ignore the profound difference Robertson saw between the pagan culture of Hinduism, and the Christian civilization of modern, Protestant Europe (see S. J. Brown, "William Robertson, Early Orientalism, and the *Historical Disquisition* on India of 1791," *Scottish Historical Review* 88 [2009], 289–312). See Thomas Ahnert, "Fortschrittsgeschichte und Religiöse Aufklärung. William Robertson und die Deutung außereuropäischer Kulturen," *Geschichte und Gesellschaft,* Sonderheft 23, "Die Aufklärung und ihre Weltwirkung" (2010), 101–122. Recently, Joshua Ehrlich has argued that Robertson thought of the moral world in Newtonian terms: like the Newtonian physical universe, which required God to replenish its energy from time to time, the moral universe had to be renewed at certain intervals by divine intervention, of which the message of Christ was one example (Ehrlich, "Wiliam

Robertson and Scientific Theism," *Modern Intellectual History* 10 [2013], 519–542). There are, however, two problems with this interpretation. Although Robertson certainly knew the writings of Newtonians like Colin McLaurin, there is no evidence that he drew an analogy between the Newtonian physical universe and the moral world. Second, the idea that the Gospel was just one of many moral renewals overlooks the fact that, for Robertson, the Gospel was a unique divine revelation, and not comparable to the events of the Reformation, for example. Like so many other events these may have in some way reflected the designs of divine providence, but they were different from the Gospel because they did not involve the revelation of any divine truths to humankind.

57. George Anderson, *A Remonstrance against Lord Viscount Bolingbroke's Philosophical Religion* (Edinburgh, 1756), p. 372.

58. John Witherspoon, "Sermon I. Man in his natural state," in *The Works of John Witherspoon*, vol. 4 (Edinburgh, 1804), p. 21.

59. Anderson, *A Remonstrance*, p. 331.

60. John Witherspoon, "Lectures on Moral Philosophy," in *The Works of John Witherspoon*, vol. 7 (Edinburgh, 1805), p. 41.

61. "Cum igitur mentis qualitates, cogitatio nempe, & ratiocinatio, actusque spontanei, notis qualitatibus materiae omnino contrariae esse videantur, concludere licet, mentem humanam esse aliquod a corpore prosus diversum" (John Witherspoon, *Disputatio Philosophica de Mentis Immortalitate* [Edinburgh, 1739], p. 2).

62. "Optimae ac elegantissimae res materiales nihil sunt, praeter partes materiae diversimode conjunctas" (Witherspoon, *Disputatio*, p. 3).

63. "Simplex & indivisa animi natura perire igitur nequit, nisi in nihilum redigatur, quod cum causarum quarumlibet naturalium vires superet, affirmare licet mentem humanam esse sua natura immortalem" (Witherspoon, *Disputatio*, p. 4).

64. "Imo haud raro cernimus hominum sceleratissimis omnia prospere evenire, dum boni innumeris premuntur malis" (Witherspoon, *Disputatio*, p. 4).

65. John Witherspoon, "Lectures on Moral Philosophy," in Witherspoon, *Works*, vol. 7, p. 49.

66. Witherspoon, "Lectures on Moral Philosophy," p. 49.

67. Witherspoon, "Lectures on Moral Philosophy," p. 42.

68. George Anderson, *An Estimate of the Profit and Loss of Religion, personally and publicly stated* (Edinburgh, 1753), p. 241.

69. Anderson, *An Estimate*, p. 241.

70. John Witherspoon, "Sermon XV. The Absolute Necessity of Salvation through Christ. Preached before the Society in Scotland for Propagating Christian Knowledge, in the High Church of Edinburgh, on Monday, January 2. 1758," in *Works*, vol. 4, p. 245.

71. Witherspoon, "Sermon XV. The Absolute Necessity of Salvation through Christ," p. 243.

72. Witherspoon, "Sermon XV. The Absolute Necessity of Salvation through Christ," p. 242.

73. Witherspoon, "Sermon XV. The Absolute Necessity of Salvation through Christ," footnotes pp. 259 and 267–268.

74. Witherspoon "Sermon XV. The Absolute Necessity of Salvation through Christ," p. 268.

75. Robert Walker, *Sermons on Practical Subjects*, 3rd ed., vol. 1 (London, 1783), pp. 142–143.

76. Walker, *Sermons on Practical Subjects*, 3rd ed., vol. 1, p. 147.

77. Walker, *Sermons on Practical Subjects*, 3rd ed., vol. 1, p. 148.

78. Robert Walker, *Sermons on Practical Subjects*, 4th ed., vol. 3 (Edinburgh, 1784), p. 338.

79. Walker, *Sermons on Practical Subjects*, 4th ed., vol. 3, p. 346.

80. David Hume, *A Treatise of Human Nature*, II.iii.3, p. 415.

81. Hugh Blair, "Sermon X. On Devotion," in *Sermons*, vol. 1 (Edinburgh, 1777), p. 274.

82. Henry Home, Lord Kames, *Essays on the Principles of Morality and Natural Religion* (Edinburgh, 1751), p. 12.

83. Henry Home, Lord Kames, *Essays on the Principles of Morality and Natural Religion* (Edinburgh, 1751), pp. 19–20.

84. Henry Home, Lord Kames, *Essays on the Principles of Morality and Natural Religion*, p. 76.

85. Henry Home, Lord Kames, *Essays on the Principles of Morality and Natural Religion*, p. 61.

86. Henry Home, Lord Kames, *Essays on the Principles of Morality and Natural Religion*, pp. 63–64.

87. Henry Home, Lord Kames, *Essays on the Principles of Morality and Natural Religion*, p. 65.

88. Henry Home, Lord Kames, *Essays on the Principles of Morality and Natural Religion*, p. 68.

89. There are only two short publications on secular moral thought that can be attributed to Blair. These are his undergraduate dissertation, *De Fundamentis*

et Obligatione Legis Naturae (On the Foundations and Obligation of the Law of Nature), which appeared in 1739, and his review of Hutcheson's *System* in the *Edinburgh Review* of 1755. As sources on Blair's own thought, these two texts need to be treated with a certain degree of caution. The review is mainly a summary of Hutcheson's argument, and the dissertation was written for the purposes of gaining the degree of Master of Arts, when Blair was not yet twenty-one years old. As is usually the case in early modern university disputations, it is not certain how much of this piece was Blair's own work or that of one of his teachers at the university. Yet there are good reasons for taking the 1739 dissertation seriously as evidence for Blair's views on morality. In a short account of Blair's life, published in 1801, an Edinburgh minister and professor, James Finlayson, wrote that Blair's student dissertation "exhibits in elegant Latin an outline of the moral principles, which have been since more fully unfolded and illustrated in his Sermons" (James Finlayson, "A Short Account of the Life and Character of Hugh Blair," p. 495, in Hugh Blair, *Sermons*, vol. 5 [London, 1801]). More important, the substance of Blair's arguments in his dissertation appears to be continuous with the ideas expressed in his sermons.

90. "Nihil est enim quod plus ad vitam beatam valet, quam benigni & sociales Affectus, qui nos ad aliorum bonum promovendum ducunt. Alunt semper aliquid vi sua atque natura, quod tranquillet animos: quin etiam cum successu destituuntur, jucunditate attamen magis pura, animos perfundunt, quam quae ex privatis & contractioribus oblectamentis unquam profluit" (Hugh Blair, *Dissertatio Philosophica Inauguralis, De Fundamentis et Obligatione Legis Naturae* [Edinburgh, 1739], p. 5).

91. Hugh Blair, "Sermon XV. On the Motives to Constancy in Virtue," in *Sermons*, vol. 1, p. 453.

92. Blair, "Sermon XV. On the Motives to Constancy in Virtue," p. 453.

93. John Witherspoon, *Ecclesiastical Characteristics, or, the Arcana of Church Policy. Being an Humble Attempt to open up the Mystery of Moderation* (Edinburgh, 1753), p. 27.

94. Quoted in J. A. Harris, *Of Liberty and Necessity* (Oxford: Oxford University Press, 2005), p. 52.

95. G. W. Leibniz and Samuel Clarke, *A Collection of Papers which passed between the late Learned Mr. Leibnitz and Dr. Clarke* (London, 1717), p. 385.

96. Matthew Tindal, *Christianity as Old as the Creation: or, the Gospel, a Republication of the Religion of Nature*, vol. 1 (London, 1730), p. 16.

97. William Dudgeon, *A View of the Necessitarian or Best Scheme* (London, 1739), p. 5.

98. Anderson, *An Estimate of the Profit and Loss of Religion*, p. 2.

99. Anderson, *An Estimate of the Profit and Loss of Religion*, pp. 4–5.

100. Anderson, *An Estimate of the Profit and Loss of Religion*, pp. 5–6.

101. Anderson, An *Estimate of the Profit and Loss of Religion*, p. 10.

102. Anderson, An *Estimate of the Profit and Loss of Religion*, p. 10.

103. Anderson, An *Estimate of the Profit and Loss of Religion*, pp. 10–11.

104. Anderson, An *Estimate of the Profit and Loss of Religion*, p. 11.

105. John Witherspoon, "Lectures on Moral Philosophy," in *Works*, vol. 7 (Edinburgh, 1804), p. 18.

106. Witherspoon, "Lectures on Moral Philosophy," p. 18.

107. Witherspoon, "Lectures on Moral Philosophy," p. 18.

108. Witherspoon, "Lectures on Moral Philosophy," p. 18.

109. Witherspoon, "Lectures on Moral Philosophy," p. 19.

110. Alasdair Cameron, "Theatre in Scotland, 1660–1800," in *The History of Scottish Literature*, vol. 2, ed. Andrew Hook (Aberdeen: Aberdeen University Press, 1987), 197–198.

111. John Witherspoon, *Serious Inquiry into the Nature and Effects of the Stage. Being an Attempt to show, that Contributing to the Support of a Public Theatre, is inconsistent with the Character of a Christian* (Glasgow, 1757), p. 11.

112. Witherspoon, *Serious Inquiry into the Nature and Effects of the Stage*, p. 12.

113. Witherspoon, *Serious Inquiry into the Nature and Effects of the Stage*, p. 19.

114. John Dwyer, *The Age of the Passions: An Interpretation of Adam Smith and Scottish Enlightenment Culture* (East Linton: Tuckwell Press, 1998).

115. Jerrold Seigel, *The Idea of the Self: Thought and Experience in Western Europe since the Seventeenth Century* (Cambridge: Cambridge University Press, 2005), p. 161.

116. Adam Ferguson, *The Morality of Stage-Plays Seriously Considered* (Edinburgh, 1757), p. 3.

117. Ferguson, *The Morality of Stage-Plays*, p. 10.

118. Ferguson, *The Morality of Stage-Plays*, p. 8.

119. Ferguson, *The Morality of Stage-Plays*, p. 11.

120. Ferguson, *The Morality of Stage-Plays*, p. 11.

121. Ferguson, *The Morality of Stage-Plays*, p. 17.

122. Ferguson, *The Morality of Stage-Plays*, p.18.

123. See above, pp. 86–93.

124. Thomas Reid, *Essays on the Active Powers*, ed. Knud Haakonssen and James A. Harris (Edinburgh: Edinburgh University Press, 2010), p. 46.

125. James Beattie, *Elements of Moral Science*, vol. 1 (Edinburgh, 1790), p. 204.

126. Beattie, *Elements of Moral Science*, vol. 1, p. 200.

127. Beattie, *Elements of Moral Science*, vol. 1, p. 204.

128. Beattie, *Elements of Moral Science*, vol. 1, p. 200.

129. Reid, *Essays on the Active Powers*, p. 67.

130. Thomas Reid, *Thomas Reid on Logic, Rhetoric and Fine Arts: Papers on the Culture of the Mind*, ed. A. Broadie (Edinburgh: Edinburgh University Press, 2005), p. 85.

131. Reid, *Logic, Rhetoric and the Fine Arts*, p. 87.

132. Reid, *Logic, Rhetoric and the Fine Arts*, p. 85.

133. Reid, *Logic, Rhetoric and the Fine Arts*, p. 85.

134. Reid, *Essays on the Active Powers*, p. 70.

135. Reid, *Essays on the Active Powers*, p. 69.

136. Oswald, *An Appeal to Common Sense*, vol. 2, p. 307.

137. Reid, *Essays on the Active Powers*, p. 5. See also Nicholas Wolterstorff, *Thomas Reid and the Story of Epistemology* (Cambridge: Cambridge University Press, 2001), pp. 253–254.

138. Thomas Reid, *Philosophical Orations of Thomas Reid. Delivered at Graduation Ceremonies in King's College, Aberdeen, 1753, 1756, 1759, 1762*, ed. Walter Robson Humphries (Aberdeen: The University Press, 1937), p. 20.

139. "Jam vero cum Theologi Saniores & peritiores, Theologiam depurgare et defoecare didicerint, Questiones & Disputationes Theologicas parvi habentes quae ad virtutem & Pietatem Christianum promovendam nullum momentum habent; Non minus oportet Philosophiae sordes & rubiginem Detergere, in Coenobijs per multa Secula calliginosa contractam; ut ratio Splendori Dignitati & Utilitati restituatur" (Thomas Reid, *Philosophical Orations*, p. 20).

CONCLUSION

1. In William Ferguson's phrase, Moderatism had become "little more than the Dundas interest at prayer, with nepotism and pluralism the main order of service" (William Ferguson, *Scotland. 1689 to the Present* [Edinburgh: Oliver & Boyd, 1978], p. 227).

2. See John Leslie, *An Experimental Inquiry into the Nature and Propagation of Heat* (London, 1804), p. 521 ff. On the history of the Leslie affair, see J. G.

Burke, "Kirk and Causality in Edinburgh, 1805," *Isis* 61 (1970), 340–354; J. B. Morrell, "The Leslie Affair: Careers, Kirk and Politics in Edinburgh in 1805," *Scottish Historical Review* 54 (1975), 63–82; Ian D. Clark, "The Leslie Controversy, 1805," *Records of the Scottish Church History Society* 14 (1963), 179–197; and, recently, Charles Bradford Bow, "In Defence of the Scottish Enlightenment: Dugald Stewart's Role in the 1805 Leslie Affair," *Scottish Historical Review* 92 (2013), 123–146.

3. H. Meikle, *Scotland and the French Revolution* (Glasgow: James Maclehose and Sons, 1912), p. 194.

4. William Robertson, "Sermon on the Centenary of the Glorious Revolution, 1788," in William Robertson, *Mescellaneous Works and Commentaries*, ed. Jeffrey Smitten (London: Routledge/Thoemmes Press, 1996), pp. 175–187. As Richard Sher has shown, in the 1790s Alexander Carlyle and Henry Brougham had, for very different reasons, an interest in exaggerating the radicalism of Robertson's sermon (see Richard B. Sher, "1688 and 1788: William Robertson on Revolution in Britain and France," in P. Dukes and John Dunkley [eds.], *Culture and Revolution* [London: Pinter, 1990], pp. 98–109).

5. Thomas Somerville, *The Effects of the French Revolution, with Respect to the Interests of Humanity, Liberty, Religion, and Morality* (Edinburgh, 1793), p. 89.

6. Emma Vincent Macleod, *A War of Ideas: British Attitudes to the Wars against Revolutionary France, 1792–1802* (Aldershot: Ashgate, 1998), p. 140.

7. Colin Kidd, "The Kirk, the French Revolution, and the Burden of Scottish Whiggery," in N. Aston (ed.), *Religious Change in Europe, 1650–1914* (Oxford: Clarendon Press, 1997), pp. 222–223.

8. Kidd, "The Kirk, the French Revolution, and the Burden of Scottish Whiggery," p. 223.

9. Emma Vincent Macleod, "The Responses of Scottish Churchmen to the French Revolution, 1789–1802," *Scottish Historical Review* 73 (1994), 191–215.

10. K. J. Logue, *Popular Disturbances in Scotland, 1780–1815* (Edinburgh: John Donald, 2003), p. 168.

11. H. Meikle, *Scotland and the French Revolution* (Glasgow: James Maclehose, 1912), p. 36. See also Francis Hutcheson, *Considerations on Patronages: Addressed to the Gentlemen of Scotland* (London, 1735).

12. Meikle, *Scotland and the French Revolution*, p. 35.

13. W. M. Heatherington, *History of the Church of Scotland. From the Introduction of Christianity to the Period of the Disruption,* 3rd ed. (Edinburgh: John Johnstone, 1843), p. 225.

14. Kidd, "The Kirk, the French Revolution, and the Burden of Scottish Whiggery," p. 230. Meikle, *Scotland and the French Revolution,* p. 200. See also Bob Harris, *The Scottish People and the French Revolution* (London: Pickering and Chatto, 2008), p. 30: "The fundamental source of the Secessionists' and reform presbytery's alienation from the British state was their view of its religious, not civil, shortcomings."

15. Emma Vincent Macleod, "The Scottish Opposition Whigs and the French Revolution," p. 82, in Bob Harris (ed.), *Scotland in the Age of the French Revolution* (Edinburgh: John Donald, 2005), pp. 79–98.

16. Vincent Macleod, "The Scottish Opposition Whigs and the French Revolution," p. 80.

17. On these debates, see Anna Plassart, "Scottish Perspectives on War and Patriotism in the 1790s," *Historical Journal* 57 (2014), 107–129.

18. Dugald Stewart, *A Short Statement of some Important Facts, relative to the Late Election of a Mathematical Professor in the University of Edinburgh; accompanied with Original Papers and Critical Remarks* (Edinburgh, 1805), p. 13.

19. Stewart, *Collected Works,* vol. 10, p. cxxxvii.

20. Bow, "In Defence of the Scottish Enlightenment," pp. 129, 138.

21. Stuart Semmel, *Napoleon and the British* (New Haven: Yale University Press, 2004), p. 76; Linda Colley, *Britons: Forging the Nation, 1707–1837* (London: Pimlico, 1994), p. 312. On the debate over Napoleon's religious policies within France, see Helena Rosenblatt, *Liberal Values: Benjamin Constant and the Politics of Religion* (Cambridge: Cambridge University Press, 2008), pp. 76–121.

22. J. G. Burke, "Kirk and Causality in Edinburgh, 1805," *Isis* 61 (1970), 340–354.

23. Dugald Stewart, *Collected Works,* vol. 10, ed. W. Hamilton (Edinburgh, 1858), p. cxxxviii.

24. Roger Emerson, *Academic Patronage in the Scottish Enlightenment: Glasgow, Edinburgh and St Andrews Universities* (Edinburgh: Edinburgh University Press, 2008), p. 333.

25. Dugald Stewart, for example, considered the Moderates' criticisms of Leslie important enough to publish his own rebuttal of them (see Stewart, *A Short Statement of some Important Facts*). See also Bow, "In Defence of the Scottish Enlightenment," pp. 135–137.

26. Clark, "The Leslie Controversy, 1805," p. 180.

27. Bow, "In Defence of the Scottish Enlightenment," p. 136.

28. *Scots Magazine* 68, 279–80, quoted in Clark, "The Leslie Controversy, 1805," pp. 184–185.

29. Clark, "The Leslie Controversy, 1805," p. 189.

30. Leslie, *An Experimental Inquiry into the Nature and Propagation of Heat,* p. 519. Leslie is referring to Hume's chapter "Of the Idea of Necessary Connexion" in his *Enquiry concerning Human Understanding* (see David Hume, *An Enquiry concerning Human Understanding,* ed. Tom L. Beauchamp [Oxford: Oxford University Press, 1999], pp. 134–147).

31. Leslie, *An Experimental Inquiry into the Nature and Propagation of Heat,* p. 520.

32. Clark, "The Leslie Controversy, 1805," pp. 179–197.

33. See above, pp. 96–105.

34. John Inglis, *An examination of Mr. Dugald Stewart's pamphlet, relative to the late election of a mathematical professor in the University of Edinburgh,* 2nd ed. (Edinburgh, 1806). p. 143.

35. W. L. Brown, *Remarks on certain Passages of "An Examination of Mr. Dugald Stewart's Pamphlet, by one of the Ministers of Edinburgh"; relative to Subjects nearly connected with the Interests of Religion and Learning* (Aberdeen, 1806), pp. 59–60.

36. Brown, *Remarks on certain Passages,* pp. 59–60.

37. Clark, "The Leslie Controversy, 1805," p. 194.

38. Daniel F. Rice, "Natural Theology and the Scottish Philosophy in the Thought of Thomas Chalmers," *Scottish Journal of Theology* 24 (1971), 23–46.

39. Robert Lundie, *Report of the Proceedings and Debate in the General Assembly of the Church of Scotland respecting the Election of Mr. Leslie to the Mathematical Chair in the University of Edinburgh* (Edinburgh, 1805), p. 104.

40. Lundie, *Report of the Proceedings,* p. 105.

41. Clark, "The Leslie Controversy, 1805," p. 189.

42. Anon. [A. M. Thomson], *A Letter to the Rev. Principal Hill, on the Case of Mr. John Leslie, Professor of Mathematics in the University of Edinburgh* (Edinburgh, 1805), p. 97.

43. Anon. [A. M. Thomson], *A Letter to the Rev. Principal Hill,* pp. 98–99.

44. Anon. [A. M. Thomson], *A Letter to the Rev. Principal Hill,* p. 101.

45. On Hadow, see above, p. 29.

46. Anon. [A. M. Thomson], *A Letter to the Rev. Principal Hill,* p. 102.

47. Hugh Blair, *Observations upon a Pamphlet, entitled, An Analysis of the Moral and Religious Sentiments contained in the Writings of Sopho, and David Hume, Esq; &c* (Edinburgh, 1755), p. 22.

48. Inglis, *An examination of Mr. Dugald Stewart's pamphlet*, p. 143.

49. Quoted in Alexander Campbell Fraser, *Thomas Reid* (Edinburgh: Oliphant, Anderson & Ferrier, 1898), pp. 122–123.

50. See above, p. 88–90.

51. Thomas Reid, An Inquiry into the Human Mind on the Principles of Common Sense, ed. Derek R. Brookes (University Park: Pennsylvania State University Press, 1997), 6.24, p. 197.

52. Reid, *An Inquiry into the Human Mind*, 6.24, p. 196.

53. John Wright, "The Scientific Reception of Hume's Theory of Causation: Establishing the Positivist Interpretation in Early Nineteenth-Century Scotland," in P. Jones (ed.), *The Reception of David Hume in Europe* (London: Thoemmes-Continuum, 2005), p. 335.

54. Stewart, *A Short Statement*, p. 49.

55. Stewart, *A Short Statement*, p. 49.

56. Stewart, *A Short Statement*, p. 54.

57. Brown, *Observations on the Nature and Tendency of the Doctrine of Mr. Hume, concerning the Relation of Cause and Effect*, 2nd ed. (Edinburgh, 1806), p. 182.

58. Brown, *Observations*, pp. 136–139.

59. Brown, *Observations*, p. 95.

60. Brown, *Observations*, p. 95.

61. Brown, *Observations*, p. 180.

62. Brown, *Observations*, p. 179.

63. Brown, *Observations*, p. 182.

64. Sher, "1688 and 1788," p. 106.

65. Brown, *Remarks on certain Passages*, p. 62.

66. George Hill, *The Advantages of Searching the Scripture. A Sermon preached before the Society in Scotland for Propagating of Christian Knowledge* (Edinburgh, 1787), p. 25.

67. George Hill, *Heads of Lectures in Divinity* (St. Andrews, 1796), p. 29.

68. Hill, *Heads of Lectures in Divinity*, p. 128.

69. John R. McIntosh, *Church and Theology in Enlightenment Scotland: The Popular Party, 1740–1800* (East Linton: Tuckwell, 1998), p. 234.

70. J. Sheehan, *The Enlightenment Bible: Translation, Scholarship, Culture* (Princeton, NJ: Princeton University Press, 2005), pp. 254–256.

71. Stefan Collini, "Arnold," in A. L. Le Quesne, George P. Landow, Stefan Collini, and Peter Stansky, *Victorian Thinkers* (Oxford: Oxford University Press, 1993), p. 296.
72. Quote in Collini, "Arnold," p. 298.
73. Matthew Arnold, "Literature and Dogma," in *Dissent and Dogma,* ed. R. H. Super (Ann Arbor: University of Michigan Press, 1968), p. 345.
74. Quoted in Sheehan, *The Enlightenment Bible,* p. 253.

Bibliography

UNPUBLISHED PRIMARY SOURCES

"Register of the Resolutions and Proceedings of a Society for the Reformation of Manners," Edinburgh University Library Special Collections, MS: La III.339.

Wallace, Robert, "A little treatise against imposing creeds or confessions of faith," Edinburgh University Library Special Collections, MS: La II.620 (19).

———, "The End of Ecclesiastical Splendour in the Church and of Regal or Monarchicall Authority in the State in all the Christian Nations in Europe," Edinburgh University Library Special Collections, MS: La. II.620 (15).

PUBLISHED PRIMARY SOURCES

Abernethy, John, *Religious Obedience founded upon Personal Persuasion. A Sermon Preach'd at Belfast the 9th of December 1719* (Belfast, 1720).

———, *Sermons on Various Subjects,* 2 vols. (London, 1748).

Anderson, George, *An Estimate of the Profit and Loss of Religion, personally and publicly stated* (Edinburgh, 1753).

———, *A Remonstrance against Lord Viscount Bolingbroke's Philosophical Religion* (Edinburgh, 1756).

Anon., *The Case of the Patrons of the Churches in Scotland, considered with Regard to the Bill now depending in the Honourable House of Commons* (Edinburgh, 1735).

Anon., *A Vindication of Mr Hutcheson from the Calumnious Aspersions of a Late Pamphlet. By Several of his Scholars* (s.l., 1738).

Anon. [John Hyndman], *A Just View of the Constitution of the Church of Scotland, and of the Proceedings of the last General Assembly in relation to the Deposition of Mr Gillespie* (Edinburgh, 1753).

Anon. [John Bonar], *An Analysis of the Moral and Religious Sentiments contained in the Writings of Sopho and David Hume, Esq.* (Edinburgh, 1755).

Anon., "Memoirs of Dr Wallace of Edinburgh," *Scots Magazine* 33 (July 1771), 340–344.

Anon. [A. M. Thomson]. *A Letter to the Rev. Principal Hill, on the Case of Mr. John Leslie, Professor of Mathematics in the University of Edinburgh* (Edinburgh, 1805).

Arnold, Matthew, "Literature and Dogma," in Matthew Arnold, *Dissent and Dogma*, ed. R. H. Super (Ann Arbor: University of Michigan Press, 1968), pp. 139–411.

Augustine of Hippo, *The City of God against the Pagans*, ed. R. W. Dyson (Cambridge: Cambridge University Press, 1998).

Aurelius, Marcus, *The meditations of the Emperor Marcus Aurelius Antoninus*, ed. James Moore and Michael Silverthorne; trans. Francis Hutcheson and James Moor (Indianapolis: Liberty Fund, 2008).

Balguy, John, *The Foundation of Moral Goodness: or a Further Inquiry into the Original of our Idea of Virtue* (London, 1728).

Baxter, Andrew, *An enquiry into the nature of the human soul; wherein the immateriality of the soul is evinced from the principles of reason and philosophy* (London, 1733).

Beattie, James, *Evidences of the Christian Religion; Briefly and plainly stated,* 2 vols. (Edinburgh, 1786).

———, *Elements of Moral Science*, 2 vols. (Edinburgh, 1790).

———, *Selected Philosophical Writings*, ed. J. A. Harris (Exeter: Imprint Academic, 2004).

Blair, Hugh, *Dissertatio Philosophica Inauguralis, De Fundamentis et Obligatione Legis Naturae* (Edinburgh, 1739).

———, *Observations upon a Pamphlet, entitled, An Analysis of the Moral and Religious Sentiments contained in the Writings of Sopho, and David Hume, Esq; &c* (Edinburgh, 1755).

———, Review of Hutcheson's *System of Moral Philosophy*. *Edinburgh Review* 1755.

———, *Sermons*, 5 vols. (Edinburgh, 1777–1801).

Brown, Thomas, *Observations on the Nature and Tendency of the Doctrine of Mr. Hume, concerning the Relation of Cause and Effect*, 2nd ed. (Edinburgh, 1806).

Brown, William L., *Remarks on certain Passages of "An Examination of Mr. Dugald Stewart's Pamphlet, by one of the Ministers of Edinburgh";*

relative to Subjects nearly connected with the Interests of Religion and Learning (Aberdeen, 1806).

Burnet, Gilbert, and Francis Hutcheson, *Letters between the late Mr. Gilbert Burnet and Mr. Hutcheson concerning the True Foundation of Virtue or Moral Goodness. Formerly published in the London Journal* (London, 1735).

Campbell, Archibald, *An Enquiry into the Original of Moral Virtue* (Edinburgh, 1733).

————, *The Necessity of Revelation: or an Enquiry into the Extent of Human Powers with Respect to Matters of Religion; Especially those two fundamental Articles, the Being of God, and the Immortality of the Soul* (London, 1739).

Campbell, George, *The Spirit of the Gospel neither a Spirit of Superstition nor of Enthusiasm: a Sermon preached before the Synod of Aberdeen, April 9, 1771* (Edinburgh, 1771).

Cicero, Marcus Tullius, *Tusculan Disputations,* trans. J. E. King (London: William Heinemann, 1927).

Clarke, Samuel, and Gottfried Wilhelm Leibniz, *A Collection of Papers which passed between the late Learned Mr. Leibnitz and Dr. Clarke* (London, 1717).

Cockburn, John, *Right Notions of God and Religion, together, with two Discourses for the better Conduct of the Sincere and for Correcting some prevailing Errors* (London, 1708).

Committee for Purity of Doctrine and Archibald Campbell, *The Report of the Committee for Purity of Doctrine, at Edinburgh, March 16, 1736, and Professor Campbell's Remarks upon it* (Edinburgh, 1736).

Craig, Mungo, *A Satyr against Atheistical Deism with the genuine character of a deist. To which is Prefixt, an account of Mr. Aikenhead's notions, who is now in prison for the same damnable apostacy* (Edinburgh, 1696).

Doddridge, Philip, *Some Remarkable Passages in the Life of the Honourable Col. James Gardiner, who was slain at the Battle of Preston-Pans, September 21, 1745* (London, 1747).

Dudgeon, William, *A View of the Necessitarian or Best Scheme* (London, 1739).

Erskine, John, *Theological Dissertations* (London, 1765).

Ferguson, Adam, *The Morality of Stage-Plays Seriously Considered* (Edinburgh, 1757).

Finlayson, James, "A Short Account of the Life and Character of Hugh Blair," in Hugh Blair, *Sermons,* vol. 5 (Edinburgh, 1801), pp. 491–516.

Garden, George, *Comparative Theology or, The True and Solid Grounds of Pure and Peacable Theology* (Edinburgh, 1707).

General Assembly of the Church of Scotland, *Acts of the General Assembly of the Church of Scotland, 1638–1842* (Edinburgh, 1843).

Gerard, Alexander, *Sermons,* vol. 2 (London, 1782).

Glasgow Presbytery and William Leechman, *The Remarks of the Committee of the Presbytery of Glasgow, upon Mr. Leechman's Sermon on Prayer, with his Replies thereunto &c., to which is prefix'd Historical Account of the whole Proceedings of the said Presbytery and their Committee; and of the Synod of Glasgow in that Affair* (Edinburgh, 1744).

Halyburton, Thomas, *The great concern of salvation: in three parts; viz. I. A discovery of man's natural state. II. Man's recovery by faith in Christ. III. The Christian's duty, with respect to both personal and family religion* (Edinburgh, 1721).

Hamilton, William, *The Truth and Excellency of the Christian Religion* (Edinburgh, 1732).

Heineccius, Johann Gottlieb, and George Turnbull, *A Methodical System of Universal Law, with Supplements and a Discourse by George Turnbull,* ed. Thomas Ahnert and Peter Schröder (Indianapolis: Liberty Fund, 2008).

Hill, George, *The Advantages of Searching the Scripture. A Sermon preached before the Society in Scotland for Propagating of Christian Knowledge* (Edinburgh, 1787).

———, *Heads of Lectures in Divinity* (St. Andrews, 1796).

Home, John, *Douglas. John Home's Douglas: A Tragedy, with Contemporary Commentaries,* ed. Ralph Mclean (Glasgow: Humming Earth, 2010).

Howell, T. B. (ed.), *A Complete Collection of State Trials and Proceedings for High Treason and other Crimes and Misdemeanours from the earliest period to the present time,* vol. 13 (London, 1812).

Hume, David, *Philosophical Essays concerning Human Understanding* (London, 1748).

———, *A Treatise of Human Nature,* ed. L. A. Selby-Bigge and P. Nidditch (Oxford: Oxford University Press, 1978).

———, *Essays Moral, Political and Literary,* ed. E. F. Miller (Indianapolis: Liberty Fund, 1987).

———, *An Enquiry concerning Human Understanding,* ed. Tom L. Beauchamp (Oxford: Oxford University Press, 1999).

———, *The Letters of David Hume,* ed. J. Y. T. Greig, 2 vols. (Oxford: Oxford University Press, 2011).

Hutcheson, Francis, *Considerations on Patronages. Addressed to the Gentlemen of Scotland* (London, 1735).

————, *Logicae Compendium. Praefixa est Dissertatio de Philosophiae Origine ejusque inventoribus aut excultoribus praecipuis* (Glasgow, 1738).

————, *Metaphysicae Synopsis: Ontologiam, et, Pneumatologiam complectens* (Glasgow, 1742).

————, *A System of Moral Philosophy*, 2 vols. (Glasgow, 1755).

————, *On Human Nature. Reflections on our common system of morality. On the social nature of man*, ed. T. Mautner (Cambridge: Cambridge University Press, 1993).

————, *Essay on the Nature and Conduct of the Passions and Affections*. Ed. Aaron Garrett (Indianapolis: Liberty Fund, 2002).

————, *Logic, Metaphysics, and the Natural Sociability of Mankind*, ed. and trans. James Moore and Michael Silverthorne (Indianapolis: Liberty Fund, 2006).

————, *Philosophiae Moralis Institutio Compendiaria, with A Short Introduction to Moral Philosophy*, ed. Luigi Turco (Indianapolis: Liberty Fund, 2007).

————, *Inquiry into the Original of Our Ideas of Beauty and Virtue*, ed. W. Leidhold, 2nd ed. (Indianapolis: Liberty Fund, 2008).

Hutcheson, Francis, and James Moor, *The Meditations of the Emperor Marcus Aurelius*, ed. James Moore and Michael Silverthorne (Indianapolis: Liberty Fund, 2008).

Inglis, John, *An examination of Mr. Dugald Stewart's pamphlet, relative to the late election of a mathematical professor in the University of Edinburgh*, 2nd ed. (Edinburgh, 1806).

Johnson, Samuel, *A Dictionary of the English Language*, 2nd ed., 2 vols. (London, 1755–56).

Kames, Henry Home, Lord, *Essays on the Principles of Morality and Natural Religion, in two parts* (Edinburgh, 1751).

————, *Essays on the Principles of Morality and Natural Religion*, 3rd ed. (Edinburgh, 1779).

————, *Loose Hints upon Education, chiefly concerning the Culture of the Heart* (Edinburgh, 1781).

King, William, *De Origine Mali* (Dublin, 1702).

Law, William, *Theses Philosophicae* (Edinburgh, 1705).

Leechman, William, *Sermons*, 2 vols. (London, 1789).

Leslie, John, *An Experimental Inquiry into the Nature and Propagation of Heat* (London, 1804).

Locke, John, *Two Treatises of Government*, ed. P. Laslett (Cambridge: Cambridge University Press, 1988).

————, *An Essay concerning Human Understanding*, ed. P. H. Nidditch (Oxford: Clarendon Press, 1975).

Logan, John, *Sermons*, vol. 2 (Edinburgh, 1791).

Lundie, Robert, *Report of the Proceedings and Debate in the General Assembly of the Church of Scotland respecting the Election of Mr. Leslie to the Mathematical Chair in the University of Edinburgh* (Edinburgh, 1805).

Mandeville, Bernard, *The Fable of the Bees*, ed. F. B. Kaye, 2 vols. (Indianapolis: Liberty Fund, 1988).

Morren, Nathaniel (ed.), *Annals of the General Assembly of the Church of Scotland, from the final secession in 1739, to the Origin of the Relief in 1752* (Edinburgh: John Johnstone, 1838).

————, *Annals of the General Assembly of the Church of Scotland from the Origin of the Relief in 1752 to the Rejection of the Overture on Schism in 1766* (Edinburgh: John Johnstone, 1840).

Oswald, James, *Letters concerning the Present State of the Church of Scotland, and the consequent Danger to Religion and Learning, from the Arbitrary and Unconstitutional Exercise of the Law of Patronage* (Edinburgh, 1767).

————, *An Appeal to Common Sense in Behalf of Religion*, 2 vols. (Edinburgh, 1772).

————, *The Divine Efficacy of the Gospel-Dispensation. A sermon, preached before the Society in Scotland for Propagating Christian Knowledge, at their anniversary meeting, in the High Church of Edinburgh, on Friday, June 8, 1770* (Edinburgh, 1770).

Pomponazzi, Pietro, *Tractatus de Immortalitate Animae*, ed. trans. Gianfranco Morra (Bologna: Nanni & Fiammenghi, 1954).

Pufendorf, Samuel, *On the Duty of Man and Citizen*, ed. J. Tully, trans. M. Silverthorne (Cambridge: Cambridge University Press, 1991).

————, *The political writings of Samuel Pufendorf*, ed. C. L. Carr, trans. M. Seidler (New York: Oxford University Press, 1994).

Reid, Thomas, *Philosophical Orations of Thomas Reid. Delivered at Graduation Ceremonies in King's College, Aberdeen, 1753, 1756, 1759, 1762*, ed. Walter Robson Humphries (Aberdeen: The University Press, 1937).

————, *An Inquiry into the Human Mind on the Principles of Common Sense*, ed. Derek R. Brookes (University Park: Pennsylvania State University Press, 1997).

————, *Essays on the Intellectual Powers of Man*, ed. D. R. Brookes and K. Haakonssen (Edinburgh: Edinburgh University Press, 2002).

————, *Thomas Reid on Logic, Rhetoric and the Fine Arts: Papers on the Culture of the Mind*, ed. A. Broadie (Edinburgh: Edinburgh University Press, 2005).

————, *Essays on the Active Powers*, ed. Knud Haakonssen and James A. Harris (Edinburgh: Edinburgh University Press, 2010).

Robertson, William, et al., "Reasons of Dissent from judgment and resolution of the Commission, March 11, 1752, resolving to inflict no censure on the Presbytery of Dunfermline for their disobedience in relation to the settlement of Inverkeithing," in Morren (ed.), *Annals of the General Assembly of the Church of Scotland, from the final secession in 1739, to the Origin of the Relief in 1752* (Edinburgh: John Johnstone, 1838), pp. 231–242.

Robertson, William, *The Situation of the World at the Time of Christ's Appearance* (Edinburgh, 1755).

————, *The History of Scotland* (London, 1759).

————, *The History of the Reign of the Emperor Charles V*, 3 vols. (London, 1769).

————, *The History of America*, 3 vols. (Dublin, 1777).

————, "Sermon on the Centenary of the Glorious Revolution, 1788," in William Robertson, *Miscellaneous Works and Commentaries*, ed. Jeffrey Smitten. (London: Routledge/Thoemmes Press, 1996), pp. 175–187.

————, *An Historical Disquisition concerning the Knowledge which the Ancients had of India; and the Progress of Trade with that Country prior to the Discovery of the Passage to it by the Cape of Good Hope* (London, 1791).

————, *Miscellaneous Works and Commentaries*, ed. Jeffrey Smitten (London: Routledge/Thoemmes Press, 1996).

Scougal, Henry, *The Life of God in the Soul of Man: or, the Nature and Excellency of the Christian Religion. With the Methods of Attaining the Happiness it proposes; Also an Account of the Beginnings and Advances of a Spiritual Life*, 4th ed.(London, 1702).

————, *The Life of God in the Soul of Man: or, the Nature and Excellency of the Christian Religion* (Edinburgh, 1739).

Shaftesbury, Anthony Ashley Cooper, Third Earl of, *Characteristicks of Men, Manners, Opinions, Times*, ed. L. Klein (Cambridge: Cambridge University Press, 1999).

Simson, John, and James Webster, *The Case of Mr John Simson* (Glasgow, 1715).

Smith, Adam, *The Correspondence of Adam Smith*, ed. E. C. Mossner and Ian Simpson Ross (Indianapolis: Liberty Fund, 1987).

Somerville, Thomas, *The Effects of the French Revolution, with Respect to the Interests of Humanity, Liberty, Religion, and Morality* (Edinburgh, 1793).

Stewart, Dugald, *A Short Statement of some Important Facts, relative to the Late Election of a Mathematical Professor in the University of Edinburgh; accompanied with Original Papers and Critical Remarks* (Edinburgh, 1805).

Stewart, Dugald, *Collected Works*, ed. W. Hamilton, vol. 10 (Edinburgh, 1858).

Strabo, *The Geography of* Strabo, 8 vols., trans. Horace Leonard Jones (London: William Heinemann, 1917).

Tindal, Matthew, *Christianity as Old as the Creation: or, the Gospel, a Republication of the Religion of Nature*, vol. 1 (London, 1730).

Turnbull, George, *A Philosophical Enquiry concerning the Connexion betwixt the Doctrines and Miracles of Jesus Christ. In a Letter to a Friend* (London, 1731).

———, *Christianity neither false nor useless, tho' not as old as the Creation: or, an Essay to prove the Usefulness, Truth, and Excellency of the Christian Religion; and to vindicate Dr Clarke's Discourse concerning the Evidences of Natural and Revealed Religion, from the Inconsistencies with which it is charged by the Author of Christianity as old as the Creation* (London, 1732).

———, *Principles of Moral and Christian Philosophy*, ed. A. Broadie (Indianapolis: Liberty Fund, 2005).

Walker, Robert, *Sermons on Practical Subjects*, 3rd ed., 2 vols. (London, 1783).

Wallace, Robert, *The Regard due to Divine Revelation, and to Pretences to it, considered. A Sermon preached before the Provincial Synod of Dumfreis, at their Meeting in October 1729. On 1 Thess. V. 20, 21. With a Preface containing some Remarks on a BOOK lately publish'd, Entitled, Christianity as Old as Creation*, 2nd ed. (London, 1733).

Wishart, William, *The certain and unchangeable Difference betwixt Moral Good and Evil* (London, 1732).

———, *Answers for William Wishart, Principal of the College of Edinburgh, to the Charge exhibited against him before the Rev. Synod of Lothian and Tweeddale* (Edinburgh, 1738).

———, *Discourses on Several Subjects* (London, 1753).

Witherspoon, John, *Disputatio Philosophica de Mentis Immortalitate* (Edinburgh, 1739).

———, *Ecclesiastical Characteristics, or, the Arcana of Church Policy. Being an Humble Attempt to open up the Mystery of Moderation* (Edinburgh, 1753).

————, *Serious Inquiry into the Nature and Effects of the Stage. Being an Attempt to show, that Contributing to the Support of a Public Theatre, is inconsistent with the Character of a Christian* (Glasgow, 1757).

————, *The History of a Corporation of Servants* (Glasgow, 1765).

————, *The Works of John Witherspoon*, 9 vols. (Edinburgh, 1804–1805).

Wollaston, William, *The Religion of Nature delineated* (London, 1722).

SECONDARY SOURCES

Ahnert, Thomas, "Pleasure, Pain, and Punishment in the Early Enlightenment: German and Scottish Debates," *Jahrbuch für Recht und Ethik* 12 (2004), 173–187.

————, "The Soul, Natural Religion and Moral Philosophy in the Scottish Enlightenment," *Eighteenth-Century Thought* 2 (2004), 233–253.

————, *Religion and the Origins of the German Enlightenment: Faith and the Reform of Learning in the Thought of Christian Thomasius* (Rochester, NY: Rochester University Press, 2006).

————, "Clergymen as Polite Philosophers: *Douglas* and the Conflict between Moderates and Orthodox in the Scottish Enlightenment," *Intellectual History Review* 18 (2008), 375–383.

————, "Epicureanism and the Transformation of Natural Law in the Early German Enlightenment," in N. Leddy and A. Lifschitz (eds.), *Epicurus in the Enlightenment*, Studies on Voltaire and the Eighteenth Century (Oxford: Voltaire Foundation, 2009), pp. 53–68.

————, "Francis Hutcheson and the Heathen Moralists," *Journal of Scottish Philosophy* 8 (2010), 51–62.

————, Fortschrittsgeschichte und Religiöse Aufklärung. William Robertson und die Deutung außereuropäischer Kulturen," *Geschichte und Gesellschaft*, Sonderheft 23, "Die Aufklärung und ihre Weltwirkung," (2010), 101–122.

————, "The Moral Education of Mankind: Character and Religious Moderatism in the Sermons of Hugh Blair," in Thomas Ahnert and Susan Manning (eds.), *Character, Self, and Sociability in the Scottish Enlightenment* (New York: Palgrave, 2011), pp. 67–84.

Asselt, Willem J. van, *The Federal Theology of Johannes Cocceius (1603–1669)* (Leiden: Brill, 2001).

Bahlman, D. W. R., *The Moral Revolution of 1688* (New Haven: Yale University Press, 1957).

Barlow, Richard B., "The Career of John Abernethy (1680–1740): Father of Non-Subscription in Ireland and Defender of Religious Liberty," *Harvard Theological Review* 78, 3/4 (1985), 399–419.

Batty, Margaret, "Campbell, Archibald (1691–1756)," *Oxford Dictionary of National Biography* (Oxford: Oxford University Press, 2004), http://www.oxforddnb.com/view/article/4476, accessed 14 November 2013.

Beiser, Frederick, *The Sovereignty of Reason. The Defense of Rationality in the Early English Enlightenment* (Princeton, NJ: Princeton University Press, 1996).

Blackbourn, Simon, "Morality without God," *Prospect,* April 2011.

Bosbach, Franz, *Monarchia Universalis: ein politischer Leitbegriff der frühen Neuzeit* (Göttingen: Vandenhoeck & Ruprecht, 1988).

Bow, Charles Bradford, "In Defence of the Scottish Enlightenment: Dugald Stewart's Role in the 1805 John Leslie Affair," *Scottish Historical Review* 92 (2013), 123–146.

Broadie, Alexander, *A History of Scottish Philosophy* (Edinburgh: Edinburgh University Press, 2009).

Brooke, Christopher, *Philosophic Pride: Stoicism and Political Thought from Lipsius to Rousseau* (Princeton, NJ: Princeton University Press, 2012).

Brown, S. J., "William Robertson (1721–1793) and the Scottish Enlightenment," in S. J. Brown (ed.), *William Robertson and the Expansion of Empire* (Cambridge: Cambridge University Press, 1997), pp. 7–35.

———, "William Robertson, Early Orientalism, and the *Historical Disquisition* on India of 1791," *Scottish Historical Review* 88 (2009), 289–312.

Buckle, Stephen, *Hume's Enlightenment Tract* (Oxford: Oxford University Press, 2001).

Burke, J. G., "Kirk and Causality in Edinburgh, 1805," *Isis* 61 (1970), 340–354.

Burson, Jeffrey, *The Rise and Fall of Theological Enlightenment. Jean-Martin de Prades and Ideological Polarization in Eighteenth-Century France* (Notre Dame, IN: Notre Dame University Press, 2010).

Cameron, Alasdair, "Theatre in Scotland 1660–1800," in *The History of Scottish Literature,* vol. 2, ed. Andrew Hook (Aberdeen: Aberdeen University Press, 1987), pp. 191–205.

Carabelli, Giancarlo, *Hume e la Retorica dell' Ideologia* (Florence: La Nuova Italia Editrice, 1972).

Carey, Daniel, *Locke, Shaftesbury, and Hutcheson: Contesting Diversity in the Enlightenment and Beyond* (Cambridge: Cambridge University Press, 2006).

Cassirer, Ernst, *The Philosophy of the Enlightenment*, trans. Fritz. C. A. Koelln and James P. Pettegrove (Boston: Beacon Press, 1966).

Clark, Ian D., "From Protest to Reaction: The Moderate Regime in the Church of Scotland, 1752–1805," in N. T. Phillipson and Rosalind Mitchison (eds.), *Scotland in the Age of Improvement*, 2nd ed. (Edinburgh: Edinburgh University Press, 1996), pp. 200–224.

———, "The Leslie Controversy, 1805," *Records of the Scottish Church History Society* 14 (1963), 179–197.

Clarke, Tristram, "The Williamite Episcopalians and the Glorious Revolution in Scotland," *Records of the Scottish Church History Society* 24 (1990), 33–51.

Coffey, John, and Alister Chapman, "Introduction: Intellectual History and the Return of Religion," in Alister Chapman, John Coffey, and Brad S. Gregory (eds.), *Seeing Things Their Way: Intellectual History and the Return of Religion* (Notre Dame, IN: Notre Dame University Press, 2009), pp. 1–23.

Coleman, Charly, "Resacralizing the World: The Fate of Secularization in Enlightenment Historiography," *Journal of Modern History* 82 (2010), 368–395.

Colley, Linda, *Britons: Forging the Nation, 1707–1837* (London: Pimlico, 1994).

Collini, Stefan, "The Idea of 'Character' in Victorian Political Thought," *Transactions of the Royal Historical Society* 35 (1985), 29–50.

———, "Arnold," in A. L. Le Quesne, George P. Landow, Stefan Collini, and Peter Stansky, *Victorian Thinkers* (Oxford: Oxford University Press, 1993), pp. 193–326.

Corneanu, Sorana, *Regimens of the Mind: Boyle, Locke, and the Early Modern Cultura Animi Tradition* (Chicago: University of Chicago Press, 2011).

Davidson, Nicholas, " "Le plus beau et le plus mechant esprit que ie aye cogneu": Science and Religion in the Writings of Giulio Cesare Vanini, 1585–1619," in Ian Maclean and John Brooke (eds.), *Heterodoxy in Early Modern Science and Religion* (Oxford: Clarendon Press, 2005).

Davie, George, E., "Berkeley's Impact on Scottish Philosophers," *Philosophy* 40 (1965), 222–234.

Drummond, A. L., and J. Bulloch, *The Scottish Church, 1688–1843: The Age of the Moderates* (Edinburgh: The Saint Andrew Press, 1973).

Dwyer, John, *The Age of the Passions: An Interpretation of Adam Smith and Scottish Enlightenment Culture* (East Linton: Tuckwell Press, 1998).

Ehrlich, Joshua, "William Robertson and Scientific Theism," *Modern Intellectual History* 10 (2013), 519–542.

Emerson, Roger, *Academic Patronage in the Scottish Enlightenment: Glasgow, Edinburgh and St Andrews Universities* (Edinburgh: Edinburgh University Press, 2008).

Ferguson, William, *Scotland: 1689 to the Present* (Edinburgh: Oliver & Boyd, 1978).

Force, Pierre, *Self-Interest before Adam Smith: A Genealogy of Economic Science* (Cambridge: Cambridge University Press, 2003).

Fraser, Alexander Campbell, *Thomas Reid* (Edinburgh: Oliphant, Anderson & Ferrier, 1898).

Gaskin, J. C. A., *Hume's Philosophy of Religion*, 2nd ed. (Basingstoke: Macmillan, 1988).

Gay, Peter, *The Enlightenment: The Rise of Modern Paganism* (New York: W. W. Norton, 1995).

Giles, Paul, "Enlightenment Historiography and Cultural Civil Wars," in S. Manning and F. Cogliano (eds.), *The Atlantic Enlightenment* (Aldershot: Ashgate, 2008), pp. 19–36.

Graham, Gordon, "The Ambition of Scottish Philosophy," *The Monist* 90 (2007), 154–169.

Graham, Michael, *The Blasphemies of Thomas Aikenhead: Boundaries of Belief on the Eve of the Enlightenment* (Edinburgh: Edinburgh University Press, 2008).

Greene, Donald, "Latitudinarianism and Sensibility: The Genealogy of the 'Man of Feeling' Reconsidered," *Modern Philology* 75/2 (1977), 159–183.

Grote, Simon, "Hutcheson's Divergence from Shaftesbury," *Journal of Scottish Philosophy* 4 (2006), 159–172.

———, "Religion and Enlightenment," *Journal of the History of Ideas* 75 (2014), pp. 137–160.

Haakonssen, Knud, *Natural Law and Moral Philosophy. From Grotius to the Scottish Enlightenment* (Cambridge: Cambridge University Press, 1996).

———, "Natural Rights or Political Prudence? Francis Hutcheson on Toleration," in *Proceedings of the British Academy* 186 (2013), 183–200.

Harris, Bob, *The Scottish People and the French Revolution* (London: Pickering and Chatto, 2008).

Harris, James A., "Answering Bayle's Question: Religious Belief in the Moral Philosophy of the Scottish Enlightenment," *Oxford Studies in Early Modern Philosophy* 1 (2003), 229–254.

————, *Of Liberty and Necessity* (Oxford: Oxford University Press, 2005).

————, "Religion in Hutcheson's Moral Philosophy," *Journal for the History of Philosophy* 46 (2008), 205–222.

Harris, Tim, *Revolution: The Great Crisis of the British Monarchy, 1685–1720* (London: Penguin, 2007).

Heatherington, W. M., *History of the Church of Scotland. From the Introduction of Christianity to the Period of the Disruption*, 3rd ed. (Edinburgh: John Johnstone, 1843).

Henderson, G. D., *Mystics of the North-East* (Aberdeen: The Spalding Club, 1934).

Herdt, Jennifer, *Putting on Virtue: The Legacy of the Splendid Vices* (Chicago: University of Chicago Press, 2008).

Heydt, Colin, "Practical Ethics in Eighteenth-Century Britain," in James A. Harris (ed.), *The Oxford Handbook of British Philosophy in the Eighteenth Century* (Oxford: Oxford University Press, 2013), pp. 369–389.

Hirschman, Albert O., *The Passions and the Interests: Political Arguments for Capitalism before Its Triumph*, 2nd ed. (Princeton, NJ: Princeton University Press, 1997).

Hochstrasser, Tim, *Natural Law Theories in the Early Enlightenment* (Cambridge: Cambridge University Press, 2000).

Holden, Thomas, *Spectres of False Divinity: Hume's Moral Atheism* (Oxford: Oxford University Press, 2010).

Hoppit, Julian, *A Land of Liberty: England, 1689–1727* (Oxford: Oxford University Press, 2000).

Howe, Daniel W., "John Witherspoon and the Transatlantic Enlightenment," in Susan Manning and Frank Cogliano (eds.), *The Atlantic Enlightenment* (Aldershot: Ashgate, 2008), pp. 61–79.

Hudson, Wayne, *The English Deists: Studies in Early Enlightenment* (London: Pickering and Chatto, 2009).

————, *Enlightenment and Modernity: The English Deists and Reform* (London: Pickering and Chatto, 2009).

Hundert, E. J., *The Enlightenment's Fable: Bernard Mandeville and the Discovery of Society* (Cambridge: Cambridge University Press, 1994).

Hunter, Michael, "'Aikenhead the Atheist': The Context and Consequences of Articulate Irreligion in the Late Seventeenth Century," in M. Hunter and D. Wootton (eds.), *Atheism from the Reformation to the Enlightenment* (Oxford: Clarendon Press, 1992), pp. 221–254.

Israel, Jonathan, *Radical Enlightenment: Philosophy and the Making of Modernity, 1650–1750* (Oxford: Oxford University Press, 2001).

————, *Enlightenment Contested: Philosophy, Modernity, and the Emancipation of Man, 1670–1752* (Oxford: Oxford University Press, 2008).

————, *Democratic Enlightenment: Philosophy, Revolution, and Human Rights, 1750–1790* (Oxford: Oxford University Press, 2011).

Jackson, Clare, *Restoration Scotland, 1660–1690: Royalist Politics, Religion and Ideas* (Woodbridge: Boydell Press, 2003).

Jacob, Margaret. C., *The Radical Enlightenment: Pantheists, Freemasons and Republicans* (London: George Allen & Unwin, 1981).

Kail, Peter J., "Hutcheson's Moral Sense: Skepticism, Realism, and Secondary Qualities," *History of Philosophy Quarterly* 18 (2001), 57–77.

Keohane, Nannerl, *Philosophy and the State in France: The Renaissance to Enlightenment* (Princeton, NJ: Princeton University Press, 1980).

Kidd, Colin, "Religious Realignment between Restoration and Union," in J. Robertson (ed.), *A Union for Empire: Political Thought and the Union of 1707* (Cambridge: Cambridge University Press, 1995).

————, "The Kirk, the French Revolution, and the Burden of Scottish Whiggery," in N. Aston (ed.), *Religious Change in Europe, 1650–1914* (Oxford: Clarendon Press, 1997), pp. 222–223.

————, "Conditional Britons: The Scots Covenanting Tradition and the Eighteenth-Century British State," *English Historical Review* 117 (2002), 1147–1176.

————, "Subscription, the Scottish Enlightenment and the Moderate Interpretation of History," *Journal of Ecclesiastical History* 55 (2004), 502–519.

————, *Union and Unionisms: Political Thought in Scotland, 1500–2000* (Cambridge: Cambridge University Press, 2008).

Kleer, R. A., "Final Causes in Adam Smith's *Theory of Moral Sentiments*," *Journal for the History of Philosophy* 33 (1995), 275–300.

Knox, R. Buick, "Establishment and Toleration during the Reigns of William, Mary and Anne," *Records of the Scottish Church History Society* 23 (1989), 330–360.

Lachman, David, *The Marrow Controversy, 1718–1723: An Historical and Theological Analysis* (Edinburgh: Rutherford House, 1988).

Lafond, Jean, "Augustinisme et Épicurisme au XVIIe Siècle," in Jean Lafond, *L'Homme et son Image: Morales et literature de Montaigne à Mandeville* (Paris: Honoré Champion, 1996), pp. 347–458.

LaVopa, A. J., "A New Intellectual History? Jonathan Israel's Enlightenment," *Historical Journal* 52 (2009), 717–738.

————, "The Not-So Prodigal Son: James Boswell and the Scottish Enlightenment," in Thomas Ahnert and Susan Manning (eds.), *Character, Self and Sociability in the Scottish Enlightenment* (New York: Palgrave, 2011), pp. 85–104.

Landsman, Ned C., "Evangelists and their Hearers: Popular Interpretation of Revivalist Preaching in Eighteenth-Century Scotland," *Journal of British Studies* 28 (1989), 120–149.

————, "Witherspoon and the Problem of Provincial Identity," in R. Sher and J. Smitten (eds.), *Scotland and America in the Age of Enlightenment* (Edinburgh: Edinburgh University Press, 1990), pp. 29–45.

Leidhold, Wolfgang, *Ethik und Politik bei Francis Hutcheson* (Freiburg: Karl Alber, 1985).

Logue, K. J., *Popular Disturbances in Scotland, 1780–1815* (Edinburgh: John Donald, 2003).

MacInnes, Allan, "Jacobitism in Scotland: Episodic Cause or National Movement?" *Scottish Historical Review* 86 (2007), 225–252.

Maclean, Ian, "Heterodoxy in Natural Philosophy and Medicine: Pietro Pomponazzi, Guglielmo Gratarolo, Girolamo Cardano," in Ian Maclean and John Brooke (eds.), *Heterodoxy in Early Modern Science and Religion* (Oxford: Clarendon Press, 2005).

Macleod, Emma Vincent, "The Responses of Scottish Churchmen to the French Revolution, 1789–1802," *Scottish Historical Review* 73 (1994), 191–215.

————, *A War of Ideas: British Attitudes to the Wars against Revolutionary France, 1792–1802* (Aldershot: Ashgate, 1998).

————, "The Scottish Opposition Whigs and the French Revolution," in Bob Harris (ed.), *Scotland in the Age of the French Revolution* (Edinburgh: John Donald, 2005), pp. 79–98.

Malcolm, Noel, "Hobbes, Ezra, and the Bible: The History of a Subversive Idea," in N. Malcolm, *Aspects of Hobbes* (Oxford: Clarendon Press, 2002), pp. 383–431.

Manning, Susan, *Poetics of Character: Transatlantic Encounters* (Cambridge: Cambridge University Press, 2013).

Matheson, Ann, "Hugh Blair's Sermons," in Stephen W. Brown and Warren McDougall (eds.), *The Edinburgh History of the Book in Scotland,* vol. 2: *Enlightenment and Expansion* (Edinburgh: Edinburgh University Press, 2012), pp. 471–475.

McBride, Ian, "The School of Virtue: Francis Hutcheson, Irish Presbyterians and the Scottish Enlightenment." In Robert Eccleshall, D George Boyce, and Vincent Geoghegan (eds.), *Political Thought in Ireland since the Seventeenth Century* (London: Routledge, 1993), pp. 73–99.

———, *Scripture Politics: Ulster Presbyterians and Irish Radicalism in the Late Eighteenth Century* (Oxford: Clarendon Press, 1998).

McIntosh, John R., *Church and Theology in Enlightenment Scotland: The Popular Party, 1740–1800* (East Linton: Tuckwell, 1998).

Mclean, Ralph, "Introduction," in John Home, *John Home's Douglas: A Tragedy, with contemporary commentaries,* ed. Ralph Mclean (Glasgow: Humming Earth, 2010), pp. ix–xix.

Meikle, H., *Scotland and the French Revolution* (Glasgow: James Maclehose and Sons, 1912).

Mijers, Esther, *"News from the Republick of Letters": Scottish Students, Charles Mackie and the United Provinces, 1650–1750* (Leiden: Brill, 2012).

Monod, Paul Kleber, *Jacobitism and the English People, 1688–1788* (Cambridge: Cambridge University Press, 1989).

Moore, James, and Michael Silverthorne, "Introduction," in Marcus Aurelius, *The Meditations of the Emperor Marcus Aurelius,* trans. Francis Hutcheson and James Moor, ed. James Moore and Michael Silverthorne (Indianapolis: Liberty Fund, 2008).

Moore, James, "Hutcheson's Theodicy: The Argument and the Contexts of *A System of Moral Philosophy,*" in P. Wood (ed.), *The Scottish Enlightenment: Essays in Reinterpretation* (Rochester, NY: Rochester University Press, 2000), pp. 239–266.

———, "Presbyterianism and the Right of Private Judgement: Church Government in Ireland and Scotland in the Age of Francis Hutcheson," in R. Savage (ed.), *Philosophy and Religion in Enlightenment Britain* (Oxford: Oxford University Press, 2012), pp. 141–168.

Moriarty, Michael, *Disguised Vices: Theories of Virtue in Early Modern French Thought* (Oxford: Oxford University Press, 2011).

Mulsow, Martin, *Moderne aus dem Untergrund: radikale Frühaufklärung in Deutschland 1680–1720* (Hamburg: F. Meiner, 2002).

Niedermann, Joseph, *Kultur: Werden und Wandlungen des Begriffs und seiner Ersatzbegriffe von Cicero bis Herder* (Florence: Bibliopolis, 1941).

Norton, David Fate, *David Hume: Common-Sense Moralist, Sceptical Metaphysician* (Princeton, NJ: Princeton University Press, 1982).

———, "Hutcheson's Moral Realism," *Journal of the History of Philosophy* 23 (1985), 397–418.

O'Regan, Philip, *Archbishop William King of Dublin (1650–1729) and the Constitution in Church and State* (Dublin: Four Courts Press, 2000).

Oslington, Paul (ed.), *Adam Smith as Theologian* (New York: Routledge, 2011).

Parkin, Jon, *Science, Religion and Politics in Restoration England: Richard Cumberland's* De Legibus Naturae (Woodbridge: Boydell & Brewer, 1999).

Phillipson, Nicholas, "James Beattie and the Defence of Common Sense," in Bernhard Fabian (ed.), *Festschrift für Rainer Gruenter* (Heidelberg: Winter, 1978), pp. 145–154.

———, "Providence and Progress: An Introduction to the Historical Thought of William Robertson," in S. J. Brown (ed.), *William Robertson and the Expansion of Empire* (Cambridge: Cambridge University Press, 1997), pp. 74–91.

———, "The Making of an Enlightened University," in Robert D. Anderson, Michael Lynch, and Nicholas Phillipson, *The University of Edinburgh: An Illustrated History* (Edinburgh: Edinburgh University Press, 2003), pp. 51–101.

———, *Adam Smith: An Enlightened Life* (London: Allen Lane, 2010).

Plassart, Anna, "Scottish Perspectives on War and Patriotism in the 1790s," *Historical Journal* 57 (2014), pp. 107–129.

Pocock, J. G. A., "Enthusiasm: The Antiself of Enlightenment," in Lawrence E. Klein and A. J. LaVopa (eds.), *Enthusiasm and Enlightenment in Europe, 1650–1850* (San Marino, CA: Huntington Library, 1998), pp. 7–28.

———, *Barbarism and Religion*, vol. 1: *The Enlightenments of Edward Gibbon, 1737–1764* (Cambridge: Cambridge University Press, 1999).

———, *Barbarism and Religion*, vol. 5: *Religion: The First Triumph* (Cambridge: Cambridge University Press, 2010).

Porter, Roy, *Enlightenment: Britain and the Creation of the Modern World* (London: Penguin, 2000).

———, *Flesh in the Age of Reason* (London: Allen Lane, 2003).

Raffe, Alasdair, "Presbyterians and Episcopalians: The Formation of Confessional Cultures in Scotland, 1660–1715," *English Historical Review* 125 (2010), 570–598.

———, "Presbyterianism, Secularization, and Scottish Politics after the Revolution of 1688–90," *Historical Journal* 53 (2010), 317–337.

Raphael, David Daiches, *The Moral Sense* (London: Oxford University Press, 1947).

Redwood, John, *Reason, Ridicule and Religion: The Age of Enlightenment in England, 1660–1750* (London: Thames and Hudson, 1996).

Rice, Daniel F., "Natural Theology and the Scottish Philosophy in the Thought of Thomas Chalmers," *Scottish Journal of Theology* 24 (1971), 23–46.

Riley, Patrick, *Leibniz's Universal Jurisprudence: Justice as the Charity of the Wise.* (Cambridge, MA: Harvard University Press, 1996).

Rivers, Isabel, *Reason, Grace, and Sentiment: A Study of the Language of Religion and Ethics in England, 1660–1780*, vol. 1: *Whichcote to Wesley* (Cambridge: Cambridge University Press, 1991).

———, *Reason, Grace, and Sentiment: A Study of the Language of Religion and Ethics in England, 1660–1780*, vol. 2: *Shaftesbury to Hume* (Cambridge: Cambridge University Press, 2000).

———, "Doddridge, Philip (1702–1751)," *Oxford Dictionary of National Biography* (Oxford: Oxford University Press, 2004), http://www. oxforddnb.com/view/article/4476, accessed 14 November 2013.

———, "Scougal's *The life of God in the soul of man:* The Fortunes of a Book, 1676–1830," in R. Savage (ed.), *Philosophy and Religion in Enlightenment Britain: New Case Studies* (Oxford: Oxford University Press, 2012), pp. 29–55.

Robbins, Caroline, *The Eighteenth-Century Commonwealthman* (Indianapolis: Liberty Fund, 1987).

Robertson, John, *The Case for the Enlightenment: Scotland and Naples, 1680–1760* (Cambridge: Cambridge University Press, 2005).

Rosenblatt, Helena, *Rousseau and Geneva: From the* First Discourse *to the* Social Contract, *1749–1762* (Cambridge: Cambridge University Press, 1997).

———, *Liberal Values: Benjamin Constant and the Politics of Religion* (Cambridge: Cambridge University Press, 2008).

Ross, Ian S., *The Life of Adam Smith* (Oxford: Clarendon Press, 1995).

———, "The Natural Theology of Lord Kames," in P. Wood (ed.), *The Scottish Enlightenment* (Rochester, NY: University of Rochester Press, 2000), pp. 335–351.

Russell, Paul, *The Riddle of Hume's Treatise: Skepticism, Naturalism, and Irreligion* (Oxford: Oxford University Press, 2008).

Schmitz, Robert M., *Hugh Blair* (New York: King's Crown Press, 1948).

Schröder, Winfried, *Ursprünge des Atheismus: Untersuchungen zur Metaphysik- und Religionskritik des 17. und 18. Jahrhunderts* (Stuttgart-Bad Cannstatt: Frommann-Holzboog, 1998).

———, "Natürliche Religion und Religionskritik in der deutschen Frühaufklärung," in Hans-Erich Bödeker (ed.), *Strukturen der deutschen Frühaufklärung* (Göttingen: Vandenhoeck & Ruprecht, 2008), pp. 147–164.

Schubert, Anselm, *Das Ende der Sünde: Anthropologie und Erbsünde zwischen Reformation und Aufklärung* (Göttingen: Vandenhoeck & Rupprecht, 2002).

Scott, W. R., *Francis Hutcheson: His Life, Teaching and Position in the History of Philosophy* (Cambridge: Cambridge University Press, 1900).

Sefton, Henry R., "Rev. Robert Wallace: An Early Moderate," *Records of the Scottish Church History Society* 16 (1966), 1–22.

———, "'Neu-Lights and Preachers Legall': Some Observations on the Beginnings of Moderatism in the Church of Scotland," in Norman MacDougall (ed.), *Church, Politics and Society: Scotland, 1408–1929* (Edinburgh: John Donald, 1983), pp. 186–196.

Seigel, Jerrold, *The Idea of the Self: Thought and Experience in Western Europe since the Seventeenth Century* (Cambridge: Cambridge University Press, 2005).

Semmel, Stuart, *Napoleon and the British* (New Haven: Yale University Press, 2004).

Sheehan, Jonathan, "Enlightenment, Religion, and the Enigma of Secularization: A Review Essay," *American Historical Review* 108 (2003), 1061–1080.

———, *The Enlightenment Bible: Translation, Scholarship, Culture* (Princeton, NJ: Princeton University Press, 2005).

Sher, Richard B., *Church and University in the Scottish Enlightenment: The Moderate Literati of Edinburgh* (Edinburgh: Edinburgh University Press, 1985).

———, "1688 and 1788: William Robertson on Revolution in Britain and France," in P. Dukes and John Dunkley (eds.), *Culture and Revolution* (London: Pinter, 1990), pp. 98–109.

Sher, Richard B., and Alexander Murdoch, "Patronage and Party in the Church of Scotland, 1750–1800," in Norman MacDougall (ed.), *Church, Politics and Society: Scotland, 1408–1929* (Edinburgh: John Donald, 1983), pp. 197–220.

Skoczylas, Anne, *Mr. Simson's Knotty Case: Divinity, Politics, and Due Process in Early Eighteenth-Century Scotland* (Montreal: McGill–Queen's University Press, 2001).

———, "Simson, John (1667–1740)," in *Oxford Dictionary of National Biography* (Oxford: Oxford University Press, 2004), http://www.oxforddnb.com/view/article/4476, accessed 14 November 2013.

———, "The Regulation of Academic Society in Early Eighteenth-Century Scotland: The Tribulations of Two Divinity Professors," *Scottish Historical Review* 83 (2004), 171–195.

————, "Archibald Campbell's *Enquiry into the Original of Moral Virtue, Presbyterian Orthodoxy, and the Scottish Enlightenment,*" *Scottish Historical Review* 87 (2008), 68–100.

Sorkin, David, *The Religious Enlightenment: Protestants, Jews, Catholics from London to Vienna* (Princeton, NJ: Princeton University Press, 2008).

Stewart, M. A., "Berkeley and the Rankenian Club," *Hermathena* 139 (1985), 25–45.

————, "George Turnbull and Educational Reform," in J. J. Carter and Joan M. Pittock (eds.), *Aberdeen and the Enlightenment* (Aberdeen: Aberdeen University Press, 1987), pp. 95–103.

————, "Principal Wishart (1692–1753) and the Controversies of His Day," *Records of the Scottish Church History Society* 30 (2000), 60–102.

————, *The Kirk and the Infidel*, 2nd ed. (Lancaster, PA: Lancaster University Press, 2001).

————, "Halyburton, Thomas (1674–1712)," in *Oxford Dictionary of National Biography* (Oxford: Oxford University Press, 2004), http://www.oxforddnb.com/view/article/4476, accessed 14 November 2013.

————, "Rational Religion and Common Sense," in Joseph Houston (ed.), *Thomas Reid: Context, Influence, Significance* (Edinburgh: Dunedin Academic Press, 2004), pp. 123–160.

————, "Hume's Intellectual Development, 1711–1752," in M. Frasca-Spada and P. Kail (eds.), *Impressions of Hume* (Oxford: Clarendon Press, 2005).

Suderman, Jeffrey M., *Orthodoxy and Enlightenment: George Campbell in the Eighteenth Century* (Montreal: McGill–Queen's University Press, 2001).

Taylor, Charles, *A Secular Age* (Cambridge, MA: Belknap Press, 2007).

Turco, Luigi, "La prima Inquiry morale di Francis Hutcheson," *Rivista Critica di Storia della Filosofia* 23 (1968), 39–60 and 297–329.

————, "Sympathy and Moral Sense: 1725–1740," *British Journal for the History of Philosophy* 7 (1999), 79–101.

Voges, Friedhelm, "Moderate and Evangelical Thinking in the Later Eighteenth Century: Differences and Shared Attitudes," *Records of the Scottish Church History Society* 22 (1985), 141–157.

Ward, W. R., *The Protestant Evangelical Awakening* (Cambridge: Cambridge University Press, 1992).

————, *Early Evangelicalism: A Global Intellectual History, 1670–1789* (Cambridge: Cambridge University Press, 2006).

Whatley, C. A., *The Scots and the Union* (Edinburgh: Edinburgh University Press, 2007).

Wigelsworth, Jeffrey, *Deism in Enlightenment England: Theology, Politics and Newtonian Public Science* (Manchester: Manchester University Press, 2009).

Winkler, Kenneth, "Hutcheson's Alleged Realism," *Journal of the History of Philosophy* 23 (1985), 179–194.

Wood, Paul, "The Scottish Philosophy: Thomas Reid and the Common Sense School," in J. A. Harris and Aaron Garrett (eds.), *Scottish Philosophy in the Age of Enlightenment* (vol. 2 of the *Oxford History of Scottish Philosophy*) (Oxford: Oxford University Press, forthcoming).

Wolterstorff, Nicholas, *Thomas Reid and the Story of Epistemology* (Cambridge: Cambridge University Press, 2001).

Worden, Blair, "The Question of Secularization," in Alan Houston and S. Pincus (eds.), *A Nation Transformed* (Cambridge: Cambridge University Press, 2001).

Wright, John, "The Scientific Reception of Hume's Theory of Causation: Establishing the Positivist Interpretation in Early Nineteenth-Century Scotland," in P. Jones (ed.), *The Reception of David Hume in Europe* (London: Thoemmes–Continuum, 2005), pp. 327–347.

Yeager, Jonathan, *Enlightened Evangelicalism: The Life and Thought of John Erskine* (Oxford: Oxford University Press, 2011).

Young, Brian, *Religion and Enlightenment in Eighteenth-Century England: Theological Debate from Locke to Burke* (Oxford: Clarendon Press, 1998).

———, "Enlightenment Political Thought and the Cambridge School," *Historical Journal* 52 (2009), 235–251.

Index

Abernethy, John, 36, 37–38, 40, 54

abstract truths, 12, 79

Act for Securing the Church in
Scotland (*1707*), 26

actions: moral, 48, 52, 83–85, 95, 114,
116–117; motives for, 12

Adam: in innocent state, 27, 108; and
Law of Works, 49, 105, 106; as
legal representative of his entire
posterity, 27, 32, 40

Adam and Eve, and original sin, 24,
27–28, 40, 106, 107

Addison and Steele, *Spectator*, 53

aesthetic beauty, perception of, 111

affections: moral, 55–60, 112, 113; role
of, 94–95, 108, 113, 116; use of
term, 95

afterlife: divine justice in, 43, 45–46,
104; educational purpose of, 24;
fear of, 43; and moral obligation,
46, 47, 50, 60, 64; and paganism,
62–63, 91, 101; punishment in, 20,
42, 46–47, 51; and revelation, 46,
62–63, 89–91, 95, 105; rewards
and punishment in, 21, 23–24, 44,
45, 47, 49, 60–61, 82–85, 89–90,
92, 100, 103–105; and salvation,

49, 85–86; skepticism about, 82,
99; understanding of, 38, 43–44,
93, 100

Aikenhead, Thomas, 19, 20, 21, 31

Anabaptist movement, 11

Anderson, George, 104, 105, 114;
*Estimate of the Profit and Loss of
Religion*, 97

Anne, queen of England, 71, 72

antinomianism, 29

Argathelians, 31

Arianism, 30, 31, 106

Aristotle, 44

Arminianism, 30, 32

Arnold, Matthew, 139–140

atheists, 1, 19–20

Augustine of Hippo, Saint, 7–8

Augustinian-Epicurean synthesis, 8

Augustinians: and charity, 8, 78; and
enthusiasm, 21–27; "hyper-
Augustinians," 42, 50–51; and
immorality, 39; seventeenth-
century, 14, 34, 136; use of term, 8

avisamentum, right of, 128

Bacon, Sir Francis, *Advancement of
Learning*, 11